MW01073704

PRAISE

better: A Teacher's Journey is created with brilliant authenticity and on-the-ground experiences with adolescents who are learning how the school can be a place of felt connection but can also be a space of significant adversity. Monte Syrie deeply understands that relationships are critical to the nervous system's development, and he has cultivated a practitioner's book that we will all benefit from as we delve into the 180-day project alongside passages like this: *I think learning is a process, a long process in which different learners arrive at different stages at different times, and our traditional practices don't honor this. In fact, I think our traditional practices unwittingly punish this.* Thank you, Monte Syrie, for gifting educators across the world with these rich passages contemplating how we are assessing students academically that is truth-filled, and honest, as you share examples of felt safety through your everyday conversations with students and parents.

Dr. Lori Desautels
Assistant Professor, Butler University's College of Education

Monte's *better: A Teacher's Journey* is a triumphant journey on the why of teaching. We are given a front seat in the daily life of teaching—navigating those day-to-day challenges—something that so many new and veteran teachers crave. We see how to establish a classroom community. We learn how to build humane assessment practices. We navigate the cognitive dissonances of teacher power and relationship building. Monte leads us through a personal journey of the hard road of teaching. This leads us to simple, caring tasks like *Smiles and Frowns* as well as deeply embedded understandings of identity-formation and purpose-finding. And from its very onset, it's clear that a path of *Do. Reflect. Do Better.* helps us all recognize why being introspective and listening to young people is so important in this profession.

Chris McNutt
Executive Director, Human Restoration Project
Nick Covington
Creative Director, Human Restoration Project

The highest compliment I can give a teacher is, "I wish my own children were in this classroom," which I kept thinking while reading Monte Syric's book, better. Since we can't have all of our children in his class, this book is the next best alternative. *better* takes you on Syric's journey from tradition to innovation and invites other educators to create spaces physically and philosophically where the teachers and students focus on learning, not grades. Since we can't bring our kids to Monte, let's bring ourselves to better.

Dr. Heather Lyon
Author of Engagement is Not a Unicorn (It's a Narwhal)
& The BIG Book of Engagement Strategies

Monte not only takes the reader on his journey to be ever better, he also shares strategies for all of us to reflect and grow in our work. This book shows us one step at a time how it's possible to empower learners through continuous inquiry, insight, and most importantly vulnerability.

Katie McFarland EdD
Technology and Instructional Leader, Western New York

Syric pens a beautiful narrative about his journey to a healthier classroom community. *better* shows us all how to create a place where students are understood for exactly who they are, allowing each and every student to thrive.

Katie Budrow
Co-Author of Moving Beyond Classroom Management: Leading a Culture of Learning

With his "affinity for the alliterative," Monte mentors us to "put down [the] sword," pick up a "walking stick," and join him on a continuous journey. His reflections are sometimes on assessment, sometimes on learning, sometimes on processes, but always on relationships, growth, and joy. His passion and humility are evident in each of his entries, and with this text designed as a journal, he invites us to do, reflect, and do better in so many aspects of classroom life. I feel like I have made great strides in my sixteen-year career, but Monte reveals (with clear models from his own classroom) how I (we) can always do better–and that we can be on this vital quest together.

Nicholas A. Emmanuele
HS ELA Teacher, Dept. Chair

better is a book that reveals the teacher's heart. It charts the triumphs and failures of one teacher's career. It relies on the gut instinct of a veteran who cares deeply for the success of every student in the class. It is a must-read for teachers who want the best for their learners. Monte Syrie is a risk-taker. He is willing to experiment and his students, because they know he cares for them, are his willing test subjects. He dares to subvert the traditional education system in ways most teachers dream and he takes the reader along for a ride that inspires. If you want to do *better*, read *better: A Teacher's Journey*. It will ignite a passion for teaching and learning and becoming the teacher you want to be.

Aaron Blackwelder
Digital Learning Coach Vancouver Public Schools
5 time High School Golf Coach of the Year
Founder Teachers Going Gradeless

better: A Teacher's Journey is a showcase of iterative and reflective practice in which Monte generously navigates his own learning journey with honesty, vulnerability, and passion. Through the relentless pursuit of his own better, Monte shows us what is possible when we reject the performative charade of schooling and instead walk alongside our students towards more authentic and meaningful learning. Towards our own better.

Abe Moore
Manager of Education for Nature Play, South Australia

Monte has done the work for those of us thinking about changing the way students learn. Through this book you will see, the research has been done for you. Monte keeps it real. He is authentic in sharing what he learned through Project 180. This work wasn't without mistakes and failing and Monte is transparent about all of it. His students discovered their strengths and areas of growth, learned to advocate for themselves, learned to make conscious decisions, made positive connections with Monte and their peers, and felt safe in the learning environment he created in his classroom. When we think about making changes, we want to see it in action. We want to see what it looks like in action. This book will provide that for you.

Charity Dodd
Content Manager, LINC, The Learning Innovation Catalyst

better: A Teacher's Journey

First edition 2022

For Sherry,

my wife, my witness.

No one knows my *better* better.

better

A TEACHER'S JOURNEY

Project 180 Book One

MONTE SYRIE

TABLE OF CONTENTS

Praise ii

Foreword 3

Preface 7

better Begins 9

Prologue 33

Year One 37

better Between 129

Year Two 203

better Between 293

Year Three 317

better Bends 399

better Builders 401

FOREWORD

The best of us in education embrace the premise, "Do the stuff that scares ya." High school teacher and blogger, Monte Syrie, not only walks that path, he's brought lanterns, climbing rope, a GPS, and trail mix for the rest of us. As J. Alfred Prufrock anti-matter, Monte dares to disturb the universe. And that eternal and snickering Footman? All he can do is palm the mug when Syrie declares, "Hold my beer," and bushwhacks into the deeper waters of teaching, fully lucid while tackling mistakes and making required revisions. In short, he is brave.

better: A Teacher's Journey is the consummate behind-the-scenes look at a modern, professional educator's decisions and discoveries while teaching adolescents. Monte is an earnest provocateur, however, sharpening his teaching acumen against the jagged edges of grades and grading. Such a contentious yet impactful whetstone forces Monte to confront systemic weaknesses as well as his own misconceptions and inconsistent practices, then change those methods to reflect modern pedagogy. This is not easy, nor is it done overnight. And that may be the best lesson we get from Monte: We're not only allowed to be imperfect in teaching, it's those imperfections and the changes in our practices that get us out of bed in the morning–and give students the best chance of success.

Here we see Monte's early bravado become something so much more by becoming less: As he says at one point, he finally learns to, "...put [his] superhero shirts in a drawer and ego on the shelf," which is something so many of us need to learn. Monte finds efficacy in doubt and promise in recognizing hypocrisy. His signature, "Smiles and

Frowns," is known internationally (I know, I've found it when working with teachers overseas), and I don't know of anyone so reflective, then so effective, as a result. He's a teacher's teacher.

Monte embraces the *Atomic Habits* (James Clear, 2018) and others' approach that sees the healthiest evolutions happen one degree or step at a time, with the journey never finishing. He embraces the, "ever-quest," (Monte's word, but I'm totally trying it on for size and it fits perfectly), becoming better with each error and its reflection, but not crumbling when outcomes aren't instantly wonderful. In this, he (we) survive the day and find teaching doable. What grace here, and what a great thing it is to never arrive!

The writing is cogent, with a conversational, almost musical tone. Descriptions and analyses are clear, personable, and compelling, revealing an exceptionally thoughtful individual trying to do his best by his students and his profession. Check out the drama, too: Just as he gets excited about one new strategy, he finds a pitfall and has to re-group; he's not as smart as he thought he was. It's a very real classroom with high-stakes outcomes for his students. They are depending on him to get it right.

What a thrill to see someone of Monte Syrie's longevity and expertise still evolving with the humility and awe of a first year teacher! Monte's subject knowledge is powerful, yes, but the real sources of oxygen in his teaching are relationships, community, student agency, cultivating hope, leading by example, and embracing the humanity of learning, including how we become stronger for the introspection. A favorite moment from the book? One of his students notes, "The best evidence that I'm learning is that I'm not making the same mistakes, I'm making new ones."

As we know, teaching is a fight against entropy, and that fight can zig-zag. Educators who require orderly schematics when teaching children, especially teenagers, tilt at pedagogical windmills, flailing about while those embracing ambiguity, fallibility, pushing against the system's hypocrisies, and the messy nature of the teaching-learning dynamo summit the far vista. Monte captures the joy, frustration, and discovery of such journeys beautifully. So much so, we wonder how much more we might be today, had we been in his classes over the years.

Yeah, let's do pedagogical 180's. There's thrill in the centrifuge, maybe even escape velocity. That's it. Monte might say, let's imperil complacency, find ourselves, and watch our students achieve better than before.

Rick Wormeli

Author of *Fair Isn't Always Equal*, 2nd Edition

PREFACE

This is not a book of answers. It's a book of betters from my own journey of chasing better across my twenty-five years in the classroom. They are my betters, the discoveries from my wonderings and wanderings in search of better for whom my betters matter most: my students. My kids, the reason I *do*, the reason I *reflect*, the reason I *do better*. So, it's just that: a book of betters to share with you. But, please know, my betters are not answers. They are not the way to do it. I have neither found nor will I ever find the answer. I have only discovered–and will only ever continue to discover–betters. And here at this twenty-fifth year, I have decided to pause and share my journey with my fellow educators so maybe my better journey inspires their own.

This is not a book of data, at least not in the more traditional sense of the term. One will find no science here to drive or validate practice. This is a book of reflection, where one will find, what I believe to be, the art of our practice, that place that drives us beyond our heads to where we discover validity in the humanity of our hearts. That is not to say that the science of teaching is not important. It is to say that the art of teaching is equally important. Science has secured its place in the literature. There are plenty of books to support the science side of our practice. This just isn't one of them.

This is not intended to only be a book about me. This is supposed to be a book about you, too. Really, it's a book about all of us–each of us on a journey to better. Yes, it contains my betters, but not because my betters are better. They are just the betters that I have discovered and decided to share. My betters are not, should not, cannot be your betters. Your betters are your betters. They have to be. They are the reflection of your own journey in the classroom. And, as you read this book, that is what I want you thinking of: your own journey. I hope my journey is no more than a vehicle for you to think about the betters you have thus far collected along your way. More, I hope it drives you to "dare *your* different" and "brave *your* better" as you chase the dreams on your own horizons.

This book is for you.

better Begins

AN INTRODUCTION TO PROJECT 180

It started on a dare. "Sy, you're gonna do this, too, right?" And though I had not planned on joining my kids in our independent learning project in the late fall of 2015, Megan Lavin's question put me on the spot, and I accepted the challenge as if I had planned it all along. "Of course," I assured her. But, as a matter of course, I didn't have a clue what I might do.

I could begin a blog. I had always wanted to, but the want of it had never been enough to get to the start of it, and in truth, I wasn't even really sure what a blog was, and more, I was quite sure that I had no idea how to begin. But, as I found myself encouraging kids to pursue their passions with our projects, I found myself moving from the want of a blog to the start of a blog, and quite unexpectedly my journey to better began. Well, my current journey. In truth, my journey–as with all teachers' journeys–began the moment I stepped into the classroom.

But it's my more recent journey, my Project 180 journey from the last five years, which will be the focus here in my first book of betters.

Project 180

My blog didn't begin as Project 180. It began simply as a daily blog to, as the name of my website suggests, "change education." At first I thought, in earnest, it was about starting and continuing conversations among the stakeholders: fellow educators, parents, students, and the public. And with that in mind, I took my very first step into the blogosphere.

THE FIRST STEP - DECEMBER 12, 2015

After *years* of thinking about it and recently being challenged to complete an independent learning project with my students, I have started my own blog, a blog dedicated to changing education-one word at a time. And while I have many words to share, I cannot do it alone. I need your help. Your words count. *Truly*. Let's do it, then. Let's change education.

And so, I began by posing questions, hoping that others would chime in, and if we could get the conversation going, then we could start the slow but important process of changing education. As such, I posed questions about what I thought were important topics to bring about necessary change in education. I began with motivation.

What will it take to truly motivate students to learn?

JANUARY 2016 TOPIC: MOTIVATION

DECEMBER 31, 2015

Why aren't students motivated to learn?

Little has vexed me more than this particular question over the course of my career. And while I have certainly sought the answers during my first two decades in the classroom, the answers elude me, and I remain certain of only one thing: for the most part, kids have little motivation to engage–truly engage–in what we call learning. This month we will explore and seek to better understand what truly motivates students to learn, hopefully turning understanding into action by doing differently in the classroom.

Is it grades? For a time, naively and stubbornly, I clung to the notion that grades motivated students to engage in learning. And so, for years, I attempted to *make* kids learn, using grades as both punishment and reward. I wasted many a year here.

Is it me? Maybe if *I* am engaging, the kids will be more engaged. And though there is some truth found in this approach, I have often wondered if the kids were really more engaged or just more entertained. Good teachers have to be engaging, but good teachers, I believe, also know that being engaging alone is not enough to truly engage all the kids in learning. At least, that has been my experience. Of course, it may be that I'm not as engaging as I think.

Is it parents? I became a more empathetic teacher when I became a parent. As a young, yet-to-have-any children-of-my-own teacher, I imagined that parents getting their children to be more committed to education simply required their telling them to do it. Just do it, right? As if. Now, with children of my own, I know and fight the nightly battles to get my children to do their homework, listening to a litany of reasons for why they don't want to do it, ranging from boredom to frustration. And sometimes-here comes the confession of the public-school teacher who's also a parent, I give in. I am human, I am a parent. I get it. And while I know that parents play a very vital role in their children's education, the answer cannot simply lie in parents' parenting. There has to be a better answer.

Is it the future? The future can be scary. And it seems we teachers count on and exploit that to motivate our students. "You have to pass the state assessment…, If you fail this class…, If you want to go to *college…, If you want to get a good job…, It will hurt your GPA…, This will be on the final…, When you get into the real world….*" Admittedly, sadly, I believe all of these scare tactics have crossed my lips over the years, especially early on, but now, thankfully, I know better, for these rarely inspire commitment and more often coerce compliance, which does not elicit engagement.

Is it students themselves? The longer I'm at it, and the more I learn, I have become increasingly suspicious that the truth of the matter lies somewhere within this realm. Yes, to varying degrees, the above considerations matter and play a role in motivating some students, but not all. And while we will continue to use them, despite their limited success, I wonder if we shouldn't instead focus our energy here. That said, I am not suggesting that we simply dump it on the kids. No, to be sure, but I *am* suggesting that maybe we need to work harder to create learning opportunities that transcend traditional approaches, which emphasize extrinsic factors and compliance, and focus instead on approaches that trigger intrinsic factors and commitment.

In the end there are no simple answers, and as with most things, the truth is probably closer to the middle than the ends, but without answers, we will never arrive at a truth. So, over the next month, let's seek some solutions, some answers to the question: *What will it take to truly motivate students to learn?*

But the conversation never really got going the way I hoped it might. People commented. But comments aren't really conversations, and I soon discovered that maybe my grand plan to "conversate" our way to change, might not be as fruitful as I'd hoped. Plus, admittedly and somewhat abashedly, my lack of participation in and ignorance of social media kept me from knowing that there were plenty of conversations going on already about changing education. As such, I discovered I wasn't providing the "present" of a platform after all. I discovered I was late to a game that had been long underway. And so, my approach changed to what I then called a Weekly Wonder.

WEEKLY WONDER: I WONDER IF OUR GRADING SYSTEM IS FAIR.
JANUARY 24, 2016
Is Our Grading System Fair?
"A zero has an undeserved and devastating influence, so much so that no matter what the student does, the grade distorts the final grade as a true indicator of mastery.

Mathematically and ethically this is unacceptable. "
Rick Wormeli

The topic this week opens a huge can of worms in education. For better or worse, in the end, it seems that everything comes down to the final grade, which generally generates a source of anxiety for kids and a source of contention among stakeholders when disagreement or confusion presents itself in regards to how the grade was determined, and perhaps most importantly, what the grade really means and if it truly indicates learning. In short, one little letter has the power to make a huge impact on a kid's life. Of course, this is nothing new. It has always been the case, and little has changed. Grades have been and remain the center point in education, for they are often accepted as the final word on learning, the final indicator of success or failure. But what if the final word is flawed? What if grades are not really true indicators of learning, success, or failure? I wonder. And though my wonders may lure me to wander into a huge realm full of questions never asked and answers oft ignored, I will stick to one worm in the can for now: zeros. We will explore the general topic of grading practices in greater depth next month.

The great majority of kids who fail do so because of the dreaded zero, which is most generally the result of a missing assignment, not necessarily an indicator of low-or-no proficiency with course content. So, invariably, zeros kill grades, often creating holes that kids cannot crawl out of, resulting in many giving up and failing a course. So, too, even kids who do not fail courses suffer the unfair penalty of zeros, which often drastically decrease their grades. So what? If they didn't want the penalty, they should have completed the assignment. *One should not get something for nothing. Kids need to learn.* Yes, they do, but some lessons make more sense than others. And zeros don't really make sense when we examine traditional grading scales.

Most grading scales roughly reflect a 10-point-increment scale, moving down the scale from "A" (100 - 90) to "B" (89 - 80) and so on. Again, this is nothing new. We all were subject to such a scale, and kids still are today. And, as we continue down the scale, it remains uniform until we get to "F" and then it abruptly dives from 59 to 0. "F's" should stop at 50. There are no "G" through "K" grades, only "F's". In terms of numbers, scores given in this range may reflect a degree of completion (a kid did 3 of 10 problems, so he gets 30%), but in terms of learning, scores given in this range whether it's 59, 34, or 17 reflect one thing: failure. When kids or parents see scores below 60, they generally understand that that indicates a performance well-below standard; students have not been successful with the content. When we start assigning numbers within this range, what are we really seeking to communicate? Let's take a 52%. Are we really meaning to suggest that this is a lesser fail than a 33%, which should then suggest a greater fail? This then continues down the scale, approaching the zero, a sign of complete and utter failure. Kids in this range for various reasons are well-below the grade-level standards that we have established in our classrooms. That's the message, generally intended and generally received. This is clear. What I wonder is if we also have to attach a punishment in the form of a sub-50-point score? Somehow, it just doesn't seem fair. Why can't we let an "F" be an "F?" We let "A's be A's" and "B's" be "B's." Why not "F's?" Why do we have to let the bottom drop out? A bottom that drops the kids off a cliff they can rarely re-climb, especially in classrooms where they cannot turn in late work or redo assignments. Is this really fair for kids? Is this ethical in an arena where the stakes are so high? I'm not sure.

Four years ago, I quit zeros. They are no longer allowed in my classroom. I still have "F's" which communicate, in number *and* learning, performances well-below standard. Kids still receive failing scores in my classroom, but I don't tack on punishment, additional insult to injury in the form of sub-50% scores; 50% is now the lowest score possible in my class. The kids know from the mark that they have failed to meet standard; I don't need to crush them more with added penalties. It makes sense to me, it makes sense to my kids, and it makes sense to parents. It's also beginning to make sense to some of my colleagues, who, too, have adopted a no-zero policy. But not all. Some of my colleagues have accused me of malpractice, suggesting I am ruining kids' lives by not teaching them a lesson. And I guess, of that, I am guilty. But I sleep at night knowing that I have given kids a fair shake, and while I may not be teaching them the harsh lessons of life, I am giving them opportunity by creating a realm of possibility in room 219.

Your turn. Is the practice of giving zeros fair? Please, join the conversation. Your words matter.

I was still posing questions; I was still seeking conversation; I was still chasing change. And the more I chased, the more my own (significant) change began to take shape. Truly. For, as I now look back, this post became a game-changer for my blog; it led to Project 180. At last, I had found my battleground with this one: grading.

It struck a nerve in those around me. It struck a chord in me. And by year's end, I was ready to fight in the arena. The plan for Project 180 had begun.

LET THE WORK BEGIN: MORNING MINUTES

AUGUST 8, 2016

Morning, all. Well, after a nearly two-month break, it's time to get back to work. I am so excited to get *Project 180* underway this year, but I have lots to do before it begins on August 31. As a first step, I submitted the article below to Edutopia this morning . For my regular readers, it is nothing new, so don't worry about reading it. It's just packaged a little differently. I eagerly look forward to reconnecting with everyone this year. Hope your summer has been and continues to be great.

Project 180 is the first step in an effort to transform education by turning it upside down-challenging the status quo and disrupting convention. For the next two years, I will set aside traditional grading practices in my high school English classroom, seeking to improve my students' experiences by making learning, not grading, the central focus.

For now twenty years, I have been unsettled by and dissatisfied with traditional and conventional grading practices, suspecting that there had to be a better way to approach learning, that grades-in the traditional sense-did little to help and, in many cases, made worse the learning in my classroom. I have dabbled in and experimented with standards-based grading and found it to be a promising alternative to tradition, but I think that-though it is radical in its own right-it is not radical enough to bring about the necessary shift in a system far too settled in the it's-how-we've-always-done-it-rut approach to education. So, in an effort to turn things upside down, I am going to give my students A's on day one. I am going to take grades out of the equation by giving them what they, their parents, and society have come to believe is the golden stamp of approval in American public education: an A. Then for the next 180 days, I am going to give them an opportunity to learn, to grow, free from the pressure and pretense of grades.

Can students learn without grades? My instincts say yes. But my critics-including the ghosts of my own self-doubt-will suggest otherwise, clinging to the deeply-seated standard of traditional grading as the way, the mark of learning. But two decades in, I am going to listen to my gut and take a monumental risk to learn and grow, and ultimately, hopefully make better the learning experiences in my classroom.

I first flirted with the idea after reading the Zanders' *The Art of Possibility*. In one of the chapters, the authors discussed the "practice of giving an A," an approach where students were given an A at the outset of the year during which they had to live into the A, proving in the end that they had earned it.

And though I found it intriguing, it never amounted to more than a casual fling, for I could not fully wrap my head around taking such a crazy path in a traditional, public-school setting. That was ten years ago, but now armed with the confidence-maybe craziness-that change not only must but can happen, I am ready to get this journey underway. We can change practice. We have to change practice. But it will happen neither easily nor expediently. It will take effort. It will take time. I am devoting both.

My original intent was not to gift A's to all my students. My original plan was to give each student a P for pass, a seemingly simple, harmless way to take traditional grades off the table. However, after discussing the idea with our lead counselor, it became clear that a "P" could be problematic on students' transcripts when it came to college entrance and/or scholarships. So, wishing to never do harm, I decided to go with A's for all, which I believe better set the desired course anyway. One, it took traditional grading out of the equation. Two, it was radical enough to call attention to the shortcomings of conventional grading practices. Thus, the stage was set. But how was I going to do it?

Below is a rough sketch of my plan. But before we get there, here is a necessary preface. Students (and parents) will be given full ownership of their learning in my classroom this year. As the lead learner in the room, I will provide opportunities for students to learn and grow in an ELA environment. I will provide direction, feedback, and encouragement, but only they can provide the motivation to learn and grow. They already have their A's for the year. Now it's their turn to live into their A's by making the experience what it should be in the first place, an opportunity to build themselves over the next 180 days, not a year-long sentence to get a grade. They will grow or they won't. I can only provide the opportunity. They have to own their learning. Here is how I plan to do it.

1. Actually, there is a possibility of two marks in my classroom. There is a qualification to the A. An A requires the signature of both students and parents on any and all "progress reports" (details below). They do not have to complete the report, but they must sign it. Failure to sign, will result in a "P," which indicates credit for the course with no effect on GPA.

2. Our work for the year will center around what I have come to call our 10 "Super-Student Standards," standards derived from not only the Common Core but also my 20 years in an ELA classroom. I basically approached it with, "these are the things that we will hang our hats on this year, the things that we will learn."

3. In addition, I came up with a "Super Student Profile" emphasizing 15 habits/behaviors of learners, things that matter, things I want my students conscious of, things I want parents to know, but things that would never be attached to a grade (in the traditional sense).

4. "Reporting" will happen frequently. Every day, students will reflect on their learning in their notebooks. Every two weeks, students will complete learning logs: self-assessments on standards and profiles (must be signed by student and parent). Every nine weeks, I will complete a progress report that is created through conferring with each student. The students will either agree with or challenge my assessment. Challenges must be supported by evidence. Nine week progress reports must also be signed by student and parent. Every semester, students will complete a student-led conference, a comprehensive review of their growth (must be signed by student and parent). For practice, I will use our online grading system to report completed practice.
5. Learning experiences will primarily occur within the context of project-based learning.

There are so many more details to share- many more, too, that I will consider and discover over this two-year project. But for now, I hope this provides a skeleton for my approach.

Why project 180? Well a few things.

One, 180 degrees turns things upside down-a necessary step for change. Two, there are 180 days in a school year-this endeavor will be the most difficult thing that I have done in my career, so I will have to take it one day at a time. Plus, I plan to share my journey one day at a time on my blog. Three, because "upside down" is uncomfortable it must be set upright again-another 180 degrees, bringing things full circle, at which point, I hope I have learned to make learning better in my little corner of the world. If you are interested, please join my journey this fall, as I daily post the stories from the adventure.

Crazy? Maybe. Determined? Absolutely. We have to change education.

Of course, I did not know back on that August day when I formally announced Project 180 to the world that I would go on to blog every morning for the next five years. At most (and I had actually forgotten this until I began going back through old posts) the plan was to document the journey for two years and turn it into two books. One, showing how I turned things upside down (Project 180), and two, showing how I set them right again by going full circle (Project 360), thinking I would have answers to deliver to the world. But, obviously, that only became a forgotten memory on the journey to here. And more–importantly–that only led me to better, for as I shared in the preface, this is a book of betters, not answers. And so here I am five years later with only my betters to share, not the least of which is knowing better that there are no answers, only betters.

better Battle

In a sense, it all began a battle. I, sword in hand, was ready to smite the status quo, to shake the great tree, and knock education on its ass. I thought it was my call to duty, my call to arms. And, in April of 2016, I answered the call with my first announcement of the 180 journey (though I didn't know its name then). I was prepared to battle the forces without, which threatened my realm within.

KNOCKING THE SLOTH ON HIS ASS: MORNING MINUTES, APRIL 13, 2016

'I hate a Roman named Status Quo!' he said to me. 'Stuff your eyes with wonder,' he said, 'live as if you'd drop dead in ten seconds. See the world. It's more fantastic than any dream made or paid for in factories. Ask no guarantees, ask for no security, there never was such an animal. And if there were, it would be related to the great sloth which hangs upside down in a tree all day every day, sleeping its life away. To hell with that,' he said, 'shake the tree and knock the great sloth down on his ass.' ~Ray Bradbury, Fahrenheit 451

It's time. Over the next several weeks I am going to begin revealing my plan for next year, a two-year journey in 219 to shake the foundation and bring down some of the edificial facades of education, challenging the status quo, ...shaking the sloth.

So, then, the Morning Minutes will now mostly be devoted to working through-*lots to think about*--revising, refining, and finalizing the blueprints for my remodeling project in 219. Excited to share the process with you and get your input and feedback along the way. The journey begins.

Happy Wednesday, all. May your eyes be stuffed with wonder.

But now, as I look back and lean on what I've learned, better is not a battle without, it's a journey within.

There are things that threaten, that reach from the outside and unsettle and unnerve us in our realms, our rooms. From district mandates, to standardized tests, to new programs promising success (if we follow with fidelity), to old programs/conventions/traditions (that don't–and never did–make sense), we are beset by threats from the outside. And when we find ourselves in this space, we fight or we withdraw. We become the pariah, the negative pain in the ass. Or we become the recluse, the apathetic go-along. I have been both, time and again. I often relished the role of fighter, imagining I was a champion for good. And, as often, I disdained the acceptance of apathy, imagining I was a victim of evil. But neither really got me anywhere. So, I sought better. And along the way, I have found it–within.

There will always be things outside our rooms that we cannot control. I am not going to win the battle against the new program that the district has spent tens of thousands of dollars on. Oh, I can rattle my saber a bit, but it's not a battle I am going to win. I have learned that. But, importantly, I have also learned that while I cannot control what's outside, I have a great deal of control over what's inside–myself and my classroom. Admittedly, I still feel the rise in my resistance when outside forces come knocking (I am still a fighter), but I am no longer available for the battle between "good and evil." I am committed to the better battle, the journey within. I have traded my sword for a walking stick and engaged in the work that really matters: better.

180

What's in a name? Why Project 180? While I am no longer exactly sure how it came to be, here's the earliest mention I could find of 180 from the "Let the Work Begin" post I shared a few pages back.

"Why project 180? Well a few things. One, 180 degrees turns things upside down–a necessary step for change. Two, there are 180 days in a school year–this endeavor will be the most difficult thing that I have done in my career, so I will have to take it one day at a time. Plus, I plan to share my journey one day at a time on my blog. Three, because "upside down" is uncomfortable it must be set upright again–another 180 degrees, bringing things full circle, at which point, I hope I have learned to make learning better in my little corner of the world. If you are interested, please join my journey this fall, as I daily post the stories from the adventure."

I think I thought at the time that the cycle would eventually stop, that the spin would settle, that the circle would complete itself, and I would have the answers. Of course, I now know there are no answers, and too, of course, I now know there is no stop, the journey continues 180 degrees at a time. There is no *settle*, only search. And it is this search, this chase that led to the essence of the 180 journey, my mantra: *Do. Reflect. Do Better*. This is the endless "ever-quest" that is our work, that is the path to better.

better

I discovered "better" quite by accident. I stumbled upon it early in my 180 work when I discovered that I wasn't finding answers. I wasn't finding "right." I wasn't finding "good." And I certainly wasn't finding "great." I was only finding "better"–one mistake, one question, one half-turn at a time. More accurately, I suppose, I was making many mistakes, I was asking many questions, and I was making many dizzy turns. And that is where I discovered better only leads to better. One *Do*. One *Reflect*. One *Do Better* at a time.

As such, better isn't about arriving; better is about moving. Better never rests. And that is why I believe better beats best. Best suggests an end, but better suggests there's better yet around the bend. Better is impermanent. And that is why you will find it written in lowercase throughout the book–even on the cover. A capital seems to "finish it," but the work is never done, and by the time we are ready to share our better, a new one's already begun. In fact, by the time you are reading this book, my book of betters, I will have already moved on to the next better. But for now, in this moment, my betters at this five year point in the 180 journey will fill the pages and chapters ahead. So why, then, would you want to read about some betters that are already behind me? Simple, so you begin your own better journey. Remember, it's really not about my betters. It's about yours.

Chapters Ahead

better began as one book. It became two, then one again. And finally it settled into two books. It had to. As it passed the 100,000-word mark, *better* became too big for one book, so I split it into two. Book One covers years one through three. And Book Two covers years four and five.

But as big as *better* is, it still only brushes the surface of the first five years of Project 180. It presents only ten percent of the nine-hundred-plus blog posts from those years. Between the two books, you will find ninety posts, which I carefully selected as "waypoints" from the journey; places marked on a map as worthy of revisiting. As you might imagine, nine hundred to ninety was no small undertaking as I retraced my steps, searching for the places that I might share with you.

Why ninety? For the sake of novelty, I chose to be creative with factors of 180 throughout the book, so I set myself the task of finding ninety.

To reach that number, I decided to go with fifteen posts per year. But that only got me to seventy-five. So I needed to find another fifteen, which I found from the summers between, during which some of my richest reflections came into being. And with that, I had my ninety.

But there had to be more to *better* than copying and pasting ninety posts into a book, ninety posts which could—and still can—be accessed for free on my website (along with eleven-hundred-some other posts). So, the "more to better" became what I came to call "180 Wraps." I have set up each post with exactly 180 words, and I have followed up the same post with exactly 180 words for a full—if you will—circle, 360-word wrap for each post. Consequently, I wrote exactly 180 words 180 times. *The price of novelty.* Here's a brief guide to how I formatted each post.

Quote

Each post opens with a quote directly from the post itself.

180°5.25.2016

The "waypoint coordinates" (180 degrees plus the original date of the post) is written with exactly 180 words to set up the post.

Post

The post is written as it was originally published (typos and all for the sake of authenticity. Please forgive the errors).

360°2021

The looking-back-five-years-later, full-circle is a 360-degree wrap up in exactly 180 words.

better Builder

Here you will find what I call a "better Builder" reflection question to consider in the context of the post for your own room, your own journey, your own better. Each chapter ends with a list of its respective "better Builders." You will also find all "better Builders" from the book at the end of the book.

There are five main chapters. And each, in keeping with the novelty of the factors of 180, has an exactly ninety-word introduction and an exactly ninety-word conclusion. I am grateful I only had to do this five times. Writing ninety words, though but half, was twice as challenging as writing one-hundred-eighty words.

There is also a Prologue, "better ~~Grading~~ Learning," which I felt was a brief but necessary nod to Project 180's roots: grading, which is, indeed, where it all began, but, as you will see in the pages that follow, Project 180 became about more—*so much more*—than grading.

To the Reader

I am honored to have you join me at this juncture of the 180 journey. And as we make our way through the pages ahead, I hope you find me a worthy guide, not in an instructive way but in an ignitive way. My humble hope is to inspire and ignite your own journey into better.

So, with that, let's go. Let's take 180 for a spin. Let's go find better together. It's there beyond the bend, where better begins.

Do. Reflect. Do Better.

Prologue

better ~~Grading~~ Learning

How can I create better learning experiences?

Really, this is where Project 180 began. Tired of playing the grade game, I wanted to find a way to make learning the focus in the classroom, not grading. So, I set off to find and chase better, which I thought meant better grading, but really it's been about finding better learning. However, before I share my learning discoveries from the 180 journey, let's first take a hike down the grading trail.

The Game of Grades

This, "The Game of Grades," I suppose, could be a book in itself–but only to be another "grading book" on the shelf. To be sure, much has already been explored, studied, and written on the topic of grading. So, with that in mind, it is not my intent to recite the literature in what is simply a prologue, but it *is* my intent to reveal some of my own experiences (which I suspect mirror many of your own) from playing the grading game over the course of my career.

Really, though, it began much earlier than that. It didn't begin when I stepped into the classroom as a teacher; it began when I entered the room and took my place at the table as a student. I "learned" the game of grades long ago. *We all did.*

Of course, I didn't think it a game when I was a student. It was serious business. These things, these marks, were permanent record. *This will go on your transcript*–as if that said it all, and to "serious it up" even more, they kept it under lock and key in a special room. *The transcript.* And the longer we played the game, the more serious it got, because when we got to high school, they fronted it with "permanent." *This will go on your permanent record.* Serious business.

And it was. So serious that many–too many–came to be permanently "fixed" with a label long before they got to the "permanent realm" of high school. But that just seemed a natural part of the game: labeling and sorting. And we learned to play our roles: smart, dumb, or average. And if ever we strayed, we regularly got a report card to remind us of our place in the grading game.

Okay, I am being a bit flip I suppose, but I think this was the sad reality for far too many of us as we learned the rules of school. Teachers were there to label us. And we were there to live the labels. And we, all of us–students, parents, society–generally accepted that the system was simply playing by the rules. After all, it was their game, and no one knew the rules better than they.

And then, in the fall of '96, I entered the classroom and found myself sitting on the other side of the table as the teacher–the grader, not the graded. And I discovered that I really had no idea what I was doing. Of course, I didn't let anyone know that. Seems no one did as I look back. We just assumed everyone else knew what they were doing, and so, we just let everyone else assume the same of us. And alone in our assumptions, we essentially ended up doing what everyone else was doing: grading the way we were graded. And the game of grades continued.

For my part, I tried to remember the rules. Assignments had points. *How many?* Tests had more points. *How many more?* Late work had to be penalized. *So many ways to punish. Sadly, I tried them all.* Grades were earned not given. *I had to be objective.* Retakes were not valid. *They had already seen the test.* Any content covered was fair game on tests. *Even the brief mentions I made from the lecture. They should have been listening.* Final grades could not be changed. *The integrity of the system was at stake*. Extra credit was a gift. *Sometimes, maybe, I could be subjective*.

And with that, I became every teacher I ever had as I tried to remember the rules, and when I couldn't or when things didn't work, I kept it to myself. I didn't want to be the one who didn't know the most fundamental, the most impactful part of the job: grading. And so, I played the game. We all did, I suppose. *Until*. Until, we didn't.

At some point, I think we all reached a point of reckoning with the rules, mostly because we discovered there are no rules. We discovered that the game is largely made up, that no one really taught us how to grade. Most of us had a three-credit "assessment" course in our training, from which we learned little to nothing about grading. So, then, when did we learn to grade? We didn't. And in this reckoning, many came to crisis as they discovered they had been complicit in keeping education's dark little secret: grading is a game.

That is not to say that we haven't done our best to do right by kids. We have. And it is that consideration, "right by kids," that likely led us to question grades in the first place. Something wasn't right, so we started to identify what was wrong, and we started to make changes to our practice. At first, quietly. We still, I think, wondered and worried about offending the Gods of Grading, so we kept it to ourselves. But, in that "keeping" we continued to be complicit on some level. *Please* know that I am not blaming teachers. I acknowledge there is real fear in our bucking the system, in our challenging the status quo. But there is also real guilt in not rectifying the wrong, so we get caught; we get stuck. We want to change. And I think we even know how. But I think we get trapped into believing that we can't. But we can. And we should. And when we know others are not only facing the same fears but also rewriting the old rules, we begin to learn it's okay. We can change.

I call it daring different and braving better. Different has to be a dare. I think we all hold a *different*–a crazy, unconventional idea, that we dare not share, and not because we don't regard it as right, but rather because we worry it might be wrong. But we have to dare our "differents." In most cases, it comes from a good place–doing right by kids. And from that conviction comes our courage, our call to brave better. It's a simple formula, really. We have a different to try. And it's *a lot different.* But it comes from a kid-centered place. And when we come from *that* place, we have to brave our better. However, we are not talking about a reckless rush into the arena. We are talking about "better" (a reasoned reflection), and the worst that can happen when we brave our betters is our next better.

Five years ago, when I started Project 180, it began as a reckoning of the rules, a challenge to that which had to be reconciled in my own practice: grading. I had reached a place where it was game over, a place where I had no choice but to dare different and brave better. So, I did.

Year One

THE YEAR OF THE A

At this point, I still had a sword in my hand. I thought I had to take a bold step into the arena, and so I decided to give all my kids an A for the year. I wanted to call attention to grading and its impact on learning. I wanted to "knock the sloth on his ass." I was convinced that if I was ever going to get to learning, I had to get past grading, which had become Cerberus, the three-headed dog, guarding the gates of my hell.

I have to face 20 years of doubt and misgivings about my own grading practices. I can no longer ignore the haunt of those ghosts.

180°8.26.2016

Of course, no one enters the arena without fear. And I suppose I was afraid. I was exposed. Well, I would be exposed–in ways that I never had before. Grades are a rather private matter among teachers (we don't want to be the one who's playing the game wrong). And now, not only would the matter be more public, it would also be more open to scrutiny, and with such a move as this, many would call me wrong. I would be upside down. But I wouldn't be unprepared. And part of that preparation was reflecting on and discovering my why. Why was I doing this? I didn't yet fully know or understand the what and how (I would learn), but I did understand the why. And of all the "why's" I held in my hand at that time, this was perhaps the most important. *"I have to face 20 years of doubt and misgivings about my own grading practices. I can no longer ignore the haunt of those ghosts."* Why? I no longer had a choice. I had to.

PROJECT 180: WHY?
AUGUST 26, 2016

Morning, all. Project 180 will officially get underway in less than a week. And while I am excited about this new adventure, I would be less than honest if I didn't also share that I am scared. And that anxiety makes me live in my head, thinking a lot about the possibilities of success and failure, especially failure. Of late, I have been thinking quite a bit about the number of conversations that I will likely be engaged in as others ask me about what I am doing, and why I am doing it. Here are some of my rehearsed responses as to the why, in no particular order. Thought I would share.

I want to learn.
I want to see if kids will learn without traditional grades.
I want to see if kids can learn better without traditional grades.
I want to challenge conventional thinking.
I want to challenge the status quo.

I want the focus in my classroom to be learning, not grading.
I got tired of playing the grade game.
I want to call attention to the absence of any real foundation for traditional grading practices.
I want to expose the incredible amount of autonomy that teachers have over their grading practices.
Am I not entitled to the same autonomy as every other teacher?
I believe education has to change.
I believe true motivation is intrinsic.
I think learning is a process, a long process in which different learners arrive at different stages at different times, and our traditional practices don't honor this. In fact, I think our traditional practices unwittingly punish this.
I believe students must take ownership of their learning, and I believe this happens through commitment, not compliance.
I have to face 20 years of doubt and misgivings about my own grading practices. I can no longer ignore the haunt of those ghosts.
I want to grow.

Happy Friday.

360°2021

Five years later, I have discovered that my why's haven't really changed–or settled me. Yes, my what's and how's have changed consistently–and necessarily–as I have learned, but my why's have remained at the center of my cycle in the 180 process of doing, reflecting, and doing better. And so, as you chase your own better, I believe it is key to know your "why's." Write them down. Have them in hand when others seek to critique the better you are chasing. It disarms people when they discover that we are not wandering on a whim. We are chasing better, and that means we know our "why"–deeply–as we seek to discover better "what's" and "how's" in our work. Above I suggested that facing 20 years of misgivings about my own grading practices may have been my most important "why," but now see I was wrong. "I want to grow." That was and is my most important. Let that be your "why," too. So, when people ask about the better you're braving, you can paint them a picture. *I want to grow.*

better Builder

In my room, why do I do what I do?

____

____

____

____

____

I hope I can find the courage to continue when the road gets rough.

180°8.31.2016

I've never begun a year more anxiously. A bit of a Nervous Ned anyway, my nerves were at their "Nediest" as I stood at my door with a gallon-sized Ziploc bag full of wooden A's to hand my kids. Already an awkward moment (greeting kids on day one), it was made all the more awkward when I pushed a handcrafted wooden letter, without explanation, into the hand of each kid.

Each passing face became a study. Did they smile? Did they frown? Was that a smirk? She looked confused. He just rolled his eyes. They think I am crazy.

And for a very real moment, I wondered if I had gone too far. I hadn't even told them what the A's meant—*would mean*—for our journey ahead, and already I was dancing with doubt on the very first step. But it was that first, novel step that I had to take, and I knew it. It's why I made the A's. And now that the kids had them in hand, I couldn't turn back. Day one of year one had begun.

GIVING AN A: PROJECT 180, DAY ONE
AUGUST 31, 2016

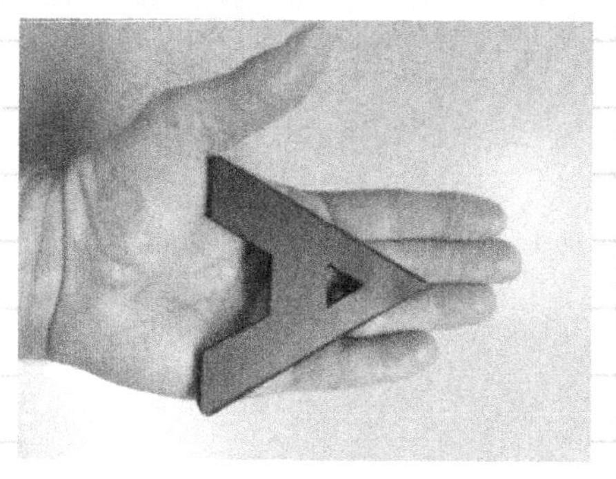

Well, probably too late to back out now. After months of thinking, writing, and talking about it, it's finally here. And while I am crazy excited to embark on this journey, I am also quite anxious as I now prepare myself to take the first step a few short hours from now. Ready or not, Project 180 is underway.

Today, I will begin the school year by giving my students an A…for the entire year. Out of desire to create something both tangible and novel, I spent a good many hours crafting 120 A's out of wood, and as my kids enter the realm of room 211 today, I will hand them what I hope comes to represent a path, a way to changing and bettering teaching and learning in American public education. Of course, as I pause on this precarious perch before taking flight into places unfamiliar, I am both thrilled and terrified by the possibilities. It is possible that I will succeed. It is just as possible that I will fail. Fortunately, my drive to succeed holds sway over my fear to fail. For now. But the two will no doubt clash time and again as the power of each rises and diminishes over the coming months, testing my conviction and fortitude. And only when the dust settles two years hence, will I see what has come. Right now, two years seems a lifetime. I hope I can find the courage to continue when the road gets rough. I hope.

Yep, too late to turn back. So, then, I will embrace the journey. Might as well. It's gonna be a long haul.

```
Happy new school year, all. Thanks for
joining me. I will need you.
```

360°2021

In many ways that fearful year remains one of the most consequential of my career. I was afraid, and so I had to be brave. That isn't intended as braggadocio. I purposefully set myself up to face failure so I would have no choice but to find success. As I mentioned previously, my "why" dwelt deeply in the well of my being. I wanted to grow. I had to grow. But to do so, I had to step away from all that I had known–for we grow not in comfort. And at that moment, I was not poised to take a little step into the unknown. I was prepared to take a giant leap. So I did.

Should you do the same? Should you make such a bold move? I don't know. I don't know your answers. But I do know that when we carry our "why's" with us, *better* answers.

Of course, it answers in myriad ways. But, regardless the response (success or failure), it always presents the possibility of growth, even when we find ourselves dancing with doubt.

better Builder

In my room, what "leap(s)" am I ready to make?

____

____

____

____

____

*In truth, I gave you nothing, but I did that,
young traveler, to give you everything.*

180°9.1.2016

I followed one letter with another letter. I wanted to make sure I formally and intentionally introduced my plan, so I carefully crafted and nervously narrated a letter to my students. I wanted them to understand what the A meant, as well as what it didn't mean. I had, in truth–literal truth–handed them their grade for the year, but I had also, in truth, handed them nothing but a symbol, for which the 180 days ahead would determine its meaning, its value. Each kid would get an A for the year, that was certain, that was cast in stone. What wasn't certain, however, was whether each kid would learn, and I wanted them to understand that that was up to them, which really became the focus of our work for year one: learning without grading. Curious–cat curious–I asked the kids to share their immediate, initial reactions to their A's on a notecard, which you will see in the post below, and you will also see that my curiosity didn't kill me. The kids were generally open to the proposed journey.

A'S DELIVERED AND ACCEPTED: PROJECT 180

DAY TWO

SEPTEMBER 1, 2016

Nervous. Surprisingly more nervous than I expected to be, but standing on a path with no return, I read with shaky voice and short breath, the letter below to introduce Project 180 to my kids yesterday.

Dear Learners:

Welcome to Honors English 10. I am beyond

excited to begin and share this journey with you. And while I am not certain about all that we will encounter and experience along our way–or even where we will land at our journey's end, I am certain that it will be unlike anything we have experienced in the past.

As you entered the room today, I handed you a wooden letter A. It is my gift to you. It is your grade for the year. No, I did not misspeak, I am giving you an A…for the entire year. It is yours to keep. I will not take it back. Promise. Cross my heart.

But, my young adventurers, take heed. For, after all, what I handed you is just what it appears to be: a wooden letter A. It is nothing. Oh, don't worry. I am not going back on my promise. I will type the A into your transcript at the end of each semester, but even that is merely a digital character, a mark on a screen. It, too, in reality, is nothing. So, before you sit back and relax with your gift and chalk me up as your "best teacher ever," consider the following.

In truth, I gave you nothing, but I did

that, young traveler, to give you everything. When I handed that A to you as you came aboard today, I really gave you ownership. I gave you the keys to your learning. I gave you choice; I gave you freedom. I gave you responsibility. And that is the essence. In the end, young friend, you are responsible for your learning. I cannot give it to you. In this arrangement that we find ourselves, I am responsible for providing opportunity and support, and I can and will give that freely and abundantly, but I am not responsible for your learning. You are. This reflects, then, the terms of our agreement for our journey.

So, we set out. 180 days from now we will set anchor in some unknown harbor. But before we set sail, pick up your A. Look at it. Feel it. Right now it is an empty gesture, a simple symbol. It won't mean anything until you give it meaning. Months from now, as we look back on the calm and storm of our journey, and you hold this symbol in your hand, what will it mean then? I can't wait to hear about your discovery. Thanks for letting me join you. I am honored.

Welcome aboard,
Syrie

Fortunately, my nerves got better with each delivery, but the first one was a doozy, as I had no idea how a new batch of learners would respond to such a radical departure from tradition. The initial response each period was suspicious silence, as I went on to explain that it was not a joke, that I was serious, that I was-hand on heart-giving them an A for the year. Still, desiring to know more, I asked each to react to the A on a note card, beseeching them to be honest. In addition, I asked them to share on the other side of the card what they wanted me to know and understand about them as learners. In general, the most common response communicated the relief they felt from the pressure of grades. I selected a range of specific responses from each class to share with you.

"I think it is a great way to make people realize how important learning really is"

"The A sounds like a great idea for students who want to learn; sadly, there will be those students who take advantage of it."

"Because of the A, I feel like I have more freedom to learn the way I need to and not the way the school wants me to."

"I really have no idea how I feel about this A. It seems cool, but my initial reaction is 'What is this?' I was always taught that nothing is free, so it worries me."

"I love this idea! I think it's very bold and I hope it works for you and me. I really hope, however, it does not at any point give me an excuse to slack, so I am going to have to work hard at that."

"I think that this is a little daring, but either way, you'll have kids that goof off and kids that work no matter what."

"Not stressed."

"I love it. I appreciate you giving us a chance to learn calmly without stressing about grades. I will most likely do a better job on the work because I won't be scared to make mistakes."

"I am excited because it's a new innovative approach to learning, and I want to see where it goes."

"I am split on the decision. It 'll help my test stress, but I am worried I won't push myself hard enough , and next year I will be unprepared."

"My reaction at first was kind of like 'Yes! don't have to do anything,' but it's kinda like being able to control your own learning."

"Shocked. Surprised. A little suspicious."

"I was relieved, but it made me want to work harder because I haven't really earned it yet."

"Where's my A+? Also, my dad's going to be confused."

In general, this represents my kids' reactions to their A's. At the moment, I am feeling good about it, but we have a long way to go, and I have a lot "proving" to do. I expected my inbox to be full of parent emails this morning, but so far no calls to have me fired. My next anxious moment will be at open house next week when I meet parents in person. I just hope they are able to place their faith in me. I just hope they are willing to give me a chance.

So, day one's done. A's delivered and generally accepted. I told the kids yesterday that they did not need to keep their wooden A's, that they could leave them on their desks if they did not want them. Three students left A's behind. And that's fine. No harm. No foul. After all, they're just silly symbols, empty gestures-nothing.

Happy Thursday, all.

360°2021

Five years later, though I am no longer literally handing kids nothing in the form of wooden letters, I am still, in practice, devaluing the place of grades in the learning environment. I still believe (I still communicate to kids) that I can give them grades, but I cannot give them their learning.

We often hear it expressed as "the teacher gave me (insert grade)," as if there was nothing to be done about it, as if, indeed, grades are given. But that's a student view. Teachers, many anyway, would likely suggest that grades are earned, not given. So, who's right? Both. Neither. Either. It depends, I suppose, on the rules of the game being played in our rooms.

For my room, then—and now—the rule remains: I can give you a grade. I cannot give you your learning. And this simple premise has guided me on my journey of many paths, which have led to one sacredly held certainty in the 180 classroom: Kids must be the caretakers of their learning. The ways have changed, but the goal has remained.

better Builder

In my room, what are the rules for grading?

____

____

____

____

____

I no longer have the power of grades to wield and wave in front of my kids.

180°9.15.2016

I lost power. But, I gained greater clarity, which led me to one of the first and biggest revelations from the Project: Without grades, I had little power. Of course, I knew (at least on some level) that grades were used to control kids before beginning the Project. I had certainly used them as such previously, but now (only ten days in), I truly came to know and understand that power when "the lights went out"...well, really when the light came on.

Influence is greater than power. With grades gone and the power vacuum that followed, I was forced to turn to that which I had discovered long ago but heretofore had never used like I would have to now: relationships. *Influence.* I would have to use my connections with kids to foster their commitment. I would no longer be able to use grades to force their compliance.

I cannot overstate the importance of this early aha in the project. My influence, made manifest by my connections with kids, became everything along the way. And *everything* it still remains.

PROGRESS REPORT: PROJECT 180, DAY 11
SEPTEMBER 15, 2016

Ten days behind us. Here are three "from-the-inside-looking-out" thoughts on the progress of Project 180.

Influence is greater than power. I no longer have the power of grades to wield and wave in front of my kids. In many classrooms, either directly or indirectly, grades are used to motivate students academically and control them behaviorally. I no longer brandish that sword. I am armed only with the connections I have made with my students and the culture I have created with them. Throughout my day, I often find myself wishing for witnesses (outsiders looking in) to observe our learning community, to see that kids can and will perform academically and manage themselves behaviorally in the absence of traditional grades. But it doesn't happen by accident. It comes down to what it's always come down to-with or without grades. Relationships. Establish this and all else will follow.

Kids will do work-hard work-that is not for points. I have more "complete" practice in my grade book at this time of the year than I ever did in the past. Granted, the kids still know that I report completed practice to parents and that may play a part in their motivation; additionally, they may still not trust that they have the freedom to not do the work if they choose, so they still do it, either out of habit or fear. Either way, at present they are doing the work I give them. Yesterday, they diligently dove into their writing and reading stories not only working hard but also worrying about the outcome, seemingly intent on creating quality, not just doing it to get done. Fingers-crossed, with a knock on wood, I believe I'm on my way to bucking the belief that kids won't work without grades. Perhaps worth noting, my seniors, with whom I still maintain a traditional grading approach, have far more missing assignments than my sophomores with gifted A's. Of course, there are a lot of factors to consider and it is not a direct comparison, but I am getting more out of my sophomores, much more-without grades to motivate them. Just sayin'.

Stressed brains aren't our best brains. There's certainly a research base out there to support that stress impairs learning. But I don't really need science to back up what I already know. We should not use stress to force kids into compliance, to create a fear of failure if we want them to learn best. That is not to say that all stress is bad. Performance anxiety presents itself even to the most prepared. It's normal. But that stress is generally born out of one's desire to do his or her best. Yesterday, there was indeed a measure of stress around the room as kids attempted to make a first impression on me with their writing. As the end of the period approached, stress was on the rise as it became evident that not all were going to finish. So, I stepped in, pushing the "pressure-release valve," and promised more time. Why wouldn't I? This is important. I want them to make their best attempt at the challenges I place in front of them. And, if and when I can give more time, I most certainly will. Teaching is not only about challenging kids; it's also about supporting them. Real challenges require support.

Support alleviates stress. Less stress equals better learning. Another worthy note, I asked the kids how they thought things were going with the approach, and the number one response was less stress-in and out of class. Music to my ears. Truly.

Overall, I am very pleased with the progress of the project. Thank you for the support. Knowing you are watching-even if from a distance-helps me sustain the necessary strength to manage the self-inflicted stress from this mad journey. Thank you. Happy Thursday.

360°2021

I'm still without power. Off the grid, so to speak. I am no longer tethered by the lines of the industry's power source: grading. I am tapped into a power more pure: learning. And that source wells from the place where I meet each of my kids, where I connect with them, where the energy of authenticity buzzes to life from the feedback/response cycle of our work (about which I will write more extensively later in the book). For now, suffice to say, this discovery (influence over power) remained and continues to be at the center of the Project 180 classroom.

Kids are still working for learning, not for points. No points for practice, only better from practice. I will discuss the evolution of the "what" and "how" of practice as we make our way through the years of the project, but the "why" remained largely unchanged for the duration of the journey: authentic learning is a choice, a commitment.

I want kids to work because they find value in the work for *learning*, not in points for *grading*.

better Builder

In my room, do I teach from a position of power or influence?

____

____

____

____

____

Trust me, it breaks my heart to not see it fully through, but I believe, in the end, I am making the best decision for my kids...

180°1.23.2017

Of all that I expected from the journey, I did not expect heartbreak. But by the time I had reached the midpoint of year one, despite my vow to never return, I found myself in a place where I needed to compromise my convictions, where I needed to correct our course. In short, I offered a return to those who chose. In truth, I was scared as hell, for I worried I would be abandoned so far from home, and that would break my spirit, break my heart.

But I believed I had no choice. It, afterall, had become much to ask of kids who were so accustomed to the traditional approach. For many, the approach had been liberating, and they had discovered something about learning and themselves. But for others, there had been little discovery, and they longed (not sure that's really the right word) for a return to the familiar. So, I offered a path back for the next semester. For those families who chose, I would provide a more traditional approach to see them through the year.

COURSE CORRECTION: PROJECT 180, DAY 83
JANUARY 23, 2017

A little heavy-hearted this morning. After too much deliberation, I have decided to make some midpoint adjustments to Project 180. And though I know I will no doubt disappoint some that I was unable to continue the good fight or "soldier on," I am not giving up; I am not quitting. I am adjusting. Trust me, it breaks my heart to not see it fully through, but I believe, in the end, I am making the best decision for my kids, for I am giving them the option to find success in the way that works best for them, even at the cost of compromising my principles.

Here is the letter that I will send home today with my kids.

Dear Parents/Guardians,

We live. We learn. After much consideration and reflection on my current approach to grading, I have decided to provide an option for those who desire it. It was not a decision lightly made, for I earnestly believe in what I am doing, but I also acknowledge that, for some, Project 180 has not provided the necessary motivation for them to grow and succeed. In the end, I want all kids to grow, and if some need a return to tradition for that to happen, then I am willing to make adjustments to my approach.

But that's not as simple as it seems. First and foremost, I made a promise. I promised all my kids that I would give them an A, no matter what, and while I am not necessarily going back on my word, for that offer still stands, I do feel like my sincere sentiments then are shallow sentiments now. And that will take me some time to reconcile-with the kids and with myself. Second, I will now have to juggle two different approaches, which is fine, but it will take more time and effort. But if that's what's required, then it's time and effort well spent. Third, I am compromising my convictions. I really do believe that we must and can do education better. I do not believe that we should maintain the status quo because of its familiarity. And while it does not sit comfortably with my spirit, my convictions are ultimately secondary to the primary concern: supporting kids. All kids.

And so, I offer a choice, a choice that needs to be a family decision. In that regard, I hope this is something that you and your child consider carefully. I would hope that it would be an opportunity for your child to reflect back on his/her performance this past semester, letting that somewhat guide the decision moving forward. As many know, the Project 180 approach has been successful. Many of your children have taken ownership and responsibility for their learning through the 180 opportunity, and I hope in earnest that you allow them to continue to be successful as they continue down this path. But ultimately the choice is yours. For those who choose to return to tradition, I completely understand, and I welcome your decision. Again, if it will help your child grow, then that's all that really matters. Truly.

Thank you for your time and attention with this matter. Thank you, too, for allowing me to live, learn, and grow. If you have any questions, please email me.

____ We would like to continue with the Project 180 grading approach for spring semester.

____ We would like to change to a traditional grading approach for spring semester.

Student Name (print):

____

Student Signature:

____

Parent/Guardian Signature:

____

Please return by Monday, January 30, 2017

Gotta admit, I am feeling a wee lost at this juncture in the journey, but I'll get back on track. In moments like this, I have to trust my compass: kids. The dial directed me here, and I am going to trust its direction. I am sorry for disappointing any of my faithful. I hope you find some sense in my decision. I will continue to fight and soldier on for what I-we-believe in; the front line has just shifted a bit. Turns out to be a battle with many fronts. The journey continues.

Happy Monday, all.

360°2021

Looking back (and as you will soon see, ahead), it was an important moment in the project's history; it was also an important moment in my own development, for I had chosen choice.

We talk a lot about offering kids choice and its impact on the authenticity of experience, but we talk less about the impact of our choosing to offer choice. There's a commitment. We have to let go. We have to trust. We have to honor. We have to be true.

Here I was at risk of my entire journey coming to an end. I am not sure what I would have done had the vast majority of my kids chosen the traditional trail (spoiler, they didn't), but if they had...well, I likely would have seen the light and taken them home. It *was* a risk. All choices invite risk, even the choice to give choices.

Consequently, this moment stuck with me, and choice (voice) has become a ritual risk in the Project 180 classroom. It has become the necessary by-product of escaping compliance and embracing commitment.

better Builder

In my room, what does choice look like?

____

____

____

____

____

In an odd, rather unexpected sorta way, I am at peace.

180º1.24.2017

By the next day, better had begun, and I found myself unexpectedly at peace with the decision I had made to offer an option to my kids. Of course, it also helped that many of the project's followers chimed in with their support, and I discovered that though I was, indeed, a "wee lost," all was not lost, and I was not alone. My supporters had not abandoned me, and in my initial interactions with kids, I was discovering that they, too, would likely and largely remain. My broken heart would mend more quickly than I imagined, and what had seemed a terrible defeat the day before, had now begun to materialize as an important moment for all of us to pause and ponder our place in the project.

It created conversations between the kids and me–real conversations, honest conversations. And, as well, it generated conversations at home. The "decision" it seemed would ultimately do more good than harm, for it invited introspection and reflection as each kid, as each family, came to consider what course would benefit them most.

SPIRIT INTACT: PROJECT 180, DAY 84
JANUARY 24, 2017

Morning, all. Thank you for all the check-ins, well-wishes, and words of support yesterday. It always means the world to me to know that you're "there." Truly. It's nice to know that so many have tuned in to the project. It's nice to know that so many care about the progress of the journey. But, of all, it's nicer to know that so many simply care about me. Thank you. And to put your minds at ease, I am fine. Really, I am great. In an odd, rather unexpected sorta way, I am at peace. And I think that's because I trusted my gut, I listened to my heart, and I followed my compass. I made a "kid decision."

And while it will be a week before I know and subsequently share the decisions of my kids and their families, some interesting conversations have already begun with my kids. Here are a few from yesterday. Names changed.

#1
John: Hey, Sy. Can I get my portfolio?
Me: Sure. What's up?
John: I want to show it to my dad. I want to show him what I have done, how I have grown. I wanna stay with 180.
Me: He wants to go traditional?
John: Yeah. He doesn't think I am doing anything.
Me: Okay. Well, make your case, kiddo. If he wants any input from me, have him or mom email me, and I will support you.

#2
Layla: Sy, whatcha think I should do?
Me: Lay, I think you are in a perfect position to continue with 180. It would

break my heart, if you went the traditional route. You have taken full responsibility and ownership of your learning. You're a poster child for 180, girl.
Layla: You really think so?
Me: Absolutely. I am so proud of all that you have accomplished so far this year. Can't quit now.
Layla: Okay, Sy. I got you.

#3
Michael: (leaning on the edge of my desk, Gary standing beside) Sy, I wanna stay with 180. I know. I know. I have kinda screwed up this semester. I started off well, but then I got lazy. But I can do this.
Me: You think you can reload and make it happen?
Michael: For sure.
Me: How will the conversation go at home? Can you convince your folks to stay with 180?
Michael: Oh, yeah.
Me: So you're going to own this?
Michael: Yep.
Gary: (jumping in) Me, too. I messed up. I got lazy, and it kinda became a habit.

Michael: (interrupting) And we're gonna be

like this, spreading his fingers apart.
Me: You're not gonna sit together?
Michael and Gary: Nah. (chuckling) We can't sit together, Sy.
Me: Huh, ya think? Okay, boys. Let's see if you can redeem yourselves.
And by the end of the day, I was feeling okay. I didn't find the decision a smudge on the project. I found it to be what it was intended to be: another option for kids. And my spirit can live with that. Journey on!

Happy Tuesday, all.

Again, thank you for being there. Really.

360°2021

Turns out, this moment was more momentous than I had imagined, for I found the compass, a symbol which would come to present a number of pivotal points in the project, paths of possibility for correcting course. It gave me the courage and confidence to change direction, which I have done numerous times for various reasons (as you will see) over the course of the five-year journey. And that's the burden of better. It's not easy to break new trail all the time. But it's also the beauty of better, for I have had the opportunity to view many vistas in my explorations, to make many discoveries in my days. And at this particular juncture in the journey, I had discovered the magic of a magnetic pull: kids.

And this opened up a whole new territory to be explored as I came to distance myself from conventional compass points (set to the status quo) and explore more broadly and search more diligently for the elements which would create better learning experiences for kids.

I had found my compass of courage.

better Builder

In my room, what helps me find my way when I get lost?

____

____

____

____

____

And while I am pleased with this result,
it gives me pause as I wonder what it really means.

180°2.1.2017

The numbers were in. The project would proceed as planned (with a few exceptions). And I *was* pleased, but not satisfied–well, not settled, and not by the few, the two, who chose to return to tradition. I was somewhat unsettled by not knowing or understanding fully the reasons for why the majority elected to stay. Yes, they had indicated their preference as requested, but I did not know the rationale for their reason. In retrospect, I wish I had asked for an explanation. I am not sure why I didn't. *Maybe I was afraid.* But regardless the reason, I wanted to know what it meant at that moment, so I surmised some possible purposes on my own (as you will read in the post).

Of course, what I did know, fortunately, was why my two decided to return to tradition, for they felt compelled to explain, which wasn't required but certainly appreciated.

Interestingly, some of my more vocal critics of 180 chose to stay with the A. And this, too, perplexed–and even hurt–me some. And the hurt had just begun.

MAKING SENSE: PROJECT 180, DAY 89
FEBRUARY 1, 2017

With all but five returned, 81 of the 83 (97%) in so far have elected to stay with the 180 option. And while I am pleased with this result, it gives me pause as I wonder what it really means. Here are some initial thoughts as I continue to process the outcome.

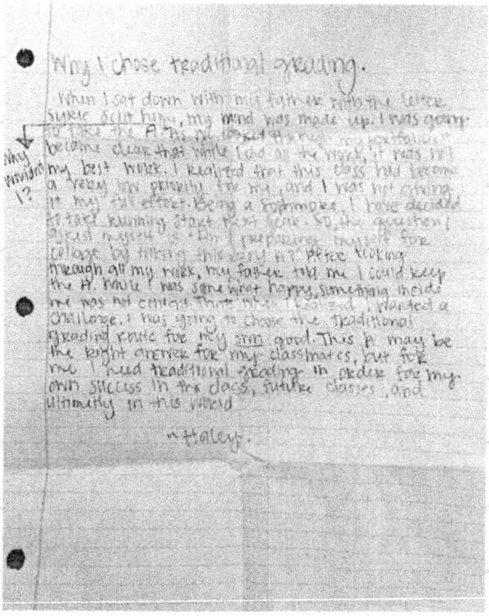

It was the path of least resistance. It's become the "new familiar," so folks stayed. I get it.

It's a "free" A. Regardless of one's feelings about 180, an A on a transcript looks better than a C. But nothing is free. One parent brought the word "nothing" into play with her comment at the bottom of a returned letter. In short, she made it clear that they were NOT in support of 180, that my approach had given her son the green light to do nothing, and that reality would be on my shoulders, my conscience. My response to her is below (name changed).

Good afternoon. Thank you for returning the parent letter indicating your preference for the approach I take with grading Justin. Thank you, too, for your frank feedback regarding 180. When I gave the A to Justin at the beginning of the year, it was certainly not intended to be an invitation for him to do nothing. On the contrary, I had hoped that it would motivate him to take greater responsibility for his learning. Unfortunately, my grand plan has not worked for Justin as it has for others. And that is why, mid-year, I presented the option to return to tradition. That said, I think that if it would better motivate him, we should return to tradition. His doing nothing is not okay, and if that is his plan for the rest of the year, I do not think it's a wise choice on his part. I told him 4 months ago when I gave him the A, I was giving him nothing. It was up to him to make it something. So, of course the choice is yours, and it seems you have made it, but I wonder if we shouldn't reconsider for Justin's sake. Again, thank you for your candid comment.

Monte Syrie

So, it makes me wonder, then, about the motivation to stay with 180 in this case. If it is the cause of "nothing," then why continue? Is it because they know he would not likely earn an "A" with a traditional approach? Is the grade more important than the learning? Is this representative of what the system has done to condition students, parents, and society to place too much emphasis on grades instead of learning? How many others made the choice for the same reason? One wonders. It is of particular interest to me that all my most-vocal critics stayed with 180. Hmmm.

The 180 approach has reduced stress. I have a hunch that for some families this was a key factor in their decision. And this makes me happy for that is certainly something I sought to achieve. Stressed brains cannot learn.

The 180 approach is working. I am certainly

not suggesting that is working for all, but it is for many. I hope at least that this was a factor in some of the decisions.

I may have been duped. It's likely that a small handful of returned letters had forged or not fully-informed signatures. It's what it is.

Okay, but what about the two who opted to return to tradition? What was their motivation?

Student #1: He needed the extra challenge of tradition. Mom and I had several face-to-face conversations about Jason's (name changed) experiences in my class and their family's breakfast-and-dinner-table discussions about character, learning, and the future, and for them, a return to tradition made the most sense. And so, after reassuring me that she believed in what I was trying to do with 180, she informed me that tradition was the better choice for them. I am happy to oblige. I love that they did not take this situation lightly. I love that they had deep, sustained conversations about learning. Love it.

Student #2: I will let Haley's letter speak for itself (see above). I am so proud of her for taking charge of her learning, for making the choice that was best for her, and I am pleased to provide a culture of possibility that allows for such a choice. Choice is commitment. I have no doubt that Haley is committed. I hope those who elected to stay with 180 are as committed as she. So proud of this young lady.

Happy February, all. Come on spring!

360°2021

I am not sure, now, if I ever made certain sense of this moment in the project. At the time, I didn't see selection as validation. I was skeptical (as is hopefully noted in the post) about what it meant. And while the skepticism was a familiar feeling, not completely unlike the feeling from traditional grading (and what it really meant for their learning), it was different. It felt different. Yes, I was unsettled, but I was not undone (that place where I had found myself with traditional grading). This *was* different. And I think this is why.

It was something that I did *with* kids, not *to* kids. Previously, with traditional grading, I always imagined kids felt like grades were something I did to them, not with them. And I always felt an apathetic acceptance–*there was nothing I could do*. But *this* was something I had done with kids. Of course, I would never really know their reasons, but I would always remember my reasons. We have to work *with* kids. It is with them we find our way.

better Builder

In my room, how can I work ***with*** *kids?*

____

____

____

____

____

And as I go about my days, I encounter those who do not see the thread, and I have to explain.

180°2.6.2017

What's a story without a little drama? And though it seems little now, it felt big then. The recent decision and discussion regarding the "traditional option" had opened the door to outside criticism to which I was compelled–even challenged, I suppose–to respond. So, I did. And in my doing, I tried to keep hold of what a few were trying to unravel: my thread.

Two anonymous people had posted critical, even insulting, comments to my blog. Of course, they're not visible to the public until I approve them as the site administrator. I could–maybe should–have elected to let them lie, ignoring the criticism, but the same critics–I believed–had accused me of approving and making public only positive comments, which was simply not true. So, I approved and responded to them in detail (as you will see).

At the time, I was still, if I'm honest–ripe for battle. My "sword" was still in hand, and I had a penchant for conflict, but fortunately I also saw the moment for what it could be, an opportunity to clarify my "why," my thread.

THE THREAD WE FOLLOW: PROJECT 180, DAY 92
FEBRUARY 6, 2017

There's a thread you follow. It goes among
things that change. But it doesn't change.
People wonder about what you are pursuing.
You have to explain about the thread.
But it is hard for others to see.
While you hold it you can't get lost.
Tragedies happen; people get hurt
or die; and you suffer and get old.
Nothing you do can stop time's unfolding.
You don't ever let go of the thread.
~William Stafford

There is a thread I follow, a thread I latched onto a long time ago, and while that thread has gone in and among things over the years, it has not changed, and I have not let go. Can't. Won't. I cling to it desperately as I make my way day to day in a world filled with the young whom I serve, pledging my best to help them on their own ways. And as I go about my days, I encounter those who do not see the thread, and I have to explain. This past Saturday, I encountered two who do not see the thread in my ways, so I have to explain. I must. The thread brought me to them; they, then, must serve a purpose in my journey. And so, I will explain.

Comment #1

"A looks better then a C??? bro are u serious? No kidding ? U expect 16 years olds to do work when u promise them an A ? How is a child supposed to learn anything when they don't have to care ? All you are is a stupid liberal. You clearly have no brain cells."

This comment was in response to my saying in the "Making Sense" post from last week that perhaps one reason some chose to remain with Project 180 is that it was a "free" A (I will speak to how free the A really is below). It was my attempt to provide an honest analysis of the results. As for, "How is a child supposed to learn anything when they don't have to care?" Well, it is troubling that we perpetuate a system where we have to give kids a reason to care beyond the opportunity to learn and build oneself. If we have to give them a reason to care, then do they really care? Is compliance really a better sign of caring than commitment? I am not convinced, so I push my kids to care for their own sake, not for the grade carrot that I dangle in front of them.

As for your final comment, I doubt I can get you to see my "liberal stupidity" any differently, so I won't try.

Comment #2

"I have been reading your blog with interest and skepticism. It sounds like this project is more for your benefit than that of your students. I am also surprised that a school would even allow a teacher to give an automatic A to every student in the class. You made it very clear that this was a project to see what the outcome would be, like a test of a teenager's mind, instead of actually teaching them. Maybe you did it to make it easier on YOU, so you wouldn't have to work so hard and give a test to see how good you actually taught them. You are angry at a student because he chose the A and now you want to start grading him? This is what YOU wrote: I told him 4 months ago when I gave him the A, I was giving him nothing. So if you are admitting to giving 'nothing', what makes that child interested in doing 'something'? He hasn't been given a guideline as to what you even expect if you are giving nothing. You as a teacher, are not doing this in the best interest of the student. You should be teaching them that hard works get the rewards, it doesn't happen automatically. And then to change it midstream? Really? How will you teach a class where some want a grade and some don't? What will the students with the automatic grade do while the others are being tested? In this life, there is no job, anywhere, where the boss says, I will give you a wage to come every day to work. You just decide what to do with your time, because I have nothing to tell you that I expect of you. That is ridiculous! You did not earn a teaching degree by winging it and the collage just passed you. You had to work hard to earn that degree! That is what you should be teaching these students. That is what they go to school for. Otherwise, they could stay home. You would not be needed. People pay taxes and expect their children go to school to learn."

Given the length of this comment and the variety of concerns raised, I will attempt to present my response in a point-by-point manner. Here goes.

"It sounds like this project is more for your benefit than that of your students… Maybe you did it to make it easier on YOU,

so you wouldn't have to work so hard and give a test to see how good you actually taught them." Easier on me? This has been by far my most challenging year of teaching in my 20 years of service. It has been incredibly difficult to step away from a traditional approach, where I could wield the power of grades to extrinsically motivate kids, trading it instead for mere influence to inspire kids to be intrinsically motivated. I have not taken the easy road, and I have not an easy destination.

"A test to see how good you actually taught them"? The Smarter Balanced Assessment is right around the corner, an assessment that all students must pass in Washington State to graduate, and while that is supposed to be a shared K-10 responsibility for all teachers with whom a child has come into contact, in reality, the finger gets pointed at he/she who stands at the end of the road. I am at the end of that road for my kids. We will see how well I have taught them then. Ironically, I was at school preparing a model introduction on a Sunday to help with a performance task when I read your comment. Sunday. Day off. At school. Typing in my coat because the heat is off. Easier on me indeed. The "test" is coming. And though sadly some will not pass, those who do will be the ones who have committed to learning. Each kid is leaving a trail behind him, a record of what they have done or not. At the end, those who do not pass probably will be the ones who have not left much of a trail.

"I am also surprised that a school would even allow a teacher to give an automatic A to every student in the class." So glad you raised this concern. Part of my motivation for doing Project 180 was to expose a dirty little secret in public education. I did 180 because I can. I say that not out of arrogance, but rather, I say it out of my own astonishment that there are no real checks and balances to a teacher's grading approach. In essence, we can do what we want. As a default, most teachers employ the traditional percentage-based approach, but they do that mostly because it's what was used with them. Teachers take a 3 credit course on assessment in college that deals very little with grading approaches. So, as a default, teachers employ the traditional percentage-based approach to grading. We use it because it exists. There is no evidence base to support its effectiveness. We cling to it for its familiarity, not its wisdom. Unconvinced that the approach truly fostered real learning in the classroom, I abandoned it. I got tired of playing the grade game. I may have swung the pendulum too far the other way, but it had been stuck for far too long on the other end. So, I took an extreme approach. I did it to get people talking. I wanted people-mostly my colleagues-to raise objections, so we could come to the table and have a serious discussion about grading practices, a discussion that is long overdue. Hopefully our exchange will nudge us closer to that reality.

"You are angry at a student because he chose the A and now you want to start grading him? This is what YOU wrote: I told him 4 months ago when I gave him the A, I was giving him nothing. So if you are admitting to giving 'nothing', what makes that child interested in doing 'something'? He hasn't been given a guideline as to what you even expect if you are giving nothing. You, as a teacher, are not doing this in the best interest of the student." At this point, I will offer that you are a parent of a student in my class.

That said, I will take you back to the first day of school this year where I sent two letters home. One to you. One to your child. I will let them speak for the nothing that you speak of in your comment. As for angry, I am not sure you know me very well. My post last week expressed my confusion and concern over a student and family opting to stay with something of which they were so critical, confusion and concern over not choosing what I thought would be a preferable option. I wonder how many other teachers out there are willing to provide personalized options?

(from the parent letter)Imagine, for a moment, that in my class you and your child will not have to play the grade game. You will already know the grade for the rest of the year, so now instead of asking about the grade, you can ask about the learning. And that is the essence: learning. An old teacher adage suggests that "grades are earned, not given," but that is simply not true in the vast majority of classrooms. Grades in many cases and in many ways are given, and so I am doing as most do, giving a grade-granted it's an A, but a grade is all I can give. I can't give learning.

Learning truly is earned. I really only provide the opportunity.

Dear Learners:
Welcome to Honors English 10. I am beyond excited to begin and share this journey with you. And while I am not certain about all that we will encounter and experience along our way-or even where we will land at our journey's end, I am certain that it will be unlike anything we have experienced in the past. As you entered the room today, I handed you a wooden letter A. It is my gift to you. It is your grade for the year. No, I did not misspeak, I am giving you an A…for the entire year. It is yours to keep. I will not take it back. Promise. Cross my heart.But, my young adventurers, take heed. For, after all, what I handed you is just what it appears to be: a wooden letter A. It is nothing. Oh, don't worry. I am not going back on my promise. I will type the A into your transcript at the end of each semester, but even that is merely a digital character, a mark on a screen. It, too, in reality, is nothing. So, before you sit back and relax with your gift and chalk me up as your "best teacher ever," consider the following.In truth, I gave you nothing, but I did that,

young traveler, to give you everything. When I handed that A to you as you came aboard today, I really gave you ownership. I gave you the keys to your learning. I gave you choice; I gave you freedom. I gave you responsibility. And that is the essence. In the end, young friend, you are responsible for your learning. I cannot give it to you. In this arrangement that we find ourselves, I am responsible for providing opportunity and support, and I can and will give that freely and abundantly, but I am not responsible for your learning. You are. This reflects, then, the terms of our agreement for our journey.So, we set out. 180 days from now we will set anchor in some unknown harbor. But before we set sail, pick up your A. Look at it. Feel it. Right now it is an empty gesture, a simple symbol. It won't mean anything until you give it meaning. Months from now, as we look back on the calm and storm of our journey, and you hold this symbol in your hand, what will it mean then? I can't wait to hear about your discovery. Thanks for letting me join you. I am honored. Welcome aboard.~Syrie

"How will you teach a class where some want a grade and some don't? What will the

students with the automatic grade do while the others are being tested?" Actually, rather easily. The content and teaching approach remains the same, regardless the choice for the grading approach. For the three who have opted for the traditional approach, I have met with them, and we have created a personalized grade book to help them keep track of their grades. The assignments will be the same, the assessments will be the same, the tests will be the same. The only difference is the grading preference.

"You should be teaching them that hard work gets the rewards, it doesn't happen automatically…In this life, there is no job, anywhere, where the boss says, I will give you a wage to come every day to work. You just decide what to do with your time, because I have nothing to tell you that I expect of you. That is ridiculous! You did not earn a teaching degree by winging it and the [collage] just passed you. You had to work hard to earn that degree! That is what you should be teaching these students. That is what they go to school for." Okay, I lumped this all into the "something-for-nothing" concern that you have raised. Of course, I hope that the letters above address this to some degree, but I will offer more. No thing is free. Nothing on the other hand is freely and cheaply given because it is…well, nothing. But the thing that I offer is an opportunity for kids to learn the value of commitment and responsibility, a thing that cannot be faked or copied from a peer's assignment, a thing that is not defined by some teacher's arbitrary approach to grading. As products of the public education system and the traditional-grading approach that comes with it, we have all played the grade game, sometimes getting A's for nothing learned, sometimes not getting the grade we think we deserved based on the subjectivity of the teacher. And in the end, as we look back, and if we are honest, and we take the "grade" out of the mix, we got out of school what we put into school, just as we have gotten out of life what we have put into life. I have not taken that important life lesson away from my kids. I have taken away the pretense that too often exists in their formative years. In reality, in my class, they can only get out of it what they put into it. For I only offer opportunity. And with that opportunity comes an abundance of support and encouragement. But I cannot do it for them. Isn't there a lesson in that? Yes, I worked very hard in college, but only because I pushed myself. In reality, the "real world" allows too many opportunities for us to skate along and take the easy road. I could have skated through college; I could skate through teaching, but I don't. I can't. I won't. And that is because I have learned to push myself, for myself. I cannot trace it back to a grade, but I can trace it back to the people who instilled self-worth in me. That is what I want for my kids. A real opportunity to discover their own power, real power, not the artificial, compliance-creating, short-term power that comes with grades.

"People pay taxes and expect their children to go to school to learn." Yep. And those people who pay taxes need to question-they have the duty to question-what is going on in our schools. As a taxpayer, you are doing your duty. But I hope that your questions continue. I hope that as you begin to take a more critical view of your child's education, you ask the same questions of all his teachers. I am on your radar because what I offer is different, because I make public-EVERY day-what goes on in my classroom. It's too bad that that which is familiar seldom comes across the screen, and it is accepted as fine because it's always been there, but I wonder what lurks beneath. I wonder if one dug what she would find.

2861 words later and sadly the thread is likely no more apparent than when I began. But it is there. I feel it. Always have. I am sorry that you cannot see it.

Happy Monday, all. Follow your thread.

360°2021

From here, the drama declined. I think we had a few more exchanges but they were as icky as insubstantive, so I let it lie, let it die. I had done what I could by explaining the thread, and she was going to see what she saw. I could not change that. It was time to move on. I had already given it more energy than it warranted. I had a thread to follow.

And I am still following it. It indeed goes "among things that change," even—especially—in the Project 180 classroom, where things are always changing as I am always chasing better. But it, the thread, the "why," never changes.

Earlier, in the first post, I talked about the importance of knowing our "why"—*deeply*—so when push came to shove, we could show others what we were following—our thread, even if they couldn't (or wouldn't) see it.

And that is what I discovered from this unfortunate but invaluable experience: the universe gave me a test, an opportunity to know and show my "why."

Daring different and braving better follow "why."

better Builder

In my room, how can I use criticism to help me grow?

____

____

____

____

____

If I do not see it through and continue along the present course, will I miss an opportunity to truly turn it upside down, to provide a better learning experience for my kids?

180°3.30.2017

A time for reckoning was approaching. Would I continue year two by giving kids an A, or would I present a different path? I didn't know. And by the end of March that first year, I was truly in a quandary. On one hand, I had removed grades from the experience and made learning the focus. *I had done what I set out to do.* On the other hand, I had leapt to an extreme end. *I had done what I set out to do.* But had I gone too far?

It was a time of doubt, but it was also a time of discovery. I was discovering that others were doing similar work, removing grades from their classrooms. And while I did find comfort in this, I also found consternation on the eve of my making a decision for year two. *Was I giving in? What had happened to the sword-wielding, system-smiting Sy who'd begun the journey?*

I didn't know. I was at a crossroads. Had it all been for nought? Was there a way ahead? I didn't know.

SCRATCHING MY HEAD: PROJECT 180, DAY 129
MARCH 30, 2017

"The research quite clearly shows that kids who are graded - and have been encouraged to try to improve their grades - tend to lose interest in the learning itself, avoid challenging tasks whenever possible (in order to maximize the chance of getting an A), and think less deeply than kids who aren't graded," Kohn explains. "The problem isn't with how we grade, nor is it limited to students who do especially well or poorly in school; it's inherent to grading.

"That's why the best teachers and schools replace grades (and grade-like reports) with narrative reports - qualitative accounts of student performance - or, better yet,

conferences with students and parents."
Cindy Long - neaToday

Already facing a tough decision, my coming across articles like the one above will not make it any easier. At present, I am leaning towards swinging the pendulum back to the center, employing a modified standards-based approach next year instead of going gradeless again. But then I read articles like this, especially with comments like the one above, and I pause. I wonder. Am I on to something here? If I do not see it through and continue along the present course, will I miss an opportunity to truly turn it upside down, to provide a better learning experience for my kids? I don't know. Questions lead to questions. Answers are elusive. Certainty hides. And I am consumed.

The next 51 days will reveal much. I will have some data to help me in my current quandary. I will have the SBA results. I will have formal feedback from the kids in the form of surveys and reflections. But I will also have my own reflections. And, I will also have my guts, my instincts, which I cannot discount for they helped lead me here in the first place. Admittedly, it has not been a place that all are willing to see or accept, for, in many ways, it runs counter to convention, it smacks of crazy. And I cannot suggest that it is neither conventional nor crazy. It is. But it is not exclusive. Others feel, practice, and share their crazy unconventionality, too. And I cannot ignore that. Can't. But for all the comfort it brings, it also brings trepidation as I work through the uncertainty of the path ahead. But I'll find my way. The journey continues. Always does.

360°2021

A moment of truth for a moment of truth. I was afraid. And though I had presented a genuine quandary, I was being a bit disingenuous, for I had made up my mind, I now believe, to abandon the A in year two. I just hadn't quite come to grips with having to make public that I had "lost the battle." Of course, though I think that's truly how I felt then (losing the battle, selling out, etc.), I now know that was my ego talking in the face of my fear and insecurity. I had rattled my saber, if you will, and now I would have to endure the walk of shame.

But that was really a bunch of self-imagined, melodramatic hooey. There would be no walk of shame, no sell out, no lost battle. I just didn't know it yet. My fear was having its moment at the mic. But reasoned reflection would soon follow, and as it turned out, so would better, for I now think this is where Do, Reflect, and Do Better were first born.

better Builder

In my room, how do I respond to my own fear and insecurity?

____

____

____

____

____

And though I knew that I would have to push the pendulum past center, I never expected to shove it clean to the other end.

180°5.2.2017

A month later, I was ready to reveal that I had made up my mind. I would not continue down the give-all-an-A path in year two. I would present an easier path to follow–for my students and my fellow educators. It *had* been a leap too far. And it wasn't too late to pull back and take a jump less-giant. I had found a bridge to better, which would allow others to join the journey.

The project had gotten some attention. A number were interested in what I was doing. But their interest was held in check by the extreme swing of the pendulum. And why wouldn't it be? Who'd want to experience and defend that end? I got it. I had lived it. So, I changed it. And that was enough to bring my grade-level team on board for year two of Project 180.

Along with my colleagues Jenna Tamura and Madeline Alderete, I would begin bringing the pendulum back to a "saner" center, where the focus would still be on learning, not grading.

My pendulum was at peace.

BACK TO CENTER: PROJECT 180, DAY 147
MAY 2, 2017

A year ago, I began scheming and dreaming. I wanted to make a bold move against tradition and convention in our public schools. I wanted to challenge the status quo, especially in the area of grading. So, I devised a bold plan. I wanted to challenge the perception that kids won't do, that kids can't learn without grades. In earnest, I believed differently, so I decided to take grades off the table. And though I knew that I would have to push the pendulum past center, I never expected to shove it clean to the other end.

My initial plan did not include giving everyone an A. It was a late development stemming from my learning that my plan of giving everyone a "pass" may prove problematic for college entrance and scholarship opportunities, so I went with plan B. I decided to take grades completely off the table by awarding an A to each student so as to make the focus learning, not simply earning. But I also sought to call attention to my approach by making a radical move, a move that I was certain would warrant strong opposition from my peers, opposition that would hopefully lead to a deep dialogue around grading practices and policies. However, astonishingly, that opposition never manifested as I thought it might. Not even a little bit. And I'm not sure why. I have my guesses of course, but I'm not certain that airing them will matter now anyhow, so I will let them lie. It's time to move forward. It's time, as I planned all along, to let the pendulum swing back to center.

Next year's plan for grading is currently under development. I have taken what I have learned thus far from the 146 days of 180 and begun to construct an approach that still bears the core principles of 180 but presents a far-less radical approach to rebuffing convention and tradition. Oh, there's still plenty of "rebel" in it-I'm still me, but it is not so crazy as not to discourage others from joining the journey. In fact I am honored to announce that the other sophomore LA teachers Jenna Tamura and Maddie Alderete have already signed on to creating a unified approach to grading for all tenth-grade language arts courses, regular and honors. I am so excited to collaborate with these exceptional educators. They have been staunch 180 supporters from the beginning and now they are jumping on board. I will reveal the plan over the coming weeks. The swing back to center has begun. Excited. Truly.

Happy Tuesday, all.

360°2021

And I was at peace. Right or wrong, I had settled on a plan for year two. But really, it was bigger than right or wrong, it was better. It was a reasoned reflection. I had done. I had reflected (extensively—maybe obsessively). And now, I would do better, until I again knew better. And then, I would do better, again. And that's really what Project 180 has become: an endless examination of present practice, a "reasoned reflection" to my next better.

Of course, this is my looking back on it through 20/20 eyes. I'm not going to suggest I had arrived at a clear understanding of the 180 cycle at that time, but I'm going to suggest that I had begun to understand "better" the "better battle," the journey within. It wasn't—it was never—about giving A's till the end of time as the answer to my questions about grading's impact on learning. It was simply a first step into a journey without an end. For as I then discovered and now know, there's always a better around the bend.

better Builder

In my room, do I push the pendulum?

And while we certainly do not claim to have arrived at 'the' way to grade, we do feel as if we have come up with an approach that more accurately communicates student growth and proficiency.

180°5.30.2017

It was time to finally reveal what year two would look like. The "A-Way" was no longer a possible path. "Select-and-Support" would become our main thoroughfare. Influenced by my crossing paths and discussing possibilities with Aaron Blackwelder (co-founder of Teachers Going Gradeless), I—along with my grade-level team members Jenna Tamura and Maddie Alderete—had settled on an approach that empowered kids to choose and defend a final grade, which I would come to call "Select-and-Support" grading (my affinity for the alliterative).

Importantly, the journey had been joined. The serendipitous encounter with Aaron Blackwelder came at a critical time for me. His and the other folks' work at Teachers Going Gradeless inspired and emboldened me to continue pushing down the path of seeking better learning experiences for my kids. I owe him much.

But I also owe a great deal to the two young teachers who were willing not only to take a risk but also to do the hard work of braving better. Together, we had charted out our route, and, together, we would learn. *Together*. I was no longer alone.

SNEAK PEEK: PROJECT 180, DAY 166
MAY 30, 2017

Here is a preview of our grading policy that we will implement next year in all sophomore language arts courses, both regular and honors. Of course, the Focus Standards will vary some between regular and honors courses, but our grading approach will be uniform. And while we certainly do not claim to have arrived at "the" way to grade, we do feel as if we have come up with an approach that more accurately communicates student growth and proficiency. We are excited to learn and grow with our kids next year, and we feel that this is a great launching point to do so. We would love any feedback that you are willing to offer.

Biggest change from Project 180? I am no longer handing kids an "A" as they walk through the door next year. Why? Well, it was never my intention to continue down that path. My giving an "A" this year was what I felt to be a necessary, radical move to take grades off the table and swing the pendulum to the opposite end, calling attention to the myriad issues surrounding traditional grading practices. I wanted to discover if kids would work, if kids could learn without the threat of a grade hanging over their heads. And while my anecdotes and Smarter Balanced Assessment (SBA) results (96.5%) are not scientifically conclusive, they do point to the possibility that we can step away from tradition, that we can take risks and kids can still learn.

But next year will be different. Following a hunch and advice from Aaron Blackwelder, I decided to let kids self-select and defend grades at the end of a term. I wish now that this is what I had done this year, but we live and we learn. And I learned a lot this year. Another factor that influenced my decision to abandon the "gifted A" was that I wanted to provide a path for others to follow, and for most it was a leap too long, so I closed the gap, and others can now follow with more confidence. More to come on how this year has influenced the path ahead, but for now, I am pleased to announce that my grade-level team has joined the journey to turn grading upside down. Welcome aboard Jenna Tamura and Maddie Alderete.

Happy Tuesday, all. A special thank you to Aaron Blackwelder for his courage and wisdom. And another special thank you to Jenna and Maddie for their hard work and dedication.

Cheney High School Grade 10 English Language Arts Grading Policies

Overview

The tenth-grade ELA teachers at CHS utilize a non-traditional grading approach. Our desire is not only to provide a system that more accurately communicates achievement and progress but also to provide a system that empowers students to take greater ownership and responsibility over their learning. The details of our approach are outlined below.

Focus Standards

Each semester there will be 10 - 12 Focus Standards adapted from the Common Core State Standards that will be at the center of our work for the grading period. 4 - 6 of the Focus Standards will be designated as "Must-Meet" standards.

Must-Meet Standards

Each semester there will be 4 - 6 Must-Meet Standards that students must meet to earn credit. If they do not demonstrate proficiency by the end of the grading period, they will be given an Unsatisfactory until they demonstrate proficiency with these standards. Students will earn credit once they meet Washington State Proficiency Levels on the Smarter Balanced Assessment at which time their grades will be changed to Satisfactory, giving them credit for the course with no effect on their GPA.

Final Grades

Students who meet the designated Must-Meet Standards will select and defend a grade at the end of the term. Students will present their grade selections and evidence (see below) during an end-of-term conference with their teacher. The students will answer two central questions during the conference.

What evidence do you have that you met the focus standards?
What evidence do you have that you achieved growth with the focus standards?
Students who do not meet the designated Must-Meet Standards will be given an Unsatisfactory until they demonstrate proficiency (see above).

Evidence

Our grading approach relies heavily upon

evidence that students collect over the term to demonstrate proficiency and growth with the term's focus standards. Students will maintain an "evidence portfolio" that houses all major assignments and assessments. These documents will be the necessary formal evidence for students to defend their selection of grades. However, this is not the only form of evidence that students may use to defend their selected grades.

Skyward

Skyward will be used as a means to report progress. Progress will be presented in two ways: Completion and Performance.

Completion will be used to report on practice. It will be presented with a 3-point scale.

3 = Complete. 2 = Near Miss. 1 = Far Miss. 0 = Missing

Performance will be used to report on proficiency. It will be presented with a 3-point scale.

3 = Proficient. 2 = Near Miss. 1 = Far Miss. 0 = Missing

Mid-term Grades

Mid-term grades are simply a formal progress report. As with final grades, students will select and defend a grade, but unlike the final grade, there will not be time for a conference. However, there will be a formal mid-term progress report, which students will complete and share at home. A parent signature will be required.

Key Terms

Proficiency - demonstrates success with standard

Growth - demonstrates continued progress with standard

Mastery - consistently demonstrates progress above standard

Practice - informal feedback opportunities designed to develop the skills necessary to achieve proficiency with the focus standards

Performance - formal feedback opportunities designed to demonstrate proficiency with the focus standards

Satisfactory grade - Under teacher discretion, a student may be given an "S" (Satisfactory) grade that awards credit for the class, but does not impact a student's GPA in a positive or negative way. If a student progresses through a class and displays effort and adequate understanding of content, but due to a variety of circumstances, would not be able to earn a passing grade, an "S" grade may be given. (Cheney High School Grading Policy)

Unsatisfactory grade - Under teacher discretion, a student may be given a "U" (Unsatisfactory) grade that does not award credit for the class, but also does not impact a student's GPA in a positive or negative way. If a student does not progress through a class, display reasonable effort, and adequate understanding of content, a "U" grade may be given. A "U" grade may be changed to a letter grade, including an "S" grade, when a teacher determines that a student has adequately completed the class. (Cheney High School Grading Policy)

360°2021

I had found my better around the bend, but as I now know–and embrace, I had not found my end. And that, again, is the beauty–and burden–of better. It never ends. And that's to be embraced–the beauty as well as the burden.

We have to expect and accept the burden. Chasing better is work, and more, it's work we must leave behind. *Must?* Yes, I believe so. Of course, at the end of year one, I'm not sure I knew this. But I know this now. And I want you to know this, too. You will not arrive. You will leave behind the betters you build. Not every bit of your better. You will keep parts, but my experiences have led me to expect, accept, *and* embrace this as the better journey.

And though I didn't expect to leave behind what I had created going into year two, I did leave most of it behind, and as I look back now, much of what I had discovered then feels like a new discovery again. I'm far from where I began.

better Builder

In my room, what am I willing to leave behind as I move on to better?

___

___

___

___

___

When was the last time a traditional grader made public his policies for scrutiny?

180°5.31.2017

I sought feedback. I got feedback. Aaron Blackwelder, answering the call, posed a few questions about our plan, which I, in turn, used as an opportunity to further clarify our approach.

But before, I did. I saw and took an opportunity to discuss the hardworking frontier folks who seek out better in the beyond, which not only means more work but also more scrutiny, for we have to explain our explorations and discoveries. And that's okay. Here, for me, it was okay. I wanted to talk about my discoveries, even if I had to make myself vulnerable. I believed in my better, not belief in the sense that it would succeed but belief in the sense that I knew the work behind it. Better is work, honest work. We can't find better without being honest about what needs to get better. And that means we have to then go beyond, go into the frontier, and that's a life not of luxury. It's a lonely life of learning, and when we find others, we welcome the opportunity to share our stories.

OUT HERE ON THE FRONTIER: PROJECT 180, DAY 167

MAY 31, 2017

Yesterday, I offered a glimpse of our grading plan for next year, asking for feedback, and I was pleased to have fellow gradeless frontiersman and Washington State teacher Aaron Blackwelder pose a few questions about our work. Thank you, Aaron. I have attempted to address your questions below. I am not sure how well I did, and I probably wandered a bit, but it was a great opportunity to walk through our thinking. Sorry it's so long.

As I was working through this lengthy explanation, I was struck by how much thought we frontiersmen and frontierswomen put into our work in an attempt to improve teaching and learning in our classrooms. And I also thought about those critical of the movement, and I wondered how frequently those folks post their work and seek feedback. When was the last time a traditional grader made public his policies for scrutiny? Ever? But, I guess if he were to do so, he'd have to join us out here on the frontier, where things are hard won. But that's why we are here out on the frontier. We believe that nothing worthwhile is easy. We believe that there exists a better way. And we embrace the hard work necessary to build a better world for those we serve. We are frontiersmen.

Happy Wednesday, all. Big shout out to all my fellow frontier men and women. We can do this. We are doing this.

Q1: At what point do you determine if a student can simply make up/revise work to meet proficiency to earn credit or require him repeat the class? My colleagues and I are currently wrestling with this concept now.

Great question. We, too, grappled with how to address this issue in our approach. Here is our present thinking around using SBA results for students to demonstrate proficiency and earn credit when they have not done so within a grading period.

Our Must-Meet standards will closely align with the high frequency, emphasized targets found on the SBA. For instance, CCSS.ELA-LITERACY.RI.9-10.1, "Cite strong and thorough textual evidence to support analysis of what the text says explicitly as well as inferences drawn from the text," is central to the SBA. It is also central to our classrooms. Focus Standard #4: "I can integrate cited text evidence into my writing to support my thinking." With that in mind, when a student passes the SBA, we will have a measure of confidence that he/she has satisfied our requirement for the Must-Meet standard. At present, SBA scores are still linked to graduation, so we feel this is a fair trade. Of course, if the SBA scores are delinked from graduation, we will have to rethink this.

Must-Meet "proficiency" must be demonstrated on Performance Opportunities, formal opportunities designed to demonstrate proficiency with the standards. While kids may always make-up/revise Practice as a means to make progress, this will not be considered for Must-Meet proficiency. Of course, this means that we will have to recreate some Performances so kids have continued opportunities to demonstrate proficiency.

Our district does not allow students to retake classes. If students fail a class, then they have an opportunity to retrieve credit in our after-school or summer-school credit-retrieval programs. However, the other grade 10 teachers and I do not necessarily have a lot of faith in this being a fair trade, which is another reason for why we settled with the SBA. Since kids will not have an opportunity to be with us again the following year, we were forced to find an acceptable alternative for them to earn credit once they have left us.

We anticipate very few students being in this boat. Must-Meet means high expectations. And this is as true for us as it is for our kids. So, just as we set must-meet expectations for them, we will also set high-support expectations for ourselves, which requires a concerted effort to provide the necessary supports and opportunities for the kids to achieve proficiency. Our goal for each term is that every kid demonstrates proficiency with the Must-Meet standards. For the few who do not, we, again, think passing the SBA is a fair trade.

But, that said, and this is not something that we will necessarily advertise, we did discuss that there might be some situations where we can and will make some exceptions. For instance, if a kid has met 3 of the 4 Must-Meet standards and is really close with the fourth, then we imagine personalizing a plan for them to demonstrate proficiency either the next semester if they are still with us, or the next year as long as we are able to create the right conditions with the next year's teacher. But this is where we felt like we were beginning to wade into the mud, which is why we settled with the SBA plan. We wondered here, too, if we would then let the kid self-select a grade or if he would just get a "Satisfactory." And again, it started to feel muddy, so we settled with the latter. What's more, we figured that the few who do actually find themselves in this boat will be more worried about earning credit than selecting a grade.

Q2: Why differentiate between "Near Miss" and "Far Miss" if either is going to require a student to make up/redo/revise work? Do you have clear descriptors of the two levels?

Another good question. Couple of things going on here with our thinking. I'll do my best.

We have found "Near Miss" and "Far Miss" to be student and parent friendly. But we have also found it to be teacher friendly, allowing our professional judgment to come into play with each individual performance, more fluidly addressing the things that don't always fit neatly into rubric cells. Really, we only provide clear, descriptive criteria for the target. From there, with each attempt, we want kids to know how close they are to the target if they don't hit it. The articulation of this through feedback calls attention not only to the target but also to what needs to happen to help move them closer to the target. The distinction between "near' and "far" relies on professional judgment, which is supported by the language in the target descriptors. Again, the goal here is to help kids see where they are in relation to the target.

Skyward, our online grading system, is our most consistent, continuous form of communication with parents. Because there will be no "grades" to report all semester, we want a consistent way to meaningfully communicate progress to parents. Regardless of whether the "redo" is required or optional, we want to communicate to kids and parents where the attempt landed.

For Practice, we want parents to know the level of completion. Our hope, here, is that parents and kids begin to see a connection between practice and performance. And while we would never penalize a kid for incomplete practice, we do hold that practice is generally consequential to one's performance. Thus, by keeping record of completed practice, we believe we help provide a piece of history of sorts for kids to reflect on as they analyze their learning journeys over the term, hopefully making a connection between practice and performance.

For Performance, we want parents to know how kids are performing relative to the standards. Our hope, here, is that parents utilize performance scores as a catalyst for either making contact with us and/or encouraging their child to actively seek retake opportunities. We really need parents to be partners, so our hope is that we provide a simple but meaningful way to communicate progress.

We are striving for consistency. Admittedly, "near" and "far" fit Performance better than Practice. Certainly, "near miss" and "far miss" more clearly connect with the idea of hitting a target, but as for Practice and completion, the connection is less clear. Still, we believe it works, and we ultimately settled for consistency over clarity. We are gambling that parents and kids will "get" that, for completion, a near miss indicates "mostly complete" and a far miss indicates "mostly incomplete." It's not perfect. But it's what we're going with for now. If it doesn't work, we will change it.

360°2021

Better, as I have said, is a reasoned reflection. It is not of whim. It is from why. My why? To build better learning experiences for kids. We, as I also said earlier, must know our why. And from our why, we build our what and how, which will change necessarily as we wander and wonder, but our why remains. It is the path, the thread we follow.

And my why has not changed. But, as I look back on this now, my what and how have changed considerably, which I acknowledged in the previous post. And though I left them behind, as better requires, I have not forgotten them. They were necessary steps to here. And more, with this particular post, a record remains of my reasoned reflections with another pioneer on the frontier.

At this juncture, I was a little intimidated I think by Aaron and the rest of the TG2 group. Oh, not for anything they had done. They were super supportive. I was just a little insecure and still caught up in the "right" of things.

better Builder

In my room, what frontiers am I exploring?

____

____

____

____

____

She didn't need IT, for it was never "it" to begin with; it was her. It was her all along.

180°6.14.2017

We ended where we began. I suppose it was in the true 180 fashion, coming back full circle. And at that place (the end where we began), I wanted to know. I needed to know. *What had they discovered here at the end? What had they learned about learning? What had they learned about themselves?* I needed to know. So, I asked.

It became our final, our fitting final, for what had the year been about if not discovery? So, I took them back to the beginning by reading them the same letter I had read them on day one when I handed them the A (literally) for the entire year. And it was with that in mind that I asked them to consider their own journey over the course of the year to capture and share what they had discovered. That would be the final, for they would have the final word. They would tell the story. That was the plan. But I wasn't the only one with a plan. Abby had a plan, her own finale to perform.

THE MOST IMPORTANT FINAL I HAVE EVER GIVEN:
PROJECT 180, DAY 178
JUNE 14, 2017

Last fall before saying anything to my new group of kids, I began handing out wooden A's that I had made over the summer. Along with the A, I gave and read to them a letter.

Dear Learners:
Welcome to Honors English 10. I am beyond excited to begin and share this journey with you. And while I am not certain about all that we will encounter and experience along our way–or even where we will land at our journey's end, I am certain that it will be unlike anything we have experienced in the past.

As you entered the room today, I handed you

a wooden letter A. It is my gift to you. It is your grade for the year. No, I did not misspeak, I am giving you an A…for the entire year. It is yours to keep. I will not take it back. Promise. Cross my heart.

But, my young adventurers, take heed. For, after all, what I handed you is just what it appears to be: a wooden letter A. It is nothing. Oh, don't worry. I am not going back on my promise. I will type the A into your transcript at the end of each semester, but even that is merely a digital character, a mark on a screen. It, too, in reality, is nothing. So, before you sit back and relax with your gift and chalk me up as your "best teacher ever," consider the following.

In truth, I gave you nothing, but I did that, young traveler, to give you everything. When I handed that A to you as you came aboard today, I really gave you ownership. I gave you the keys to your learning. I gave you choice; I gave you freedom. I gave you responsibility. And that is the essence. In the end, young friend, you are responsible for your learning. I cannot give it to you. In this arrangement that we find ourselves, I am responsible for providing opportunity and support, and I can and will give that freely and abundantly, but I am not responsible for your learning. You are. This reflects, then, the terms of our agreement for our journey.

So, we set out. 180 days from now we will set anchor in some unknown harbor. But before we set sail, pick up your A. Look at it. Feel it. Right now it is an empty gesture, a simple symbol. It won't mean anything until you give it meaning. Months from now, as we look back on the calm and storm of our journey, and you hold this symbol in your hand, what will it mean then? I can't wait to hear about your discovery. Thanks for letting me join you. I am honored.

Welcome aboard,

Syrie

Today and tomorrow (we have a block schedule for finals), I, wooden A in hand, will read the letter again. And then, I will ask the kids to briefly pen their discoveries. It will be their final.

Yesterday, Abby got the jump on me.

She had stopped by earlier in the morning, and though she obviously had something on her mind, there were two other teachers in the room, and so, she told me it could wait. Later, in 2nd period when I had her in class, I asked her about it, and she looked around the room full of students, and again, she told me it could wait. Day got on. I got busy. I forgot about it.

After school. Abby, backpack in hand, looking a little anxious entered my room, stopping before she got to me to dig something out of her backpack. It was an A. A black wooden A. And she approached my desk, stopping in front of me, taking a deep breath.

"Sy, I have carried this in my backpack all year. And I want to give it back to you now because I feel like I have earned it."

"You don't want to keep it?" I asked.

"No, I'm good. I want you to have it back."

"You, know," I continued, "I was thinking

about you the other day, thinking about your year, and how you turned it around at the midpoint, and how strongly you've ended the year. I agree. You have earned it. I am so proud of you."

We high-fived, and she left. And as I sat there, A still in hand, I wondered why she didn't want to keep it. It was a gift, handcrafted. Admittedly, I was a little hurt. Until. Until, I reviewed the letter this morning and remembered. It was nothing. It was an empty gesture, a simple symbol. She didn't need IT, for it was never "it" to begin with; it was her. It was her all along. What a discovery.

Happy Wednesday, all.

360°2021

It's not about me. I'm still learning that. I will always be learning that, for it's hard to separate one's self, one's ego, from the work. It has to be about *them*, for it *is* them. I just offer opportunity and serve support. So, are we, then, simply humble servants? Yes, I think so. Admittedly, for me, that took some time to sink in. And that momentous moment with Abby five years ago finally hit it home.

Of course, if it is about them, then I have to make it about them. And that means I have to let go, and that really, I now think, was what happened with the handing-of-the-A that year. I had to let them have it. All of it. They had to own it. And I had to let them, which meant we had to trade in the compliance car for a new model: the commitment car. And, importantly, I'd no longer be the driver. Abby showed me that. And my kids have continued to show me. I've become a better passenger. A better teacher.

better Builder

In my room, how can I be a better passenger?

____

____

____

____

____

...they uncovered the very things that I hoped they might; they discovered things about themselves that I hope they will cherish for the rest of their lives.

180°6.15.2017

We I am not sure now why I chose "booty." Kinda cringey as I come back to it. At the time, the play on words seemed clever, but now it seems more cringe than clever. Maybe I took the treasure talk a bit far, but I did not overplay, I think, the true treasure that my kids discovered at the end of their journeys, and I wanted to share the bounty of better they had uncovered from their year of digging into learning, reaching into themselves to find what could be when grades were left behind.

For me it was pure gold. They had indeed "uncovered the very things that I hoped they might." No, not all. But many–even, I daresay, most–learned something about learning, learned something about themselves. And that is what I wanted for them. I wanted them to have the freedom to seek and search out what it's all about. Well, maybe not "all about," but I wanted them to unsee for a period of time all they'd been forced to accept within the narrow world of tradition.

BOUNTY OF BOOTY: PROJECT 180, DAY 179
JUNE 15, 2017

Wanted to share some of the students' responses from yesterday. And while I will not pretend that all of my kids made epiphanous discoveries from their 180 experiences, many did, and the few I selected captured the essence of what I hoped they would discover on their journey.

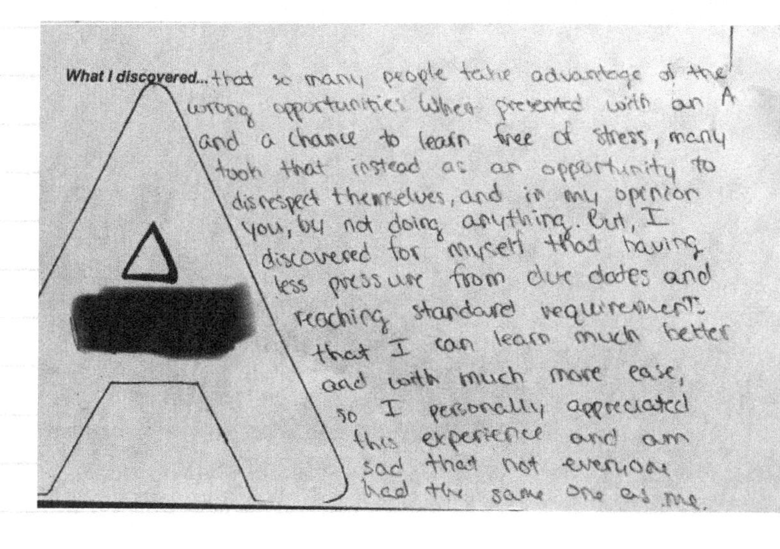

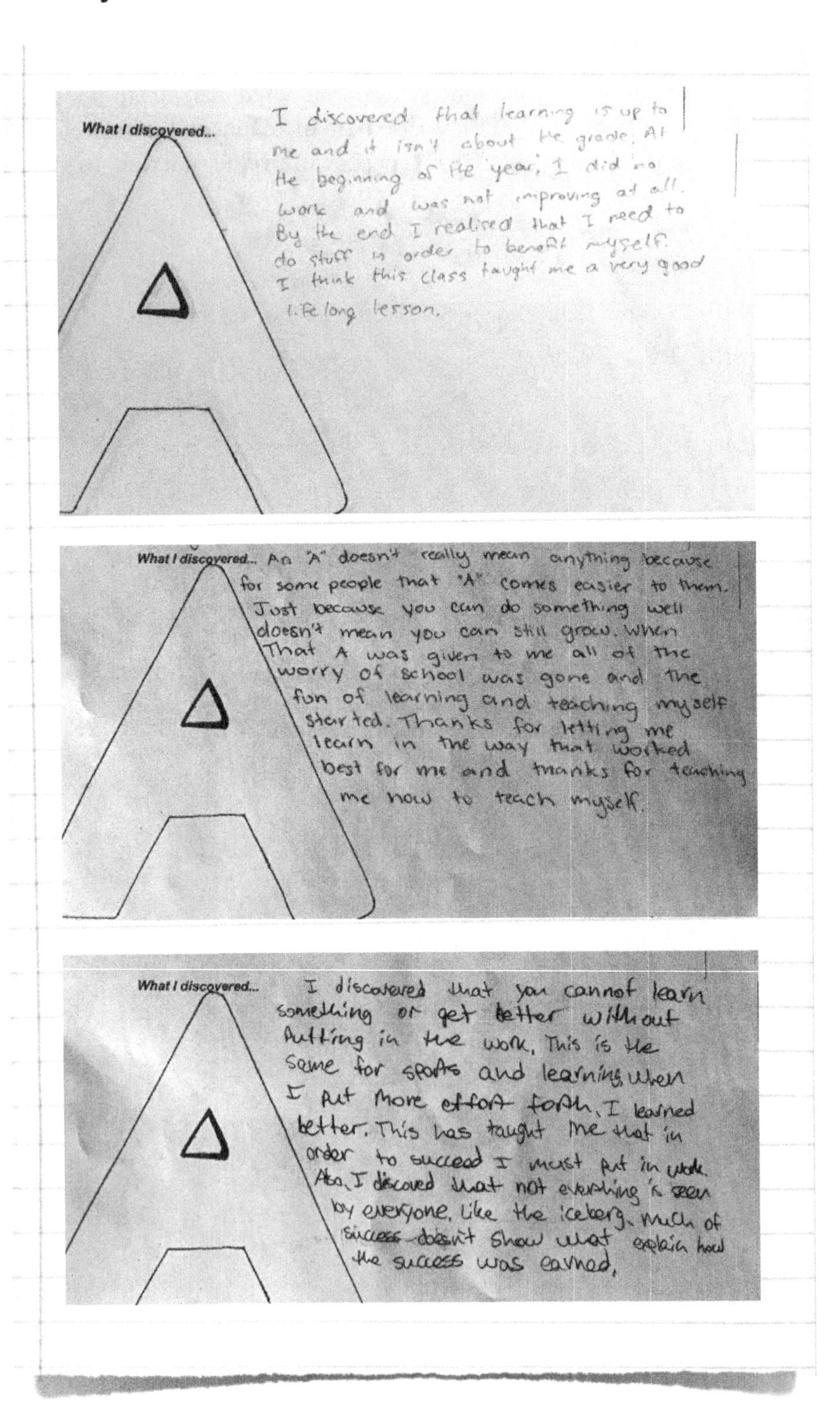
What I discovered...
I discovered that learning is up to me and it isn't about the grade. At the beginning of the year, I did no work and was not improving at all. By the end I realised that I need to do stuff in order to benefit myself. I think this class taught me a very good life long lesson.
What I discovered...
An "A" doesn't really mean anything because for some people that "A" comes easier to them. Just because you can do something well doesn't mean you can still grow. When That A was given to me all of the worry of school was gone and the fun of learning and teaching myself started. Thanks for letting me learn in the way that worked best for me and thanks for teaching me how to teach myself.
What I discovered...
I discovered that you cannot learn something or get better without putting in the work. This is the same for sports and learning. When I put more effort forth, I learned better. This has taught me that in order to succeed I must put in work. Also, I discoved that not everything is seen by everyone. Like the iceberg. Much of success doesn't show what explain how the success was earned.

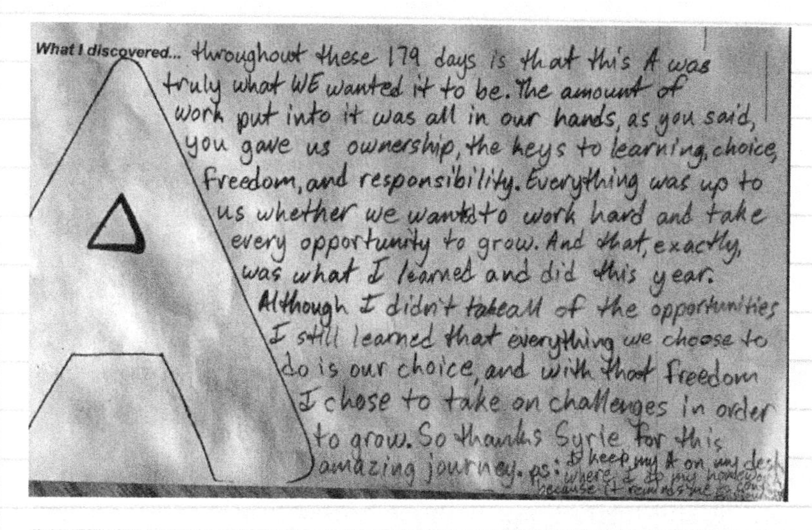

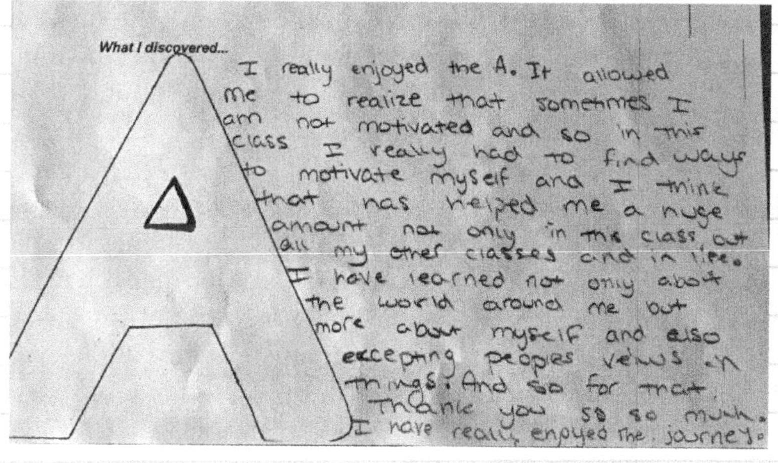

Two more sets of finals today. Eager to see what the rest of my kids found. Sad that not all discovered treasure along the way. But for those who did, they uncovered the very things that I hoped they might; they discovered things about themselves that I hope they will cherish for the rest of their lives. And who knows? Maybe those who did not reveal any discovered treasure are just

```
hiding their booty. Maybe they have it
tucked away.  Hard to imagine they got
nothing from the bounty.  But, I guess, in
the end, it's their booty. Not mine.

Happy Thursday, all. I will share more
treasure later today.
```

360°2021

Treasure is still turning up: with each new Project 180 journey, new discoveries, new bounties. They may not have quite the brilliance of the golden ***A***ge (year one), but the shine and shimmer continue as, each new year, kids pull off the cover of convention and make discoveries about learning, about themselves.

And as I think now about the years behind and the years ahead, I see that much of the work has truly been and will be about kids' making discoveries about learning and themselves. And for that, I have had to get out of the way, which meant I first had to get out of my own way. I had to let loose the confines and constraints of convention that have held me hostage for too many years.

That first step was a doozy. But from that first bold step, I learned much. I gained much—mostly the courage to continue, based on the belief that there was—there is—gold out there, which I call "better." Better is out there. And I'm still out here chasing it. I have to.

better Builder

In my room, how can I help kids discover the "treasure" in themselves?

____

____

We have a choice, and if we have the courage, we can change the world. I believe that. I really believe that.

180°6.16.2017

I'm not sure what I expected at the end really—except it wasn't the end. It was simply a pause, an opportunity to reflect on all that was behind so I could build better ahead.

I had certainly turned my wee wedge of the world upside down. Well, in truth, I had turned myself upside down—time and again—so I was forced to find my feet. As such, I came to imagine myself a turtle, flipping myself over onto my shell, seeking and embracing the challenge to set myself right again, each turn a chance to learn.

Exhausting? Yes. But if there is such a thing, it was an exhilarating exhaustion. Kind of like that good tired we get at the beginning of a school year when we invest that incredible amount of human energy into our kids to set the stage for the journey ahead. *That* exhaustion.

Never having been comfortable with the way things were, I had discovered perpetual potential energy in the turn. 180 degrees at a time. Never would I be comfortable again, even here at the end.

AS THE TURTLE TURNS: PROJECT 180, DAY 180
JUNE 16, 2017

And then it was over. No big fanfare. No

bells. No whistles. No fireworks. No welcoming committee. Just a weary traveler 180 days farther down a road without end, coming to a quiet rest, so he may reflect and recharge for that which still lies ahead. And as he looks back on the road less traveled, he remembers the times when he was lost, alone, and far from home, asking himself, "What the hell am I doing?" But he remembers, too, the times when the path was clear and others were present, and he wondered, "Am I changing the world?" But that is all behind, now only food for thought, as he replenishes his stores, preparing for the next turn, where he will walk in circles without knowing, for the landscape changes with each cycle, a mirage of promise, ever luring him around the bend. And so, here he is, come to rest 180 degrees from where he began, upside down, inside out, a turtle on a perpetual path, tipping and turning, trying to find his feet, so he can find his way.

Not entirely sure what I expected with this latest half turn, but in the end I did learn. And I will take what I have learned and use it to make even better the gradeless experience for my kids next year. And while things are still coming together on what that will look like exactly, one thing is clear: I will never go back to traditional grading. What's more, I will use what I have learned-and seek to continue learning-to convince others that we can do differently, that we can do better. We have a choice, and if we have the courage, we can change the world. I believe that. I really believe that.

Signing off for the summer. Will post on occasion. Thank you all for your support over the past several months. Could not have done it without you. Thank you for believing in me.

360°2021

I can't ride the "spinny" rides at the carnival. Heck, I can't even swing on the swings at the park. Such motion makes me sick. So, it comes as a bit of a surprise to me to find myself a motion junkie at my day job, where five years later, I'm still after the thrill of the 180 cycle. I'm still chasing better. ~~I am still trying to.~~ *I am still changing* the world. One turn at a time.

Wow, that's quite the boast, Sy. Fair enough. I almost didn't write it. I didn't–I don't–want to come across as arrogant. But I did–I do–want to come across as confident. Confident in better.

I can't walk the walk without the talk, and I can't talk the talk without the walk. I believe in better. I want you to believe in better. That's why

I am writing this book, for I believe—truly believe—better can and will change the world. Yes, it may only begin with our "wee wedge of the world," but better begets better, and the spin begins—to change the world.

better Builder

In my room, how confident am I that I can change the world?

____

____

____

____

____

With Year One done, I had put down my sword and picked up my walking stick. Better was not a battle to be won, but a journey to be joined. I had no need to fight from fear (my sword a crutch); I had a need to move, to explore, to discover. Braving better and daring different had become a way of being, so I committed to continuing my being (better) one step at a time. I'd finally found my path, which, of course, had really been there all along.

better Builders

1. In my room, why do I do what I do?
2. In my room, what "leap(s)" am I ready to make?
3. In my room, what are the rules for grading?
4. In my room, do I teach from a position of power or influence?
5. In my room, what does choice look like?
6. In my room, what helps me find my way when I get lost?
7. In my room, how can I work with kids?
8. In my room, how can I use criticism to help me grow?
9. In my room, how do I respond to my own fear and insecurity?

10. In my room, do I push the pendulum?
11. In my room, what am I willing to leave behind as I move on to better?
12. In my room, what frontiers am I exploring?
13. In my room, how can I be a better passenger?
14. In my room, how can I help kids discover the "treasure" in themselves?
15. In my room, how confident am I that I can change the world?

better Between

SUMMER 2017

When one commits to better, one commits to reflection. And reflection becomes one's reality. And here in this first summer between, reflection was on high. I was high on reflection. My brain was buzzin' after the Year of the A, and with so many doors open now, since I was past the guards at grading's gate, I could reflect on a new reality. I was free, and in that new found freedom, I would continue reaching beyond for better, which, in turn, inspired a series of summer posts: reflection's reality.

I have to face 20 years of doubt and misgivings about my own grading practices. I can no longer ignore the haunt of those ghosts.

180°8.26.2017

To do or not to do? That seems the question. *And if they do, is it true?* That seems the better question. Kids do or don't do. I have found this true no matter what I do. It was true before I started 180. It would be true in Year One of 180, and it would be true in all the years that followed. Kids do. Or, kids don't.

Of course, it was the latter of which I was warned when I schemed the "give-em-all-an-A" dream. And while I can try to suggest I was undaunted, such admonitions taunted, and I wondered and worried about the journey ahead. In truth, it was almost a non-starter. *What if the kids did nothing all year?* But more (and this was the shove I needed), *what if they did?* What if they did do? Wouldn't that be something?

Turns out (as you now know) they did. But here at the end, there was more on my mind as I reflected on Year One. I had found and now faced the *Dilemma of Do.*

THE DILEMMA OF DO
JUNE 23, 2017

Reflection's Reality: A Summer Series from the Project 180 Classroom

"They won't do anything. You can't just give kids an 'A' and expect them to do something." Though I heard lots of reasons why I shouldn't move away from traditional grading by giving kids an "A" for the year, this objection, raised by teachers, students, and parents, prevailed. Basically, boiled down, the sentiment was, "You can't give to get." Wait. What? Isn't that what we were raised to believe? That if we wanted something, we had to give something? I wanted something. And I was willing to give a lot-everything-to get it. So I started thinking.

Education tends to stress an over-reliance on the to-get-a-grade-you-have-to-do-work approach. You work. I give a grade. Makes sense. But my 20 years of experience with this transactional approach wasn't producing the learning realities that I desired for my kids. I wanted more. So I kept thinking. What if I flipped it? What if instead I took the I-give-you-a-grade-and-you-do-work approach? Would it work? Could I simply give kids an A for the year and find what I was looking for?

So I started to float the idea among my colleagues and students. Some thought it was great. Others thought it was absurd and were quick to point out the flaws in the approach, again admonishing, "They won't do any work." Of course, I heard them-couldn't help but; they told me countless times, enough that it began to sink in and self-doubt chipped at my resolve. Fearing, then, the non-start, I jumped. I did it. I gave them an A. I believed they would do. And I also believed their "do's" would be true. The do's would stem from commitment, not compliance, for there was no grade to get, so I placed my bet, gambling that kids would do for the sake of learning, that they would enter a contract of commitment. I had already spent 20 years working from the compliance contract, but I often wondered and worried about the true of that do. So I took a risk, embarked on a yearlong journey, and made some discoveries about "doing" along the way.

The Do of Compliance

If you do the work, I will give you a grade. If you don't do the work, your grade will suffer. Fear. I know this is a blanket statement, which does not fully cover the body of traditional grading, but it is the pervasive logic in most traditional classrooms. "You don't get something for nothing." In this there is truth. In my first 20 years of teaching, my kids did, and I gave. A lot of grades. And in those 20 years I made a lot of observations of kids' doing.

Copy. *The did-you-do-the-homework do.* If I have seen it once over my two decades of being in the classroom, I have seen it a million times. Okay, maybe not a million, but it is a near-daily occurrence: kids copying each other's work. And not to pick on math, but more frequently than not, it is math homework. Sorry math.

Do the minimum. *The if-I have-to do.* Whether it's getting the D, being content with the

C, or securing the A, these are the kids who always want to know, "What do I have to do to get…"

Cheat. *The dirty do.* This is the get-a-grade-or-get-caught-trying approach. When fear is a factor, even "good kids" can get sucked into this.

Do for the grade. *The transcript do.* These are the kids who have to have an A on their transcript. They don't always care about learning; they are often minimum doers, too.

Don't do/Won't do. *The no do.* These are the kids who, despite any risks or rewards, just never seem to muster a do.

Do to avoid trouble. *The hell-to-pay do.* These are the kids for whom trouble is a reality if they do not meet the trouble threshold at home. These kids range from the just-get-a-D to the must-get-an-A.

Do Sunday. *The procrastinator do.* These are the wait till Sunday night kids, which often turns into Monday morning, which then turns to during lunch, which finally…well, we know how this generally turns out.

Do for the growth. *The true do.* These are the few who see all work as an opportunity to grow, even the busy work that they're fed. They place a great amount of trust in the teacher, and do every bit of the work with fidelity.

The Do of Commitment

I already gave you a grade. You may choose to do the work. If you don't do the work, you may miss an opportunity to grow. Choice. "You don't get something for nothing." Still rings true. In my first year of Project 180, my kids did, and I gave. A lot of feedback. And in that first year, I made some observations.

No copy, no cheat. There's no point, for there is no benefit. And in this, too, there is choice. Early on, I had a couple of kids trying to pull one over. I simply told them it was their choice. If they wanted to get feedback for someone else's work, then I was okay with that. It didn't take long to sink in.

Do what I can. Not completely unlike the "minimum" above, but in the 180 classroom there was a distinct difference. The work was discriminately challenging, meaning the work found the kids where they were along the continuum, which revealed their being in different places. And as such, I would encourage the kids to do what they could. An honest attempt yielded authentic feedback. Sometimes the challenge was such that it was beyond any "do," but even honesty here gave us an entry point into the learning, allowing me to provide the necessary support for that kid, even if it meant starting over. Honesty is key here.

No grade. Did this intentionally. Gave them an A, so they would forget about grades. Even so, it was hard for kids to unlearn their grade-mongering behaviors. Later in the year, it became a joke. "It's not like I'm gonna take your A away." Or. "Man, I'm gonna give you an A for that."

Don't do/Won't do. Not sure there is an approach out there that will ever fully resolve this issue. But, my approach pushes no penalty, only responsibility. My kids have the responsibility to own their choices. I tell them that they need to make big-boy and big-girl decisions.

Still trouble. I can't control the trouble threshold at home. As a means to keep parents "in the know," I would report practice completion and performance scores in Skyward, our electronic gradebook. So, missing work yielded some trouble for some kids. This I believe is a remnant of traditional grading where missing assignments could often be catastrophic in the form of zeros.

No Sunday stress. Since there was no penalty for late work, the Sunday-night-turned-to-Monday-morning-until-time-ran-out approach vanished. I would take it whenever they finished it. But this was also a result of my carefully crafting practice, so that, regardless of when it was completed, there was benefit. No penalty. Just opportunity.
Do for growth. This was the sweet spot this past year. The desired, this-is-what-it's-all-about culture that I was looking for. This is what I got for giving. This is where we operated for the majority of the year. Kids did grow. Yes, it took them awhile to get there, but once they got there, most-not all-did the work, and in that doing, they grew, for there was really no other reason for them to do. My risk reaped the reward.

The Do Dilemma

"They won't do anything. You can't just give kids an "A" and expect them to do something." My critics were neither wrong nor right. Some kids did not do. Some kids took advantage of my "give," and I did not "get" what I wanted for all. But the majority of my kids took the gift of freedom and did what I hoped they might: they took responsibility for their learning. Still,

Project 180 was not a success for every kid in the room. But, as I reflect back on my first 20 years of traditional grading, the same was just as true; it was not a success for every kid in the room. What's more, I was not-and still am not-convinced that the "success" of my kids was not suspect. Were they really learning? Were they really growing? Were they committing? Or were they simply complying? Not sure. But I was suspicious, so I made the leap to learn.

In the end, with either approach, there is doing and there is not doing. No escaping that. And while that has been the dilemma in traditional circles forever, with too much emphasis on the don't and won't do's-the impetus for my critics' admonishment-there is perhaps a different dilemma to ponder. How true is the do? And if our wonder leads us to suspect the do is not as true as we'd like, then we are faced with another dilemma. Do the same? Or do different?

I chose to do different. I chose to take a risk. And I would encourage others to do the same. However, I am not suggesting that you leap as far as I did with the give-em-all-an-A approach. I never intended to stay on that far end of the pendulum swing. I expected and desired that it should find its way back to the middle. I only did the "A thing" as a radical first move to call attention to our grading practices, to take grades completely off the table.

Next year, I am moving to a select-and-defend-a-grade approach, an approach that still gives my students the keys to their learning, an approach that still allows them to make big-boy/girl decisions about what they do and don't do. Of course, I want them to do everything. But more, if they do, I want it to be true. That is the culture I want for my kids. I can *give* them that.

360°2021

Still a dilemma–ever a dilemma, I suppose. I have done much to do different over the last five years to make their *do* more true. I set out in search of creating better learning experiences for my kids, and I am still searching–ever searching, I suppose. For, I am still not there.

But I am not *where,* either. I am not where I began to do new (do different). I have come far from the "Do of Compliance" as I have come nearer to the "Do of Commitment." For one simple reason: I am committed to commitment. I am duly diligent in the different I do to reach that place where their do is more true. And that place, I have discovered, is messy, for that place is human. And as such, it's not nearly as orderly as the compliance classroom. Things aren't black and white (do or did not). There are hues to the do's in the commitment classroom, for we meet each in the medium of their own learning, where their choices, not our penalties, determine the truth.

That first step was a doozy. But from that first bold step, I learned much. I gained much—mostly the courage to continue, based on the belief that there was—there is—gold out there, which I call "better." Better is out there. And I'm still out here chasing it. I have to.

better Builder

In my room, how do I deal with the "Dilemma of Do" (kids' doing/not doing work)?

____

____

____

____

____

For twenty years, I had used—and sadly, on occasion, abused—that power. But now it was gone.

180°7.1.2017

Sometimes to find the way, we have to lose the way, and then, and only then, will we find *our* way. I believed learning was "the way." But there was something in the way: grading, which for too many years had been *the* way. So, to get to learning, I had to first get past grading. I had to get lost. That was easy enough. I just took grades off the table. But in losing grades, I lost something more: power.

I had acknowledged as much ten days into Year One ("Progress Report," 180°9.15.2016), but now, in the stiller moments of summer, I could better distill from reality's reflection all I had learned and lost by veering off the most-traveled path. I would have to unlearn to learn, and I wanted others to learn from my loss. Things would change when/if they ever decided to get lost themselves, when/if they ever decided to step off the path of grading to discover learning. They would lose power, and they would have to learn to lose the way.

GRADELESS AND POWERLESS

JULY 1, 2017

Reflection's Reality: A Summer Series from the Project 180 Classroom

Upside down. That was my goal with Project 180 this year. I sought to turn traditional grading on its back. I expected that turn. I wanted that turn. So, with eyes on *that* road, I set out on my 180 day journey to change the grading culture in my classroom. However, shortly after I was underway, I discovered that I would take many unanticipated half-turns as I careened along, alternating between comfort and discomfort, a turtle on his feet one moment, only to land on his back the next. And though I had many feet-in-the-air moments, one of my most uncomfortable, for it was perhaps the strangest in this strange new land, was losing the power of grades. For twenty years, I had used-and sadly, on occasion, abused-that power. But now it was gone. Fine fix I had created for myself-feet in the air, indeed. How does one simply "unpower" after twenty years? I didn't know. But only a few days down the road and with many ahead, I quickly had to learn to lead a "powerless" classroom.

The Sins of My Past

Twenty years. For twenty years I relied in varying ways and to varying degrees on the power of grades. From not accepting any late work from my seventh graders my first year to protecting the "A" for two-full decades, I used, misused, and abused the power of grades, largely out of ignorance, for I didn't know any differently. In the absence of any real training, and in the absence of *any* alternative, I did what I thought was to be done, for it was done to me. I didn't know any better. And so armed with a force greater than I could understand and a well-intentioned, though misguided, approach, I released my newly bestowed power upon my world.

I would teach them the harsh realities of the real world, for at the wise age of twenty three, I knew well all the ways of a world not kind. And in the real world, there were no breaks, so I wouldn't give them any.

They would thank me later. Tough love. I would accept no late work. It was a necessary and even logical step to teach them responsibility. And after a few, this-will-teach-them zeros in the gradebook, they wouldn't *dare* miss an assignment. And I would be the hero from whom they would learn to survive in a cruel world.

I was an idiot. Zeros didn't scare them straight. And all that they were learning about the cruel world is that cruel people make it so. I was making it so, creating a culture that didn't foster learning but instead dealt in fear. Fortunately, I eventually saw the error of my ways, and I changed. But it was gradual, and only somewhat less cruel as I then explored the full spectrum of late work penalties: 10% per day, a full-grade deduction, 50% off, etc. And once again, I found myself practicing from a place of ignorance. No one showed me the right way. But that was the bottom, the place of failing. Surely, I had it right at the top. No one had to tell me or show me that excellence was to be protected at all costs. The A grade was only for a select few, and it was my right, my duty to guard that gate. *But I didn't have it right.* To be sure, my sins ranged from top to bottom, and I was paving my way to hell with what I thought were good intentions.

In a recent, informal discussion with some folks from Teachers Going Gradeless, Aaron Blackwelder, a TG2 co-founder, shared a past perception from his own experiences as a gatekeeper of grades. "I would look for ways to make sure students did not earn 100%. I felt it was my job to protect 'perfection' and make sure not all students achieved it." And in a rush, I was reminded of my former gate-keeping moments, my tell-tale heart beating 'neath the floorboards of my not-to-be-forgotten past. Without knowing, Aaron, through his own admission, had called me out, and echoes from the past haunted in whispers. *A's are not for everyone. A students don't take days off; they are on all the time. We can be flexible D to B, but we cannot be flexible with A's; we must protect the A.* I was so worried about protecting the A that I was not focusing on what really mattered: learning. And, to be honest, the A became a power play. I was not protecting the sanctity of excellence in my classroom. I was creating a culture of impossibility, based on little more than, in truth, what I alone deemed the unreachable peak. I held the power at the foot and top of the mountain, and all points in between. I got what I wanted. And if I didn't, I used-abused-my power to get it anyway. Last year, even though I had eventually over the years learned to redirect my power in ways more fair, it all came to an abrupt end. I lost the power of grades.

The Lessons from My Present

From protect-the-A to give-them-all-an-A, things definitely took a turn this past year. I flipped it all right. It *was* what I wanted-a culture of learning without the hindrance of grades. But caught with my feet in the air, it was not exactly what I expected, and I had to approach things differently. I had to learn-quickly-how to wield influence. I had to learn to motivate and inspire without the power of grades. Here are some ways I adapted this past year.

Influence of relationships. I have always believed in relationships. They are *THE* thing, the key element to success in the classroom. In the 180 classroom, I had to lean heavily on my ability to form and sustain relationships with my students. I have always believed that relationships are investments into which we have to make generous deposits so we can make the necessary withdrawals. I invested heavily last year.

Influence of choice. With grades out of the way, the kids were put in a position of responsibility, in a position of choice. Learning was up to them. They would choose to engage and do, or they wouldn't. When they were ready to meet me partway, I would be there. We would meet somewhere in the middle, but I alone could not do the walking.

Influence of words. I have always been inspired and influenced by words, so I started coming up with mantras to inspire my kids. At first, it felt a little cheesy for all of us, but after a while, it took hold, and the kids came to expect my cornball mantras. In prep for public speaking practice, I wrote the mantra in the picture above, and we all recited it together. I will use more mantras next year. *I will use more mantras next year. I will use more mantras next year.*

Influence of relevance. I tried really hard this year to point to relevance in everything that we did. Of course, some of that was academic, but much of it was "real world." I also tried to develop, through interest and choice-based assignments, my kids' abilities to discover relevance on their own.

Influence of community. Like relationships, community can be an important investment. Through activities such as Community Circle and team-based learning, the kids came to know and became accountable to the members of our classroom community.

Influence of growth. *Reflection. Reflection. Reflection.* My kids had to reflect all the time in various ways, logging their learning. This was their "look in the mirror." It was a consistent reality check, as they were forced to face their learning. It was the only thing I "forced" them to do; it was the one small string attached to their A's. They and their parents had to sign their learning logs. Completing them was optional, but if they wanted the A, they had to sign; they had to own it. If a kid and parent were okay signing a blank learning log, then, well…

Influence of example. We are more likely to follow people who walk the walk. So, as the lead learner in the classroom, I did the vast majority of the assignments along with my kids. This paid dividends in so many ways. So many ways.

Of course, these approaches are not exclusive to the gradeless classroom, most of them can be and are used in the graded classroom, but without the grade-power in reserve, they-at least for me-felt more authentic than ever. I had nothing else. And though there were some trying times that made me long for the power position of old, I find influence a far more preferable place.

The Hope for My Future

As with any look into the future, my hope is to continue to learn. I want to find more and better ways to motivate my kids to embrace the learning opportunities in my classroom. Things will be a bit different next year with my select-and-defend approach, but the same principles will apply. They will own their learning. They will make choices. And I will be there to support and influence them in this new reality, a reality where I proudly GRADE less and POWER less. Turns out, I didn't need either all along.

Do. Reflect. Do Better.

360°2021

In my weakest of moments and on my hardest of days, I sometimes feel the pull, the urge to return to the way. One–*even one as resolute as I*–does not simply unlearn the way in a day. To be sure, I walked the way for twenty years, grounded in grading's gravity. The pull doesn't go away, but it does suck less once one can pull himself out of orbit.

And that's where I've been for the last five years. Out of orbit. Gradeless and powerless. But that doesn't mean there's no power. It takes power–some days, an immense amount of power–to remain out of orbit. And I find that power in those whom I have empowered: my students. "Penpower" is the propulsion in our system. Selecting and supporting grades has become the way. The kids have the power of the pen to capture their learning stories, where comes to light that which is greater than the gravity of grades: the revolution of relationships. In that we float on and through the space of our learning, resisting the suck of grading.

better Builder

In my room, what propels the learning?

____

____

____

____

____

There is content. There are people. The content can wait.
People first. Always first.

180°7.14.2017

If one can make an intentional discovery, then I did such a thing, for it seems not quite right to suggest I discovered the power of Smiles and Frowns by accident. No, it was discovery by design: intuition to intention to innovation.

Intuition. We know before we know. I knew before I knew. Relationships matter. They have to. Ours is human work. And how the humans work together impacts the work the humans do, together. We have to come together. We have to connect. We know this. I knew this.

Intention. If we know, we have to do, on purpose, with purpose. If we know that relationships matter, then we have to make them matter every day. I knew, so I had to do.

Innovation. The outcome of joining intuition and intention. I "discovered" that if I coupled what I knew (relationships matter) with what I do (on purpose), I could elevate the relate in the room. So, I did.

I call it Smiles and Frowns. I also call it the most important decision I have ever made as a teacher. *Ever.*

REFLECTION'S REALITY: RELATIONSHIPS ARE NOT ACCIDENTS

JULY 14, 2017

Reflection's Reality: A Summer Series from the Project 180 Classroom

"Any success or failure I have experienced in the classroom has had everything to do with relationships."

This is one of the first things I tell my

classroom management course at Eastern Washington University. I then go on to tell them, with that in mind, we will spend a lot of time talking about relationships, for they are the foundation for everything. And then I continue to tell them that when I was in their seats many years ago (literally, for the desks have not changed in the 25 years since I, too, was a young teacher candidate taking the same course at EWU) no one talked to me about relationships. No, instead I was led to believe that good management was keeping kids in their seats quietly-silently-working from bell-to-bell. I have since learned that management is not about management; it's about culture. And really, it's about relationships.

Recently, I had the honor of contributing a post to the Teachers Going Gradeless website, which highlighted the gradeless classroom as an ideal setting for creating a culture of possibility. The emphasis on culture stems from my belief that great teachers are not managers of classrooms but creators of culture. And from that place, I challenge my college students to capture their dreams of their ideal cultures, so we can then set to work on discovering and implementing the practices that will help make their ideals their realities. This approach gives them not only the opportunity to develop their talks but also check their walks. In the post, I went on to share how I keep my talk and walk in balance in the culture that I seek to create in my high school ELA classroom. And, of course, my first "talk and walk" addressed that which I sell as the key component in any classroom culture: relationships.

In the post I referenced an activity that I do with my high school students to make relationships an intentional part of my classroom culture. I call it Smiles and Frowns. But I did not discover it in the classroom. Before stepping down so I could focus on Project 180 last year, I was the ELA department chair at Cheney High School for 12 years, and one of my many responsibilities was to lead our weekly collaboration meetings. Of course, there was always an agenda-there's always an agenda-but there were also eight other people sitting around the table, eight other people with whom I had to engage in the important work that we do in the ELA department at CHS. There was an agenda. There were people. The agenda could wait. People first.

So, one Friday morning on a whim, we started with a quick go-around, sharing something from our professional and/or personal lives. It took roughly five minutes. The next week, we did the same, but this time I placed it at the top of our agenda, calling it Smiles and Frowns. It remained at the top of our agenda from there on. Even now, after my stepping down, it's still at the top of our agenda every time we meet. Last year, it made it into my classroom culture as an occasional but intentional activity to foster relationships. This year it will take center stage as the daily entry task, an intentional effort to make relationships the priority.

Smiles and Frowns

Here's the basic approach.

I sit among the kids if there is an empty desk. If not, my default perch is a seat at the front of the room. I prefer to sit among the kids. My desks are generally arranged in two half circles. But arrangement varies, so we adapt accordingly. If the arrangement is not conducive to a good sharing-and-listening environment, we will all stand in a big circle around the room.

Each person has an opportunity to share a smile and/or frown from his/her school or personal life. This is the heart of the activity. This is such a great opportunity for us all to learn about each other as individuals, learning that transfers into so many other aspects of our culture over the course of the year.

Each person has the right to pass. No one is forced to share. Sadly some kids always pass. On occasion I will pass, too, to honor those kids who are exercising their rights.

Each person has the responsibility to listen. I don't want my kids to be good listeners. I want them to be great listeners. And that takes practice. For us, it begins here. My rules for listening are pretty simple. No talking while others are sharing. Make an effort to make eye-contact with the speaker (which means one may have to turn around depending on seating arrangement). Use non-verbal gestures to put the speaker at ease (nod, smile, etc.). Not much makes me grumpy as a teacher, but if kids aren't working at being great listeners, I get grumpy.

We start at random places. Often, I will ask

for volunteers to start us off. Sometimes, I will choose. Sometimes, I will begin.
It takes five minutes. Sometimes, it takes a little more, but I am the guard at that gate. If I find that there is something that the kids are excited about or have stuck in their craws, we will spend the extra time. My culture. My choice.

How I will introduce it to the kids.
We are going to learn a lot this year. A lot. I am going to push you to make the most of our opportunity together. And while the content of the course will occupy the majority of our learning experiences, it is not the most important thing we will learn together. Yes, syntax and rhetoric are important, and, yes, we will treat them as such, but they are secondary to what matters most: the people around us. Our worlds will always be full of important stuff, but they will also be full of people. And it is my belief that if we want to learn about the world and to learn about ourselves, we first have to focus on the people around us. So we, my young friends, will spend time each day learning about each other.

Relationships are key. They are not

accidents. They require intention. I talk a lot about that. And I have found that if my mouth is moving, my feet need to keep up. I have to walk my talk. And so, to that end, I make relationships a priority, and Smiles and Frowns is just one way that I am intentional about that. Yes, I have content to cover-there's always content to cover-but at any given moment in my day, there are also thirty other bodies in the room with whom I engage the important work of learning the world. There is content. There are people. The content can wait. People first. Always first.

360°2021

Still the most important "discovery" (decision) I have ever made—will ever make. There is nothing out there to be discovered that is greater than that which considers first the people in the room. And Smiles and Frowns is the simple means (magic, I believe) to that end. It is, simply, magic. I have found nothing that brings such a transformative benefit to a classroom community and culture.

But as with any benefit there's a cost. And I will not BS you here, it takes time. It costs not a dime. It requires neither curriculum nor professional development. But it will take time. It has to. Relationships and connections aren't drive-thru diets. They are—they have to be—sit-down-at-the table dinners. They are daily, full-meal deals we make with the humans in the room.

Initially, I fretted some about the time investment. And you likely will, too. But from the returns, I found reassurance that I was spending it wisely. And now, I spend it willingly. I have to. It's the only sure investment I have ever found. *Ever*. It's my only constant.

better Builder

In my room, how do I put people first?

____

____

____

____

____

I don't want learning to be a tentative transaction, a simple exchange. I want learning to be a committed connection, an exhilarating experience.

180°7.21.2017

I suppose I am a bit of a journey junkie. So many times throughout my career, even during the pre-180 years, I have jibed with journey. I have always felt that teaching, learning, living were about the journey. But here, after the first 180 year, I was jibing with journey like I had never jibed before.

Me. Them. Became us. Oh, I had never really thought of us as separate, but I never fully felt that we were together, either. The difference? Taking grading off the table. I know I keep circling back to this, but I have to. It changed the whole dynamic. It changed the whole journey. And here at this juncture in the journey, I had discovered by changing my story, I was changing their story, which meant, of course, I was changing our story.

And it was the story that came to matter most in the gradeless learning experience—the journey. But how would I, they, we capture the story? How would we journal the journey? It was time for a better, and I had an idea.

REFLECTION'S REALITY: LEARNING IS A STORY
JULY 21, 2017

Learning as Journey

Each a journey. Each a story. Each a young spirit with whom I get the privilege to experience life and learning. For 180 days each year, my students and I join journeys, and for the briefest of moments our experiences are shared, our stories are intertwined, and we are connected. We are bound by learning. That is our journey, a journey of shared responsibility in our common quest to grow as we make our way down the road. And in that bond we've each a role. My role is to provide opportunity and support. Their roles are to take ownership and responsibility. And so, with those packs snugged securely to our backs, we face feet forward and venture into the land of learning, the realm of possibility.

Okay, my flight of fancy has passed, but that *is* my ideal approach to learning. I don't want learning to be a tentative transaction, a simple exchange. I want learning to be a committed connection, an exhilarating experience. And while I have wanted that, chased that ideal for most of my career, last year I finally caught some of what I sought. *The journey.* The difference? I took grades off the table. When I did that, it was no longer my writing their stories in the gradebook. When I took grades off the table, they had to pick up the pen; they became the authors. When I took grades off the table, I opened the path to learning. I discovered the journey.

And on that first 180-day journey, I learned about learning. I learned about reflection. Oh, I had always valued reflection's role in the learning process, but last year on my trek, I stumbled onto something that I came to call learning stories. Learning stories are reflections. But they are not merely reflections: they are the moments, the chapters, the pages of one's learning journey. I only dabbled in and experimented with this last year, but my trials were revelatory. When I gave kids the ownership of their learning, they were truly capturing their experiences in the classroom. This wasn't about writing a reflection out of compliance. It was about writing a story out of commitment. A story. Her story. Her learning. Her journey.

This year it moves beyond the experimental dabble. This year, this 180 day cycle, it will become a full-fledged part of the journey. Learning stories will be a daily component for the kids and me. I am going to call them "Journey Journals." In a recent, #TG2CHAT, I mentioned "learning stories" in reference to student reflections, and some folks expressed interest in hearing more. Knowing I could not do it in 140 characters, and knowing I had to get it put together before the year started anyway, I promised a post. Here it is. Here is how I will use Journey Journals in my classroom this year.

Finding Their Stories

Most kids do not regard their lives as stories, and even fewer regard their educational experiences as stories. Sadly, I believe it's due in part to their feeling that the adults in their lives are the ones writing their stories. So, I have tried to change that. For years, one of the first things that I have my kids write is their reading and writing stories. By the time they reach me in tenth grade, they have strongly-set attitudes on both. So, I ask them to explore those attitudes by tracing back through their experiences and capturing them in a story. If a kid "hates reading," I want to know why. More importantly, *I want him to know why*. If a kid "LOVES writing," I want to know why. *I want her to know why*.

This year, this will set the stage differently than it has in the past. This year it's about recognizing where one is and having the power to do something with it. Before it was a well-intentioned activity, but it was just that. *Now it is the first page*. It settles the kids in the content and context of our journey. It is the first step, a step that is not exclusive to the ELA classroom. Every kid has a science story, a math story, a health-and-fitness story, etc. So, for those of you reading this who teach in other contents, this can be done in *any* class.

One cool thing to note is that at Cheney High School we are having all kids in all ELA classes write their reading and writing stories, and they will keep them in their 9 - 12 writing portfolios. They will revisit the previous year's story before writing the next. The goal here is for all of them to have four stories from which they can see their growth over the four years with us. A lot of work remains with this, but I am excited by the possibilities. Back to the Journey Journals.

Capturing Their Stories

How's it going to work? Based on the premise that each day, each unit, each lesson, each activity, really each interaction-academic or not-is a learning experience, here are the basic nuts and bolts of my approach.

I will provide composition notebooks for each kid. These will be our journals. I will also have one, and I will do everything that I ask the kids to do. Well, actually, I will have two: one for honors and one for regular. I believe that my doing this along with the kids is vital. If I am selling it, I have to buy it.

Our journal entries will be our exit task. Monday thru Thursday, for the last 5 minutes, we will capture a part of our day's journey. On Friday, our scheduled reflection and reading days, the kids will have more time to capture something from the week's journey.

All entries must include an entry number, date, and title.
If students are absent, then they will still be required to capture something from their day. The journey extends beyond school.
There will be no points attached. The kids will have the opportunity to bring their journals to our learning conferences to share what they select as evidence of growth. I will share from mine as well. I am looking for commitment here. I am not interested in compliance. They will also have additional opportunities to "publish" (see below).
The capture. To help my kids catch their stories, I am going to give them learning lenses through which to view their experiences. Here is the basic premise. Our experiences can be looked at in different ways, examined in different contexts. I will ask the kids to look at their experiences through five different learning lenses.
Learning Targets: These targets represent our planned route for the day. This is a relatively straightforward lens for the kids. *What'd we do today? How'd I do today?*
Growth: My hope is that this is a consistent consideration for kids. *Am I moving? Am I growing?*

Proficiency: This, too, will likely be ever-present in the kids' minds as this will represent the major milestones (standards) throughout the journey. *How's my confidence? How's my performance?*

World: Here is where I would love for kids to connect their experiences with the broader world-life, the human experience. *How does this relate to the world? What connections can I make?*

Self: Best for last. If my kids can discover the magic of the impact of on experience on self, then there is little more that I could hope for. *This* is reflection. *What did I learn about myself? Who am I?*

Pen to paper. Once the kids have considered context, it's time to start writing. To help them get started, I will provide the story stems in the graphic below. Some kids, my "natural reflectors," won't need these; they will jump right in. Other kids will need help getting started, so for them I generated questions to serve as starters, as stems for their stories. I believe these are particularly important for the daily entries, especially early on, for the kids will need help capturing moments. So, to help prevent the, "I-dunno-responses," the kids will have these to rely on. I will be capturing my own moments from the day, so I need the kids to become self-sufficient. These stems will serve as my support for that.

JOURNEY JOURNAL

Story Stems

Use one of the "story stems" below as an entry point into reflecting on your latest learning experience.

What did you learn about yourself?
What did you learn about the human experience?
What? So What? Now What?
What thrilled you?
What frustrated you?
What challenged you?
What would you change?
What will you do differently next time?
Who contributed to your learning?
What contributions did you make?
What connections did you make?
Did you find yourself in a fixed or growth mindset?
What relevance did you discover?
What's next?
How did you feel?
What do you need to learn better, to learn best?
What was your favorite mistake?
What can you celebrate?

Learning is Reflecting
Do.
Reflect.
Do better.

@MonteSyrie

Sharing Their Stories

I will never collect the kids' journals. But I will expect that they have their journals with them every single day, and I will also expect them to share from their stories every single day. Without grades to hold over their heads, this becomes my means for holding kids accountable. I will come at it from a you-are-a-member-of-this-community angle. I will further leverage this as a way to create a community of contributors. I will seek to instill the notion that as members of a community they have a responsibility to make contributions; in a learning community each member learns not only for himself but also his community. We learn with, from, and for each other. So we will share. We will contribute. Here are some ways that we will do that.

Audience: partner, group, class, teacher, parent

Share a word, a sentence, a passage. This will be our most frequent "publishing" opportunity. We will simply share aloud one of these options with either a partner, a group, or the class.

Post-it. There will be times when the kids publish a word or sentence on a Post-it and place it on the front whiteboard. I like this because other classes will get to "hear" their peers' stories.

Poster. This will be a big poster on the wall that I will occasionally ask kids to publish a word, sentence, or passage. Similar to the Post-it, but this is more "permanent."

Pass the Paper. This one will take the longest, so we will only do it a few times a semester. Here, each kid will begin with a blank sheet of printer paper. He or she will publish a word, sentence, or passage and then pass the paper. Each kid will publish onto his/her peers' papers until the paper returns to its original owner. By the time the activity is done, each kid will own a classroom published document.

Learning Logs. Every two weeks kids have to complete Learning Logs (my form of progress reports in the gradeless classroom). As part of the required information, I will ask them to quote themselves from their Journey Journals.

Learning Conferences. This one was not included in the brick wall below, but when the kids have learning conferences with me, I will ask them to select and share a passage from their journals to give me a sense of where they are in their journeys. I will also share from mine.

Journeys Join

Thus, we are bound. We are one in our journey. We are one in our learning. We become part of each other's story. That is the ideal I've sought for years, and this year I feel like my ideal finally has a chance to become my reality. I will no doubt have to make some changes along the way, but for now, it's my best "Do." I will reflect. And I will do better.

Please feel free to use and adapt to suit your classroom needs if you are interested. That is key, folks; it has to fit you, or it won't work. Good luck on your journeys this coming year.

Do. Reflect. Do Better.

360°2021

I had an idea, so I implemented an idea, and I learned from the idea. I came up with a different idea, so I implemented a different idea, and I learned from the idea...

The 180 journey isn't a restful journey; it's a restless journey. But "-ful" or "-less," it's always a journey. That hasn't changed, and it won't. But the capture, the journal, has changed, and it will. The 180 journey's never still.

Does it always change for the better? That's a tricky question for one who pushes better as the frame for teaching, learning, and living. I can't simply or definitively say "yes" or "no." It's simply not that simple. It's definitely not that definite.

If I offer, "yes," there's truth in it. At the time I made the change, it was better. There was something, I reasoned from reflection, that had to change.

If I offer, "no," there's truth in it. Now, long after the change, I'm reflecting, and I'm not sure of my reason.

The journey never and ever changes. That's the story of my learning.

better Builder

In my room, how do I capture the learning journey?

____

____

____

____

____

If they haven't discovered these things by then, I will be deeply disappointed in myself...

180°8.7.2017

There has to be more to explore than content. Yes, I want my kids to find relevance in and gain knowledge from the things we study, but that alone is not enough. I think we have to offer more when they walk through our door. And for me, that begins on day one. I don't cover the syllabus. I deliver a promise–of discovery.

I am fond of the frame. In fact, I think teachers are framers. We frame the room. We frame the work. We frame the day. We frame the year. We frame the entire experience–whether we want to or not.

The kids look to us for the frame. What we do–or don't do–decides the day. And, man oh man, is there pressure in that. But, there's also possibility–powerful possibility.

I ponder the power in possibility. I imagine what's possible (better), and I build it. And building begins with the frame when one seeks to dwell in the house of possibility.

When one talks "journey," one has to walk journey. So, one has to frame journey.

Here's the frame.

STUDENT LETTER: A PROMISE OF DISCOVERY
AUGUST 7, 2017

As many of my regular readers know, I am a believer in the journey, and that belief has certainly carried over into my classroom, where once again it has materialized as the frame for my student letter this year. Earlier this summer in my TG2 post, Gradeless: A Culture of Possibility, I made mention of my personal drive to walk my talk, to make sure that my realities follow my ideals. This letter to my kids is an attempt to do just that, to create that accountability. I am not presenting the things in this letter as mere talk. This is the reality I want for my kids, the reality that I am holding myself to creating for my kids this year. When I say, "This is what I hope you discover on this journey," I am really providing my kids with an informal contract, a guarantee that these things will present themselves and be part of their journey. Their sharing their discoveries at trail's end will be their final. If they haven't discovered these things by then, I will be deeply disappointed in myself, and I will tell them that when I read this letter to them on day one. From there, I will have 179 days to do my best.

Dear Learners,

Welcome to Honors LA 10. I am beyond excited to begin and share this journey with you. And while I am not certain about all that we will encounter and experience along our way—or even where we will land at our journey's end, I am certain that it will be unlike anything we have experienced in the past. And as we set forth to explore and experience learning, here are some things that I hope you discover along the way.

What I hope you discover on this journey.

I hope you discover the importance of relationships. *My successes and/or failures have had everything to do with relationships in my own journey. Relationships. Relationships. Relationships.*

I hope you discover the value of mistakes and the necessity of failing. *Mistakes and failing are paths that lead to learning. Follow them. You won't get lost. In truth, you'll probably find yourself.*

I hope you discover that you own your learning. *From the deepest recesses of my teacher being, I believe that this is the key to true learning. You have to own it, for when you own it, you take responsibility for it. I am responsible for joining and aiding you in your journey, and I enthusiastically own that. But you are responsible for your learning, young friend.*

I hope you discover the unique power of your voice. *Language is power, a power available to all. It is not reserved for a select few. You have language, which means you have power. I will help you find your way, but it begins with your believing that you have power. I so hope you make this important discovery this year.*

I hope you discover that literature is a rehearsal for life. *We will engage and* *embrace literature as a way to learn about the human experience. Literature is life. Life is literature.*

I hope you discover that learning is a circle that often requires redo's. *I will create no ends to your learning. You may have as many attempts as necessary. I can control that. However, I cannot control time. Over that end, I hold no control. Time expires, but learning never ends. And as long as you are in my locus of control, I will always give you another shot. Always.*

I hope you discover the power of a growth mindset. *I firmly believe that our attitude about anything means everything. With that, I would like you to add a tiny word with gigantic implications to your learning vocabulary. Yet. I hope it helps you bridge the gap between "I can't" and "I can."*

I hope you discover the power of reflection. *I hope my "forcing" you to reflect on your learning each day will help you develop this essential learning skill for life. I will use the broccoli effect for this, "Whether we like it or not, broccoli is good for us." Whether we like it or not, reflection is good for us. #sorrynotsorry #eatyourveggies #reflectionrules*

I hope you discover that feedback is the

most essential ingredient in learning. *Travelers get hungry. The need for fuel will be significant for our sustained journey of 180 days. Fortunately, I have an unlimited supply of the necessary nutrient: feedback. I will not feed you grades. I will only offer feedback. It is the stuff of learning. It is the most vital thing I can offer you. I really hope you make this important discovery as well.*

I hope you discover the value of community and the power of empathy. *Though our learning journeys are unique, we all travel similar paths. When we come to realize that through our similar trails we share a bond, we begin to understand that we are not alone, that we can learn with others, that we can learn from others. When we connect with others, we learn. When we connect with others, we can understand. We will connect. We are a community.*

So, we set out. 180 days from now we will arrive at some destination. But before we start down the trail, consider what I have said; consider what I hope you discover. I will be with you every step of the way, but you must take the steps. I cannot take them for you. Months from now, as we look back on our explorations and experiences, and you consider this list, I hope you have added them to your packs as mementos of our time together. Thanks for letting me join you. I am honored.

Let's get started,
Syrie

I am so excited to begin this next 180 day journey with my kiddos. I am eager to get to the doing, reflecting, and doing better that I so crave. I am hungry to learn. I am ready for kids.

Do. Reflect. Do Better.

360°2021

While we may frame the room, the kids fill the room, fill the frame. That's the picture (the possibility) I imagine in a different frame by the same name. The kids, their whole-human selves, must fill the frame. We must picture them. More, they must picture themselves. If kids can't see themselves in the work, then the work will never fit with them in the frame. So, to frame that fit (kids and work), I imagine the big picture as a journey of juxtaposition where kids discover not only the work but also themselves (mostly themselves). For the self endures; the work fades.

And that was and remains my hope. I've found that by framing the experience as such, I cannot unframe it–at least in my own mind. As you'll discover in "Year Three: Helping Humans," once I came to see the humans (their whole-human selves) in the picture, the frame changed forever–for better.

We are framers. We build homes of humanity. We paint the portrait of selves. And in these frames we present the promise and power of possibility.

better Builder

In my room, what do I want kids to discover?

____

____

____

____

____

I am keenly aware of the trust that you place in me for your child's care and education each day when she or he walks into my classroom.

180°8.18.2017

We call them our kids. But they are not *our* kids. They are *their* kids. We teach parents' kids. And though we care deeply for the little humans we call our kids, their parents care more deeply. And, consequently, they place a great deal of trust in our institution and us.

I have never taken that trust lightly. And now with Project 180's commitment to daring different and braving better, I was taking it less-lightly than ever. I needed their trust, and I wanted them to know what I needed them to know. To be sure, I'd be taking their kids to places perhaps previously not experienced. Things would be different, and I hoped things might also be better. So, I wrote them a letter (another frame filled with kids).

I believe parents want us to see their kids in the work, in the picture we frame. And so, I wanted parents to know that I did (that I could not *not*) see their kids in the work. I would always see their kids in the work. That's the frame.

WHAT I WANT YOU TO KNOW: MY LETTER TO PARENTS THIS YEAR
AUGUST 18, 2017

Good morning, all. Here is my parent letter for the 2017 - 2018 school year. As always, feel free to use and/or adapt to fit your needs. DM me @MonteSyrie on Twitter if you want access to the original doc. For those already in the classroom, hope your year is off to a fantastic start. For those whose starts are right around the corner, hope you are as eager as I to get going. Happy Friday.

Dear Parents/Guardians,
Hi, my name is Monte Syrie. I will be your child's language arts teacher for the 2017 - 2018 school year. I am honored to join him or her in his or her learning journey this year. This year will mark the twenty-second year of my own learning journey, and while I tend to say this every year, I truly believe that this year will be my best year ever. And as I look ahead to my "best year ever,"

here are some things I would want you to know.

What I want you to know.

I want you to know that I care about your child. *She or he is not a number. She or he is not a "seat-filler." She or he is a person, and I will treat her or him as such. I will strive diligently to get to know her or him as an individual person, so I may best help her or him as an individual learner. I believe all my students come to me at different places socially, emotionally, and academically, and I will meet them wherever they are. So, I will meet your child where she or he is, and from there we will journey forth into our learning experiences for the year.*

I want you to know that I encourage and value your role as a partner. *I have long felt that by the time students reach high school, as a system, we tend to place parents at arm's length. I think this is unfortunate. I believe that optimal learning requires a shared responsibility among teachers, parents, and students. We have to partner in this, and so with that I offer you an open invitation to be a guest in room*

211 this year. Please join us. All I would ask is that you be willing to participate in the day's activities. Ideally, you would schedule this with me, but an open invite is an open invite. You are welcome. Always.

I want you to know that communication between us is important. *Just as I presented an open-door invite above, I also offer a direct line of communication assurance. Communication is a must. If there is ever anything that you wish to address with me, please do so. My contact information is below. My preferred form of communication is email. Please never hesitate to contact me.*

I want you to know that I believe that your child owns her or his learning. *I am not passing the buck. I simply believe that if your child is going to make the most of his or her learning opportunities, then he or she must take ownership. Here is what I wrote to him or her in my letter to students. "From the deepest recesses of my teacher being, I believe that this is the key to true learning. You have to own it, for when you own it, you take responsibility for it. I am responsible for joining and aiding you in your journey, and I enthusiastically own that. But you are responsible for your learning, young* *friend."*

I want you to know that I value learning over grading. *In the past few years I have made major strides in providing an approach that places greater emphasis on learning, not grading. As such, your child will find himself or herself in a feedback rich environment, which has been made more possible with my stepping away from traditional grading practices. Please carefully read the attached documents explaining my grading policies. And, as offered above, please do not hesitate to contact me with questions.*

I want you to know that I understand the strain that homework can place on you and your child. *It is not my goal to burden your child or your family with a heavy workload outside of school. In most instances, your child will have time to do our work in class, where I am available for feedback-the ideal situation. So, consequently, he or she will not have "homework" in the traditional sense. Instead, my "homework" for the year will be asking your child for at least 30 minutes of reading each night. That is my homework for the year. I would like you to partner with me by encouraging your child to complete this homework. 7 days a week. 30* *minutes a day.*

I want you to know my approach to life and teaching: Do. Reflect. Do Better. *Twenty-two years into my journey, I do not have all the answers. I am just seeking to do better each day, each year. This year is no different. I will make mistakes, and some of my plans will fail miserably. But I expect and accept that because I know I will learn from it each and every time. This is how I approach my own learning. It is how I will ask your child to approach his or her learning.*

These are the things I would want you to know as we set out on our own journey together as the adults in the party. I am keenly aware of the trust that you place in me for your child's care and education each day when she or he walks into my classroom. I, too, am a parent, and have the same expectations for my own children. And so, please know that I take my role in your child's journey very seriously, and I will do my best to see him or her safely to our journey's end. Thank you for joining me this year. I hope it is a "best year ever" for you and your child.

Sincerely,

Monte Syrie

360°2021

Best year? Only insofar that better is best. *Better year, then?* Yes, it had to be. It began by doing better from reflecting; it continued by doing better from reflecting; and it ended by doing better from reflecting. That is, the year ended. The work never ends. There's always another better around the bend to brave, always another different to dare.

And I have found that partnering with parents is key to the better journey. There's risk in better, but it's a reasoned risk, and when we offer reassurance to parents about the safety and support of their kids, we start off and stay on the right foot to earning and keeping their trust.

As such, I have learned that communication and transparency are critical components in securing the necessary trust for the better journey. Everything to share. Nothing to hide.

I will make mistakes. In fact, I guarantee it. But as I do, through all my better-braving, different-daring, and mistake-making, I keep safe the center. And I want parents to know that. I need them to know that. Always.

better Builder

In my room, what do I want parents to know?

____

____

____

____

____

This is your most important role. I need you to be who you are.

180°8.19.2017

I believe better is beyond. This belief drives my work with ~~grading~~ learning. This belief also drives my work with classroom culture. And so, since all betters begin with a frame, I decided to reframe "rules" in my room.

I had already moved on from "rules" some time ago with a "policies-and-procedures" frame. But really, it was mostly a change in name; they were, for the most part, still rules. Even so, small moves like a change in name begins to change the frame. Kids receive and respond differently when we frame things differently. "Policies and Procedures" greets them differently than "Rules." But, in too many classrooms, on too many first days, kids are greeted with rules first. We seem to believe if we don't get rules in front of the kids immediately, we will never get the kids where we want them. I don't believe in this anymore. I did, I suppose, at one point, but at this point, I believed there was a better way to "get kids."

And here's the frame I imagined and built for better.

BEYOND RULES: RELYING ON ROLES, ROUTINES, RIGHTS AND RESPONSIBILITIES TO CREATE CULTURE
AUGUST 19, 2017

In my continuing efforts to create the culture of possibility that I desire for my kids and myself, I have decided to reframe my policies and procedures into roles, routines, rights, and responsibilities. The intent is not all that different from the old frame, but I believe the new frame better fits this current leg of my journey.

As always, if you find some value in what you see here, please feel free to use and/or adapt. If you want access to the original doc, please DM me on Twitter @MonteSyrie.

Roles, Routines, Rights, and Responsibilities

Welcome to your language arts learning journey. I will be your guide as we make our way along our 180-day path this year. But, before we get started, there are some things we need to discuss that will hopefully help you have a successful journey in room 211 this year.

Roles

Here are the various roles that I will need you to play over the course of the year. Sometimes, our day's path will require you to play one specific role; most times, our path will require that you play many simultaneously. Either way, I promise I will not ask you to stretch yourself beyond your limits. You got this.

Role #1: Yourself. This is your most important role. I need you to be who you are. I realize that the setting in which we find ourselves sometimes impacts our ability to be ourselves, but my hope is that the classroom community and culture we create during our time together will give each of us the comfort and confidence to be who we are. This is the role that matters most to me as I join you in your journey this year. I am excited to know YOU.

Role #2: Valued Community Member. This is your second most important role. At present, many of us are not well-acquainted, but we are in this together either way. And as we will spend a lot of time together both struggling and celebrating over the days to come, my hope is that we establish a community that is rich in relationships and in excess of empathy. We are a community.

Role #3: Reader. This will be one of your worker roles. Lots to read as we explore various texts along numerous paths, discovering the power in others' words. I need you to be a reader. I need you to believe you are a reader. We are readers.

Role #4: Writer. This is also a worker role. My hope is that you write more this year than you have in all your other years combined. I believe this is perhaps one of the most important skills you can develop for life now and later. I need you to be a writer. I want you to believe you are a writer. We are writers.

Role #5: Mistake Maker. Another worker role. By now, you know there are no penalties for mistakes in room 211. In fact, mistakes are enthusiastically encouraged as they are launching points into learning. Mistakes lead to learning. We will travel down many mistake paths this year, which means we'll find lots of learning. We are mistake makers.

Role #6: Reflector. Last role but no less an important one. By now you also know that I will expect you to add to your learning story each day in your Journey Journal. Each day we will end our time together, reflecting on and sharing from our day's experiences. Reflection is such an important part of learning. I really need you to become reflectors.

Routines

Our trail stretches far into the distance, and while many unknowns lie in wait, here are some things that you can come to expect on a regular basis: our daily and weekly routines. It will take some time for these to become routine, but my hope is that these common expectations will help us move along the trail with some certainty and efficiency.

Every day we will begin with Smiles and Frowns. This is our community check in, where you will have the opportunity to share what is going on in your life in the frame of a smile and/or frown. All will be encouraged to share, but no one will be forced to share. If you choose not to share, you may simply say, "pass" when it comes to you. (5 min.)

Every day we will begin our work with Mindset Mantras (see handout). I know for some of you this will be kinda corny, but I believe that if we hear it, we say it, we will believe it. Above all, I want you to believe it. Mantras will be a regular part of our journey. (30 sec.)

Every day we will take a Brain Break halfway through the period. This is a time for you to stretch, talk, walk, and check your phones. (3 min.)

Every day we will end our work with our Journey Journals (see handout). As mentioned above in the Reflector Role, we will reflect upon and share from our experience each day. (5-7 min.)

Monday is We Are Writers day (WAW). As the name suggests, we will be writing every Monday, working on either the assigned writing or our Passion Paper.

Tuesday is also We Are Writers day (WAW).

Wednesday is We Are Grammarians day (WAG). Here we will work primarily with syntax and other "needs" that we discover from your writing.

Thursday is We Are Readers day (WAR). Each week on Monday you will either receive a Life is Lit passage or an Article of the Week. It will alternate each week. Along with the text you will be given practice. The reading and practice are due on Thursday, when we will discuss both.

Friday is We Are Learners day (WAL). Friday is an extended reflection day in our Journey Journals. It will also be devoted to your personal reading.

Every two weeks on Friday, you will complete a Learning Log (see handout). This time will be devoted to your officially recording your progress with growth and proficiency. This will also be a time for portfolio updates and upkeep.

On Mondays and Tuesdays during our WAW time, we will conduct scheduled writing conferences (see handouts).

Every day your cue to leave will be my message, not the bell. I will dismiss you each day with something along the lines of, "Thank you for letting me learn with you today. Have a great day." After you hear this, you are free to go.

Rights

As a member of this community, you have the following rights.

I have the right to feel safe.
I have the right to learn.
I have the right to ask as many questions as I want.
I have the right to make mistakes and not fear penalty.
I have the right to "prove" my learning in various ways.
I have the right to feedback as an essential part of my learning.
I have the right to access Syrie for help whenever possible.
I have the right to eat and drink in class.
I have the right to express that my rights are not being granted or protected.

Responsibilities

Beyond your rights and roles and the

routines of the room, you will also have responsibilities as a member of our learning community.

I have a responsibility to get to class on time. If I am late, I will not disrupt the class. I will quietly apologize and sit down. I understand that if my being late becomes a habit, Syrie and I will have to find a solution.

I have a responsibility to know and honor the routines of this class.

I have a responsibility to monitor my behavior so I do not disrupt the learning of my community members.

I have a responsibility to self-regulate my use of electronic devices in this room. I will keep my device stored out of sight until the Brain Break or when I have been given permission to use it as a tool. I understand that if I cannot self-regulate, Syrie will ask me to keep my device on his desk during class. I may have it back during Brain Break. I will also have future opportunities to prove I can self-regulate.

I have a responsibility to be a great listener. This means, I will not talk while others are talking; I will visually track/connect with the speaker; and I will use

gestures to demonstrate that I am listening.
I have a responsibility to self-regulate my leaving the room. I may go to the bathroom when I need to, but I need to work at keeping my leaving to a minimum.
I have a responsibility to take ownership for my learning. It is my learning.
I have a responsibility to be sensitive to and respectful of others' viewpoints. In short, I have a responsibility to be kind.
I have a responsibility to clean my space before I leave for the day.

Interventions for when I do not meet the obligations of my responsibilities.
Reminder(s)
Conversation(s)
Parent Contact
Office Referral (It is unlikely that I will ever get to this point.)

360°2021

This frame has remained. Some of the routines have, of course, changed, and I have revised some of the roles, rights, and responsibilities, but for the most part, this frame has largely remained intact. Kids get it, and—as was my goal with the reframe—it gets kids.

And I believe it gets them from word one: *yourself*. **Role #1: Yourself**. Of course, saying so doesn't magically make it so. There has to be more than talk; there has to be a good deal of walk. Day one, word one is a simple step into a long journey of discovery, a journey I believe where kids must see themselves if they are to be themselves—not just on day one or week one with some get-to-know-ya activities, but each and every day. Kid-centered. Self-centered.

And that begins here. As we cover the Four R's over the first week (one per day), it is with deeply earnest intentions that I pave the path ahead with signs of self. I want the kids to know I see them so they may better see and be—themselves.

better Builder

In my room, how do I frame the rules?

____

____

____

____

____

For much of my teaching career, I have lived a lie.

180°8.24.2017

Better does not an expert make. Turns out after the Year of the A, I knew just enough to know that I didn't know enough. I was no expert in the traditional arena (the truth in the lie lived), and I was now no expert in the gradeless arena, either.

When one just hands over the A, one does not have to worry about what makes an A an A. But when one takes a turn towards and at a select-and-support approach, one does, once again, have to wonder—and indeed worry—about what makes a grade a grade. And that is where I *once again* found myself—back in the familiar and not-comfortable game of naming a grade. And as "better" goes, I was once again—*ever again*—in a place with more questions than answers. What is an A? What is a B? What is a C? What is...and the list went on. And on.

And neither least nor last in line of questions was the wonder: Who's the expert? I felt the title was not alone mine to own. I needed help.

EXPERT, EXPERT, WHO'S THE EXPERT?
AUGUST 24, 2017

For much of my teaching career, I have lived a lie. It wasn't a mean lie, as much as it was a necessary lie, necessary because I had to hide the fact that I didn't really know what I was doing. So I hid. I hid behind the mantle of expert, and as I look back on it now, especially the early years, I realize the absurdity of the lie (and it was surely more mean than I believed, for kids suffered at my ignorant hand), but it was an absurdity for which I can only accept part of the blame, for the system in which I was educated, the system in which I was trained, the system in which I have now taught for over twenty years,

Based on your experiences, offer an explanation of what you believe is required for each of the three grades below.

A

B

C

failed me. No one taught me how to grade.

Oh, I went to college. In fact I have two degrees in education, but in all that time, no one ever sat me down, and said, "Okay, here's how this whole grading thing works." Of course, now I realize that this never transpired because no one knows-I mean *really* knows. Do we? If so, I would have to believe that there would be something that we could put our hands on, something that could guide the way, a touchstone from which we could seek wisdom to prepare and provide a valid, reliable, equitable approach to that which carries so much weight in our students' present and future: grading. If it exists, I have not found it. But I seek it. I have sought it among my colleagues for over two decades. For twenty plus years, from numerous colleagues I have directly and indirectly sought "the way." But all that I have found are numerous, similar-but-never-the-same approaches to grading. Seems no one ever really taught them, either.

I have sought it among the literature, where I have found some promising possibilities but no definitive answers, other than there is little to no support for that which is commonly practiced in the form of traditional grading. And it was-and still is-that particular revelation, where I finally fully felt the burden of the lie that I had been carrying for the majority of my career. So I quit. I quit pretending that I was an expert because I was a teacher, and I started shedding my traditional grading practices. Slowly at first, I got rid of zeros; I stopped penalizing kids for late work; I even stopped failing kids. And before long, the shedding became a cascade, culminating in my completely getting rid of grades last year, a move that led me to where I am today, in the realm of the gradeless, a realm of like-minded teachers who I believe somewhere along the way, shed, too, their skin of old, in search of that which would better serve as a means to support and communicate learning. But importantly, I have not found the gradeless realm to be the place of answers. No, to be sure, it is a dimension of questions, inhabited by seekers. We do not have the answers. But we seek the answers. And that is what matters. We are here to learn. We are here to share. And as we are here to learn, we live an existence of learning; we walk a path of perpetual questions, seeking answers not to become expert, but simply to become better.

By now, most of my readers and gradeless peers know that I am always chasing better. And that pursuit is paved with questions. This past week, seeking better with my new gradeless team, we encountered some questions in our discussions that will hopefully lead to better.

Select and Support

This year, we are using a select-and-support approach to grading. At the end of the term, kids will select and support a grade in a teacher-student conference providing evidence in answer to the questions:

1. What evidence do you have that you met the focus standards?
2. What evidence do you have that you achieved growth with the focus standards?

We are happy with this. This is what we want our approach to be this year. But there's a problem, a problem that revealed itself from… questions. Damn questions, always leading to problems.

Do we need to provide delineated descriptions of grades for the kids?

Are we just going back to traditional grades if we provide what a grade has to be?

Will the descriptions just become a checklist?

Will we create a system of minimums again? Meaning, will we recreate the reality we sought to get away from where kids ask, "What do I have to do to get an A?"

What if a student asks, "How will I decide which grade to pick? What's an A?"

What if a parent asks the same question at Open House?

What is an A?

What is a B?

What is a C?

Hmmm. It all seemed so easy. Kids select. Kids support. We put the grade on the transcript. And we would move to the next grading period. Nope. Full stop. We had to come up with an answer, an answer that fit us, an answer that protected our belief that kids must own their learning, an answer that supported the kids in their taking that ownership. So, I went home and slept on it. Here's our answer.

1. We are going to ask kids to individually indicate what they believe is required for an A, a B, and a C. Before we share our grading approach for the year, we are going to hand each kid a 3×5 card (see graphic above), and ask him or her to provide information about each grade. We will ask them to write their names on the cards, and we will collect and store them.
2. At midterm, when we are required to put a grade on the report card, we will ask our kids to complete a mid-term progress report. We will not conference with the kids, but the process is essentially the same. The kids will select and support a grade with evidence. To help them in the process of selecting their grades, we will redistribute the "grade cards" they made at the beginning of the year. We will re-collect and store the cards. The

kids will take their progress reports home to share with parents. They will return them signed. And we will enter the grade.

3. At end of term, we will once again give kids their grade cards to assist them in their grade selection before conferences. During the conference we will ask the kids if they want to make any changes to their grade cards. We will keep the cards.
4. Repeat process for second semester.
5. For the final conference, we will ask kids to revisit their grade cards, and as part of their final conference we will ask them to share their reflections on grades from the year.

But, wait. Kids can't decide what a grade is. They are not experts. Teachers have to decide. Okay, let's walk down that path for a moment. Yesterday, I spent the day with my colleagues from Cheney High School. Seventy teachers and 4 administrators. Let's imagine that I had given them the same grade card I am going to give my kids, asking them to describe what is required for each of the three grades. And though I cannot claim to know exactly how it would have played out, if I had to guess, I would offer that there would be a great number of variances among answers, leading one to wonder which answers were more "expert" than the others. Oh, I am sure that there would have been some general semblance of excellent (A), good (B) , and average (C) among the responses, but I have to wonder if the kids won't arrive at the same general concept. And if so, what might that reveal? Are we trained experts on grading? Or are we just more experienced products of the system? In truth, don't most teachers-out of necessity-end up grading how they were graded? I did. I had to. There was nothing else to turn to.

So, I wonder. I wonder if kids might not learn more from the experience if I give them the opportunity to set their own standards. Of course, I don't know. But there are a lot of things I don't know. And as it turns out, I am not sure I know any better than they what an A is. Sure it's a risk, and in the end, it could prove a mistake, but I will own it. I will learn from it. I will do better from it. All I can do. I'm no expert.

Do. Reflect. Do better.

360°2021

And I'm still no expert, even *years of better* do not an expert make. But that's the road one travels when one decides the better journey to take. We don't get to "good." We only move towards better. And when we are constantly moving, we are leaving behind as much as we are getting to.

Of course, I've since moved on. I have left behind this particular practice, not because there was no value in it. The kids were, in some regards, excellent experts, but their expertise was limited by their experience–not their age, but their experience with traditional grading, which was their only experience. And as one might expect, their descriptions mirrored their experience, and more, their descriptions mirrored what I imagined my colleagues' descriptions might have been had we indeed engaged in the activity. Deeply steeped in the tradition of grading, students, like their teachers, could neither see nor move beyond the ritual ruts. So, I moved on.

At present, I'm playing with the idea of "commitment-considered criteria" to elicit the expertise of kids. It's their learning afterall.

better Builder

In my room, who's the expert?

____

____

____

____

____

This first summer turned out to be my biggest summer. There was so much to reflect on, and I attribute much of that to the new-found freedom I had discovered by my finally getting past grading. And now that I was beyond grading, I could more intentionally lean into learning, and the more I leaned, the more I learned, the more I lived. I had found my way of being in *better*, and in that place (reflection's reality), I discovered there was so much more than grading. *So much more.*

better Builders

1. In my room, how do I deal with the "Dilemma of Do" (kids doing/not doing work)?
2. In my room, what propels the learning?
3. In my room, how do I put people first?
4. In my room, how do I capture the learning journey?
5. In my room, what do I want kids to discover?
6. In my room, what do I want parents to know?
7. In my room, how do I frame the rules?
8. In my room, who's the expert?

Year Two

THE YEAR OF THE R

Most of us have heard of the three R's in education: **R**eading, w**R**iting, and '**R**ithmetic (the old standbys of a basic education). But beyond the basics, at least of late, we have also come to recognize another R as an essential basic in the classroom: **R**elationships, which many consider to be the fourth–and most important–R in education. But there are other R's in education as well. And though I certainly did not set out to discover them in Year Two, I found them everywhere I looked–truly a **year of R**evelation.

So we, my young friends, will spend time each day learning about each other.

180°9.1.2017

Relationships. The most importantest "R" there is. And this year, "The Year of the R," I would make it the mostest with Smiles and Frowns, the activity I highlighted in the "Relationships Are Not Accidents" post in the preceding "better Between" chapter.

As with most things, frames matter. And I was hyper-conscious of this as I framed our year-long commitment to Smiles and Frowns. I wanted my kids to see themselves and others differently. I wanted them to see the people in the room as the content of our community, the most important things to be learned, so I framed it as such. We would be a community, not a class. I was committed to it. It was the first thing we'd do every day. It was the most important thing we'd do every day. Every day. No matter what.

And this was strange for kids. Not on a cosmic level. They'd "broken the ice" before. But here we were not simply breaking the ice; we'd be keeping our pond ice-free for the entire year. Strange indeed. An ice-free year.

STRANGERS AMONG US: PROJECT 180, DAY 3
SEPTEMBER 1, 2017

"I hope you discover the value of community and the power of empathy. Though our learning journeys are unique, we all travel similar paths. When we come to realize that through our similar trails we share a bond, we begin to understand that we are not alone, that we can learn with others, that we can learn from others. When we connect with others, we learn. When we connect with others, we can understand. We will connect. We are a community."

Trail Talk
"Take a quick scan of the people in the room. Raise your hand if you know everyone's name in this class." I made this request in each of my five classes yesterday. And each

time, no one could raise his/her hand. A few of the kids suggested they could name most, but the vast majority of us admitted we would miss more than we'd make. I asked them what that suggested about our community.

As many teachers do, I have my kids make "name tents" on day one. I don't assign seats, so I don't have a seating chart to assist my learning their names. So, we use the name tents for the first week. Knowing names is a top priority, a non-negotiable. A must. This year, I upped the ante. In response to the severe shortage of raised hands indicating our knowledge of names, I challenged my kids to know names along with me. I gave us till next Friday. But that's not enough. Not even close. And I told them so.

We are going to learn a lot this year. A lot. I am going to push you to make the most of our opportunity together. And while the content of the course will occupy the majority of our learning experiences, it is not the most important thing we will learn together. Yes, syntax and rhetoric are important, and, yes, we will treat them as such, but they are secondary to what matters most: the people around us. Our worlds will always be full of important stuff, but they will also be full of people. And it is my belief that if we want to learn about the world and to learn about ourselves, we first have to focus on the people around us. So we, my young friends, will spend time each day learning about each other.

Yesterday, that's how I sold "Smiles and Frowns" to the kids. It is my intentional approach to daily community building, our entry task every day for the entire year. Basically, each of us shares a smile, frown, or both from our school or personal lives. Importantly, each has the option to pass. I am not going to build bonds among us through force. So, I offer the option to pass if someone is not comfortable. A lot of kids passed yesterday. And why wouldn't they? They are among strangers. And though it bums me out that we miss an opportunity to learn each time someone passes, not all learning is lost, for even if they are not sharing, they are listening. They are learning.

And so, we found a little discomfort yesterday in our travels. As I watched the kids' responses to the roll out, I saw a mixed bag. *Rick rolled his eyes and shook his head. "I am not here to learn about the people in this class. I am here to learn about English." *Sam slunk down in his chair, trying to hide. "Oh my gosh. All eyes on me. Just let me be anonymous." *Sally smiled, sitting up in her chair. "Yes! I get to talk about me." *Carla cocked her head, confused, looking at me like I was crazy. "We're doing what?" And all sorts of responses in between. And that's okay; it's what I expected. It is a strange thing among strange people, so I will exercise understanding and patience as we move forward. At the end of the semester, I will make the name request again, but I will also ask how many could share something about each person in the room. I hope we find things less strange by then. *Names not real.

Moving on. As predicted, yesterday was a cluster with pictures. It took 40+ minutes each period, so we didn't even come close to discovering what I'd hoped yesterday. And that's just how it goes out on the trail. Things don't always go as planned. And while I was a wee grumpy about it, I just adjusted our course, and we did what we could. Today will be no less "clustery" as we have Friday late start along with an hour-long pep con, resulting in only 35 minute classes today. Silly Syrie, you should know better than to plan so much for the first few days of school. Indeed, seems this is one "do better" that I will have to continue chasing.

Today's Trail

Along today's trail we will…

…build community with Smiles and Frowns

…complete our Wordles

…reflect in our Journey Journals

And that's the plan. Funny that I haven't given out any rules, grading policies, etc. Just working on building community. Oh, I guess I did share one "rule" out of necessity. Sarah asked if eating was allowed in class. Yes, Sarah. Always. We are on a journey, not a hunger strike. Eat away kid. Just pick up after yourself.

Have a great weekend, all.

Do. Reflect. Do better.

360°2021

It's still the mostest. And Smiles and Frowns has become my signature move in the room. It is the most important move I have ever made in the classroom. *Ever.* It is my die-on-that-hill "what" for my die-on-that-hill "why." It is the walk in my talk: **R**elationships. There is nothing more important than the humans in the room. And Smiles and Frowns is my daily devotion to that notion.

So, did it work? Were the kids able to say something about each of their peers by semester's end? Were things less-strange? Yes, yes, and yes. But I did come up short on one of my predictions, one of my promises. We were not a community in the end. To be sure, as the kids came to say, "We are not a community. We are a family." And they said it over and over there at the end where things were less-strange, and we were strangers no more.

But that's a lot of time to keep the ice away. Yep. A lot. A waste of instructional time? Our family didn't think so.

better Builder

In my room, how do I build community?

Put together, the parts create a crazy whole, a madman pushed to his limits, forced to confront the confounding reality that he is human after all.

180°9.22.2017

Reality. Superman shirts don't make one Superman. Asked years ago why I wear Superman shirts so frequently, I shared that I had to, that it was a reminder of the superhuman efforts necessary to sustain the support my kids needed. They needed me to be Superman, so I became Superman. Well, at least I wore the shirts, believing them transformational. I could don my shirts and assume my superhero persona. I could become Super Syrie.

But only seventeen days into year two, I was fast finding the shirts a facade. I was only human after all. And my **ideal**ity was crashing into my **real**ity. I was on a collision course. Something had to give. There had to be a better. So, I put my shirts in the drawer and my ego on the shelf. Simple Syrie was who I needed to be at this point in the journey. I didn't need to be superhuman. I just needed to be human.

And, that's all my kids needed, too. They didn't need a caped crusader. They just needed me to be real.

I, ENEMY: PROJECT 180, DAY 17
SEPTEMBER 22, 2017

Sometimes I think my mantra, Do. Reflect. Do Better., is more a convenient rationalization to my wandering than a beacon of inspiration on my horizon. In part, it's due to the allure and blur of my ideals, a mirage of confidence in my dreamt-up, drawn-up plans as I head down the trail with my not-yet-tested "better do" in hand.

In other part, it's due to my Superman-shirt-wearing-induced ego, which compels me to believe I can achieve superhuman feats. Put together, the parts create a crazy whole, a madman pushed to his limits, forced to confront the confounding reality that he is human after all.

This has been a hard week. My ideals and realities have collided, and the aftermath has placed me in a state of super stress, affecting both my professional and personal lives. And that's not okay. So I had to get better. It's all I know, and after a week of reflecting, yesterday, I found better. Yesterday, I got better.

The Problem

I bit off more than I could chew. Suffering from "Supermanshirtis," I thought I could somehow get a feedback form filled out for each of my 120 kids, indicating hits, misses, and next steps on four learning targets. FOUR. Hmmm. Well, turns out there are only so many hours in a day, and only so much energy in the human body, even for those humans who wear Superman shirts. And even an extra helping of grit did little to help the situation. So, after days of delay and spontaneous surges of "feedbacking," I found my better. Had to. The edge was near.

The Solution

It was in front of me the whole time. The kids. I was trying to do all the lifting. So, I came up with a plan to share the load.

I created a model with an example and non-example. Ideally, I would have used a student model, but this is our first go; I have not yet a bank of models.

I made the criteria for the targets as student and first-time friendly as I possibly could, reducing them down to yes/no responses.

I then shared my model, matching it against the criteria, and I asked the kids to do the same. If the answer was "yes," they wrote it on the "hit" side of the form, "no" on the miss.

I then had the kids determine their own next steps based on their own feedback.

Finally, I told the kids that if they wanted more feedback, they could submit it to the feedback folder, and I would take a look and respond. As of yet, no one has exercised this option; I hope that's a sign that our shared approach was effective.

Importantly, the kids will have an opportunity today to apply their learning to an identical practice opportunity with this week's Life is Lit text, which should reveal if growth is occurring. We'll see. If not... well, there's always my mantra.

Hard week. But a hard week full of lessons. Felt so much better yesterday after I gave myself a break. Glad I leaned on the kids. Glad, too, they leaned back. We make a pretty good team.

Have a great weekend, all.
Do. Reflect. Do Better. (for realsies this week).

360°2021

I don't wear my Superman shirts to school anymore. Well, okay, I do on occasion–I have lots of them, but they no longer serve as a symbol of superhumanness. They're just shirts. I am just human. No, scratch that. I am proudly human. I have to be. I have to be the dreamer of ideals, for it is there–in my dreams–where I find my better realities. Our ideals aren't places we seek to avoid realities but to better them.

And our realities aren't places that dash our ideals; they are where we develop them.

And that is, in a sense, the essence of Do, Reflect, Do Better. I begin in the imagination of my ideals (believing school *can* be a place kids love) until I reach the road of my realities (accepting there will always be factors to challenge my dreams) and I reconcile the two by daring different and braving better (hoping this is maybe how we make school *that* place for kids).

I live and learn in that space between. My ideals, my realities. My realities, my ideals.

better Builder

In my room, how do I reconcile my ideals and realities?

____

____

____

____

____

I tend to think that this must be a thrill to you and your peers, but I also need to consider that it's probably frightening, too.

180°10.1.2017

Reflection. Part addiction, part affliction, it's a complicated condition. It's one I have suffered from for many years. It's something I can't always live with, but it's also something I could never live without. It's terminal. As I live with it, I will die with it. I cannot escape it. I embrace it. Reflection is my condition.

I tend to wonder too much. I tend to worry too much. And as one who is fated to wander too much in search of better for kids, the wonder and worry of it all is amplified with their "lives" in my hands. Okay, that's a bit dramatic. My moment in their lives is but a blip, but it is a moment I take not lightly, especially when I know that my choices carry consequences–now and later. So, I wonder. And I worry. I reflect.

And at this juncture in the journey, I found myself in a place of deep reflection as I wondered and worried–desperately–about the consequences reflected in my choices, that place where I see myself in them, where I worry.

DEAR KIDDO: LESSONS FROM THE 180 CLASSROOM
OCTOBER 1, 2017

Dear Kiddo,
I have thought about you all weekend. I thought about you when I was riding my bike early Saturday morning. I thought about you when I was moving horse manure on my tractor Saturday afternoon. And I am thinking about you now as I sit here in the early Sunday morning hours trying to capture this past week, so I may do better this coming week. And as I do so, all thoughts turn to you.

First, I am sorry. I am sorry that my recent addition of weekly homework in the form of personal reading for 30 minutes, 5 days a week overwhelmed you. I am sorry that my attempt at empathy and my offer of an alternative approach seemed to have little effect on your near-tears, stressed-out state that you quietly revealed to me late Friday afternoon. I am sorry.

And as I sit here, and again try to settle into your shoes, I have achieved some clarity on how you must feel. One, I am taking you along a path down which you have never been by giving you the keys to your learning, a path that has landed you in a vast landscape of unfamiliar territory. I tend to think that this must be a thrill to you and your peers, but I also need to consider that it's probably frightening, too. I will do better to remember this. Two, I know you were not happy with the outcome of your first performance despite my assurances that it was one opportunity of many to come for you to demonstrate proficiency, despite my assurances that it was not a test, that it wasn't your grade, that it was just an indicator. Easy for me to say. As I am the one who charted the course, I can see the landscape, know its nuances, but you cannot and that must be scary. I will do better to remember this, too.

Last, thank you. Thank you for opening my eyes. Thank you for reminding me that there is more to guiding than walking ahead. Thank you for reminding me that leading necessitates looking back on those we lead, that leading seeks to bridge the distance between those in front and those behind. And so, here is my looking back, here is my seeking to bridge the inevitable gaps that will occur along our journey. Meet me where you can. In the end I do not care about the work I give you. I offer it as only a challenge, as simply an opportunity. And for both, I will offer support. I will meet you where I can if you promise the same. With that, then, we will meet, and that is all that really matters.

Sincerely,
Sy
Do. Reflect. Do Better.

360°2021

I never delivered the letter. I never intended to. And though it was written with a specific kiddo in mind, it was really written for all my kiddos. It is my eternal letter to them. But in my return to this particular waypoint, I have discovered that maybe it was as much a letter to myself, my own eternal letter, my ever reminder that I journey not alone, that my choices carry consequences. Those, it seems, are terms of my condition.

Five years later, reflection is still my condition. There's no cure, only treatment. The 180 cycle. It has kept me centered and sane. It got me through the last five years, and it will get me through the next five because now I know better. I know I will wander. I have to. And as I wander, I will wonder. I have to. And as I wonder, I will worry. I have to. I have kiddos tagging along. They are my anchors, my return-to's, the points of my way. Reflection returns me to kids, for in them, I see.

better Builder

In my room, what do I wonder and worry about?

____

____

____

____

____

...his anxious fears of being trapped in the land of no return diminished as he began to imagine the possibility of building a bridge and continuing his journey.

180°10.3.2017

Return. When we reflect, we return. We go back to where we began as a gauge of our growth, as a measure of our mistakes, as a level of our learning. It follows, then, that learning is returning.

And that means we have to be builders of bridges. Better is a bridge. Better is not how far we've gotten by the end, but by how many times we've returned, circled back, along the way to adjust our aim, to tilt our trajectory based on the return of our reflection. That is our better.

Seems simple enough. But in my efforts to communicate such a simple approach to my kids, I have learned, for them, it is not so simple after all, for the simple fact that it has largely not been their experience. They have been moved along the testing trail for so many years to get to the end of the curriculum that they neither conceive of much less trust the assessment ***for*** learning approach versus the assessment ***of*** learning approach.

For them, it's been about moving, not learning.

THIS IS NOT A TEST: PROJECT 180, DAY 24
OCTOBER 3, 2017

I try to avoid the "T" word in the 180 classroom. One, it creates anxiety. Two, it suggests finality. The former is not necessary. The latter is contrived. Well, at least in the 180 classroom. So, I avoid it, and I offer in its stead: performance.

The 180 experience is a cycle of practice, feedback, and performance. The kids practice. I give them feedback. They perform. I assess their performances. Together, we adjust their aims and trajectories, and we enter the next cycle. When learning is a circle and not a line it obviates the constructs of anxiety and finality. When kids know they have practiced the performance (practice looks identical to performance), anxiety is greatly reduced, for they know what to expect. This is not always the case with "tests," many of which are often the embodiment of the "gotcha game" that some teachers play under the guise of "rigor." It is no wonder, then, that kids experience anxiety, especially in high school, where they arrive with their deeply conditioned responses and continue their "conditioning" throughout most of their educational experience, up to and including college. Further, when kids know they have another shot (multiple if necessary) to demonstrate proficiency, they come to learn that assessment can and should be "for" learning. And, too, they learn that the notion of finality is really more a teacher's choice than a dictum of the system, but it has been their reality for so long they may never fully grasp the "untruth" of the nefarious notion of a test being an end rather than a bridge. And that is what I want performances to be: bridges, crossings to the next stage. I don't want them to create anxiety. I don't want them to connote finality. I want them to be natural steps along the learning journey. But that takes time, and that takes trust. I speak it. The kids hear it. But they do not yet believe it. After all, I am up against years of conditioning, so I will be patient and diligent. We will get there.

Last week, we had our first performance. And despite my communicating its purpose, the kids approached it like a test, and they responded to it like a test. Tommy was crestfallen upon learning his score: a 1 (far miss). In his mind, he failed. In my mind, he helped create an opportunity for learning. But he did not see that upon sitting down with me to discuss his performance, but after seeing his mistakes and learning that he would not only have the opportunity for "corrections" but also a retake (retakes, if necessary), his anxious fears of being trapped in the land of no return diminished as he began to imagine the possibility of building a bridge and continuing his journey.

Our next performance is on Thursday. Yesterday, I reiterated the purpose of performances, and while I believe some kids are coming around to this approach, many are still hesitant to settle into this new reality. And that's okay. They'll get there.

Trust takes time. In many ways, I am asking them to cross a great divide, and if I were them, I, too, would want to be sure of the bridge before me.

Happy Tuesday, all.

Do. Reflect. Do Better.

360°2021

"It's an invitation to build better." This is what I tell my kids now with my assessment ***as*** learning approach. From *of*, to *for*, to *as,* I have arrived at an approach that is designed to build bridges to better.

If you were to ask my kids what a .7 in Skyward means, they would tell you that it's an invitation to improve their learning based on my feedback. The goal for all is to get to a 1. My kids would tell you that one means done, that they have satisfactorily met the expectations on their Learning Check.

We walk on bridges in the 180 classroom. We live in the cycle of the feedback/response process, traveling back to and forth from the places where we began, from the places where we build better beyond.

And that's a bridge. An invitation. We have to go back. And so, I invite them. No, it doesn't happen overnight. I still have to build trust. And that still takes a lot of time. But building bridges is an investment with many returns.

better Builder

In my room, how do I create "return-to-learn" opportunities?

Regardless, I repeat. It's what I do. I am a teacher. But there's more at work here than kids not listening.

180°10.12.2017

Repeat. If I had a dime for every time I had to repeat myself…In a sense, maybe I do. Maybe I do have a dime, or a quarter, or a dollar. After all, I am getting paid to serve and support kids, and if that service and support require repeats, then maybe I am just doing my job.

It is our job. We have to repeat ourselves. I imagine that's where the "if-I-had-a-dime" saying stems from. Teaching is repeating. In the 180 classroom, I repeat. I repeat when there's confusion, but as often, I repeat when there's disbelief, for doing and daring different create contexts kids are not accustomed to, and such situations require repeats.

They don't always believe their ears. They don't always trust their ears. In short, they don't always believe or trust what I say, especially when it breaks from tradition. And why would they? It is different. It's counter to their classic classroom conditioning. As such, I expect and accept some suspicion. And, as well, I expect and accept that I'll have to repeat myself.

I MEAN WHAT I SAY: PROJECT 180, DAY 31
OCTOBER 12, 2017

"Okay, gang. Here's some optional sentence practice for tomorrow's performance. I am encouraging you to write and label fifteen sentences: five simple, five compound, and five complex. But, you need to make a big kid decision as to how many you're going to do based on your confidence level. If you feel confident with the simple sentences, don't do them. If you're not very confident, do them and get some feedback from me. You decide."

After Smiles and Frowns yesterday, this is how I opened each period. And despite leading early with the word "optional" and ending with the words "you decide," every period-with no exception-someone raised a hand asking, "So, do we have to write all fifteen?" Kids. Love 'em, but by gosh they drive me crazy sometimes. I have a beautiful voice, so I am always dumbfounded by the fact that there could possibly be anyone out there among them who did not hang on every word of my eloquent explanations. Kidding. Really, it's just job security. If not for the fact that I have to repeat myself, I may be out of a job. So, I repeat myself, and oh man, who knows how many times I have had the pleasure over the last twenty-two years. Regardless, I repeat. It's what I do. I am a teacher. But there's more at work here than kids not listening.

"Option" goes against the grain. It runs counter to years of conditioning in a carrot-and-stick system where few if any options have existed before. They are not accustomed to making decisions. They expect me to do that for them. That's the nature of their existence, so when faced with the opportunity, it feels foreign to them, and it becomes more a matter of trust than poor listening. They don't trust me…yet. But they will, and so I do not take it personally. We are out here in uncharted territory. But some day, they will believe, will trust that optional means optional. Of course, I am also weaving a web here, for with choice comes responsibility. Today, on the performance, they will learn if they made a good big kid decision. But I have options for that too: retakes. They always have the option of retakes. Always, another word that's taking some getting used to.

"Can we use our resources on the performance?" Always. Another word I oft repeat as kids are getting used to me and my odd ways.

"Always. You may always use resources."

That's the point. Resources are meant to be used, not tucked away in a binder, out of sight, lest they help kids "cheat" on an assessment. I provide and encourage resources, for I can think of few occasions in the "real world" where we don't use resources: mechanics use manuals, doctors rely on second opinions, cooks use recipes, cashiers use cheat sheets for produce codes, and the list goes on. So, in room 211, we use resources. Ironically, it is often the teachers who would never allow resources on a test who are also the very same ones who use the "real world" to scare kids and justify their own not-really-of-this-world practices. I am not interested in the learn-it-and-leave-it model, the learn-it-for-test approach. I am interested in learning. And I think there are better approaches than what we have relied on for years. But that is a hard trend to buck, and as such, as with "optional practice," the kids have a hard time trusting me when I say, "Always." But I hope at some point I earn that trust, and they come to believe that optional means optional and always means always. Always.

Happy Thursday, all. End of the week for the kids. Tomorrow I get to sit in meetings with adults all day. I will miss the kids.

Do. Reflect. Do Better.

360°2021

Five years down the road, I am still daring different. And I am still repeating myself. The different is no less-daring, so the repeats are no less-often. Kids don't always believe. Kids don't always trust. So, I patiently persist, repeating myself as many times as necessary to diminish the "dis" in their disbelief and distrust.

"You cannot fail this class." "I don't offer D or F grades." "Your grade doesn't exist until the end of the term." "You get to select and support your final grade." "Skyward is not my gradebook." "I don't care about your grades."

"Say what?" they say with suspicion. So I reassure--repeatedly--with repetition.

And I repeat. And with each repeat, I reach beyond their disbelief and distrust.

Of course, our time is so short, their conditioning to convention so complete, that I'm not sure I ever get fully "beyond" before our time's up. But, in the brief blip of our experience, I hope at least I've sown some seeds of change from the different we've dared, and in that they have come to believe and trust.

better Builder

In my room, what's worth repeating?

____

____

____

____

____

In truth, the world is real no matter our age or stage. And it's time that teachers quit posturing, quit hiding behind this facade.

180°10.24.2017

Real. Let's be. Real is now, not some imagined later, for when we wield such a stick–the threat of some future consequence–we are defending not the future's posterity; we are defending our present policies, many of which are more likely a matter of our convenience than our allegiance to the real world.

The real in our rooms cannot be denied. Ask the kids how real it feels, and they'll tell you. Well, at least, if we are looking, they'll show us. Their worlds are as real as they are ever going to get. And as we welcome them into our worlds, the feel is no less-real from the policies we present. We are, then, creators of the worlds within our walls, whether we want to be or not. That's our reality.

It's with this in mind, that I've come to let go the stick, which I, too, wielded in defense of the real world once upon a classroom. I was going to scare them to prepare them. And I did for too long. Stick gone, I now peddle possibility instead.

STOP: PROJECT 180, DAY 38
OCTOBER 24, 2017

"Syrieididntgetachancetofinishmyessayourwifi wasdownand...and..."

"Whoa, Abby. Slow down kiddo. Sounds like you are stressing about this class. Thought we talked about this?" I responded, nodding at the back table where we 'put down the glass' last week. "No stress. Shame on you. You will have time in class today, and if you need more time than that, then we'll make it happen. Quit stressing. Go to class. I'll see you this afternoon. No stress."

Abby was one of a handful of kids yesterday who, despite my efforts to ban stress in room 211, was stressed out about the due date. And, like Abby, I gave each of them the quit-the-stressin-crap chat, letting them know that life would go on, that all would be fine. They'd get it done, and when they did, I would happily take it.

But by sixth period, though she and I had

conferenced about her essay, fixing some transitions and creating a full-circle ending, and though she finally finished the draft, Ms. Abby Stressalot was back.

"Syrieiamnotgoingtohavetimetofinishthereflectionandwehaveagameinpullmantonightandwontgetbacktilllate…"

"Stop. You're killing me, kid."

"I am stressing again, huh? I can get it to you when it's done, huh? It's gonna be fine, huh?"

"Yes, Ab, it's going to be fine." I smiled. And it was. And it will be.

As you know, I am of the firm belief that we do not need to stress kids out with our policies. Our policies. As teachers we decide what's possible and what's impossible. So, whenever I can, I choose possible. And though I know some would argue that I am not preparing kids for the "real world," I am not inclined to subscribe to that line of thinking. In fact, it has been my experience that most deadlines, including tax deadlines, can be negotiated, can be extended. Teachers negotiate their evaluation/observation deadlines with principals all the time. In fact, some who wield the "real-world" stick for teaching kids responsibility are among some of the worst when it comes to asking for leniency from their supervisors. Real world, indeed. It has also been my experience that those with the harshest responses to kids' not meeting deadlines only ever offer up the real-world defense. And this suggests to me that they have not really thought their policies through, that their policies are not about the students; their policies are about them and their inability to motivate and inspire kids to learn. Any teacher can use a "stick" to make kids comply. There is nothing remarkable in that. And, too, there is no golden guarantee that just because a kid complies with a deadline that the work is worthy. In fact, it is often sub-par, because it's more about done-on-time than done-well. Oh, some kids accomplish both, but my experience suggests that when kids are forced to comply, for many, their work lacks commitment and quality suffers. But when kids are committed and self-driven, quality flourishes. And that I believe is the better real-world lesson. When you commit to something, you accomplish something worthwhile. When you half-ass something just to get it done, you generally accomplish something that's half-assed. And I believe this is true in any world. Teachers need to let go the real-world stick. It unnecessarily elevates stress, and it can also lead to an unintended decrease in quality. In truth, the world is real no matter our age or stage. And it's time that teachers quit posturing, quit hiding behind this facade. Make learning, not deadlines the focus in your classroom. Things only become impossible when we make them so. Choose possible. What's the worst that's going to happen if a kid misses a deadline?

You'll have to assess it at a different time? But weren't you going to assess it anyway?

The kids won't be ready to move on in the content? Don't we already move on whether kids are ready or not?

It won't be fair to the other kids who turned it in on time? Did they not have the opportunity to learn and benefit from the assignment? Doesn't every kid deserve that benefit? Is he really winning something over on the other kids if he does it later?

Our policies create our worlds, worlds in which we co-exist with kids for a significant chunk of their lives. They will be shaped by that experience in one manner or another. And in that time, we should not rely on threatening the real world to scare kids straight. We should rely on our worlds, over which we truly have power to influence, over which we have the control of choice. And as such, we should choose to make it a world where kids discover what really matters: themselves. We should provide that promise. We don't need a stick. And if we do, shame on us, for we have chosen to wield it. We don't have to carry it.

In my world, there is still stress. Abby was stressed yesterday, but I think it's different. I think it's the stress of commitment, not the stress of compliance. I think it's because she cares, not because she's scared. And I want to believe that's because I chose to make it that way. My world. My choice.

```
Happy Tuesday, all. Sorry for the rant this
morning.

Do. Reflect. Do Better.
```

360°2021

And it was a rant. *Still* is a rant, I suppose. It has to stop. We have to stop. But, it's not easy. It took me years to stop, for I believed I was doing the right thing, the necessary thing. The real world *would* cast its consequences, and there was no changing that. This I knew. But *did* I know? Was there no changing it because I couldn't change it or because I believed I couldn't change it? What's the difference? Everything. The difference between possible and impossible.

I saw–I see–the power of possible. I see that my kids' experiences now might make them expect more and better from their future realities. Maybe if they experience empathy and compassion now, they will live with empathy and compassion later. Maybe we can wag the dog. Maybe the indifferent, unforgiving world needs its own reality check. Maybe instead of the world making our students, they can make the world. I like that possible. I believe in that possible. I choose that possible.

We shape the world or the world shapes us.

better Builder

In my room, how do I keep it real?

____

____

____

But I have to imagine that there are three-hundred kids who feel like they may have some say in how those stories will end, for they hold the pen.

180°11.9.2017

Revolution. Sometimes, my sword hand aches, and the old fighter in me longs for more turbulent times, which I suppose is a stark contrast from the empathy and compassion ambassador I fancied myself in the previous post. But I *am* still a fighter. And though I have put down the sword for good, I have picked up the pen (for better), and I still seek to smite the status quo, still seek to knock the sloth on his ass.

And on this particular occasion, the old spirit had returned, for we had reached a milestone moment in year two: the passing of the pen. The kids would have their first chance to capture their learning stories with our select-and-support approach to grading. Kids would select their mid-term grades, a warm up for their final grade selection down the road. And with their pens in hand, they would tell their tales, and in so doing, I imagined they would have their shake at the tree. They would stamp a moment in history. No longer would grading be something done to them.

IT'S A REVOLUTION, I SUPPOSE: PROJECT 180, DAY 49

NOVEMBER 9, 2017

"I raise my flags, don my clothes
It's a revolution, I suppose
We'll paint it red to fit right in

Whoa...

...All systems go, the sun hasn't died
Deep in my bones, straight from inside

I'm waking up, I feel it in my bones
Enough to make my systems blow
Welcome to the new age, to the new age
Welcome to the new age, to the new age
Whoa, oh, oh, oh, oh, whoa, oh, oh, oh, I'm radioactive, radioactive
Whoa, oh, oh, oh, oh, whoa, oh, oh, oh, I'm radioactive, radioactive"
-"Radioactive," Imagine Dragons

Yesterday, three-hundred sophomores at Cheney High School selected and supported their mid-term ELA grades. The sky did not fall. The world did not stop spinning. And the sun did not die. *But...*

Three-hundred kids put a stamp on their learning. Their learning. They exercised their freedom and owned their responsibility, which we granted them forty-seven days earlier when they crossed the threshold of our classrooms. And in their first opportunity to exercise the agency we gave them, they made their first step forward into official ownership, discovering that we were true to our promise that they held the keys, that they were drivers. And though I can only speak directly to the one-hundred-twenty-eight drivers in room 211, they owned it responsibly, making solid, evidence-based cases for their self-selected grades. There was not once upon my entering the grades into the system that I felt a kid had made any gross inaccuracies or unfair assessments of his or her learning. I was both confident and comfortable with their choices. They did not take advantage of my trust. They took advantage of their opportunity to own it.

And next Monday, when the midterm report cards arrive home in the mail, there will be at least one mark on the sheet that they fully understand, that they can fully explain. But I am not sure that can be said with certainty for the five other marks on the page. For "my marks," I want them to feel that it was something that was done with them. I fear for too many of the other marks that they will feel like it was something that was done to them. There's a difference. I want my kids to feel we are engaged in a partnership with their learning, a shared experience, a shared responsibility. And I believe that feeling of engagement is achieved through ownership. Conversely, I think a lack of ownership, a feeling of "this is something that is being done to me," a feeling of "I have no control over the situation," leads to disengaged, disenfranchised kids.

And I think we can change that. I "feel it in my bones, enough to make my systems blow." But it takes courage. We have to believe that there are different ways, there are better ways. There were roughly seventy-eight-hundred grades entered into the system at CHS yesterday. Seventy-eight-hundred stories told. Stories. Stories about learning. And stories have power. But there is a tenuous line that divides the power to harm and the power to help. As the thirteen-hundred kids at CHS look ahead to the next nine weeks, I wonder how they read their stories; I wonder how they imagine their next chapters. Hard to know. But I have to imagine that there are three-hundred kids who feel like they may have some say in how those stories will end, for they hold the pen. And a day later, it seems that all is still well in the world. The sun hasn't died.

Happy Thursday, all. Have a great three-day weekend.

Do. Reflect. Do Better.

360°2021

I'm a bit of sap when it comes to Imagine Dragons' songs. Well, any number of songs by any number of artists that seem to ignite the revolutionary spirit in me, and when I need that ignition, I still turn to them, imagining they were written for me–my anthems. Yes, sappy. Well, silly anyway.

Over the years, I have turned most to "Radioactive," for that is my want for my kids. I want that pen power to welcome a new age in education. I want them to pave paths for those behind and those ahead. I want them to stamp–indelibly–their stories on the world, so they may come to expect more and better from their educational experiences.

Of course, revolutions don't happen overnight, or over five years. The revolution is still underway. The world hasn't changed. Yet. But there is change in the world. Kids now are discovering what they may remember as adults–as parents, as policymakers, as educators. And as they remember, may they want more and better for their kids.

That's a revolution, I suppose. A new age.

better Builder

In my room, what do I want my students to want for their own children's education?

___

___

___

___

___

...they have moved far beyond indifference. They have come to own it. It is theirs. It is mine. It is ours.

180°12.6.2017

Revolt! Sometimes, ambassador. Sometimes, fighter. Sometimes, jackass. I play many roles, wear many hats. Some hats I wear more proudly than others. And while I don't don my donkey hat very often, it does find itself to the top of my head on occasion, and I play the jackass. Not proudly.

It was time for a test. So, I popped a doozy on my unexpecting–and undeserving–kids. But I had to know, and I wanted their responses to be authentic, so I lied to them. Only a jackass would see the logic in lying to arrive at authenticity. But the hat was already on, and so was the test. I had to know. I had to know the impact of Smiles and Frowns on our classroom community.

So, I simulated a situation where I was compelled to quit Smiles and Frowns, something I vowed I would never do (see **R**elationships in the first post). But here on this day, vow be damned, I told the kids we were done. It was a jackass move that resulted in revolt. Kids weren't amused.

IT WAS ONLY A LITTLE LIE: PROJECT 180, DAY 62
DECEMBER 6, 2017

"We're done. No more. No more Smiles. No more Frowns. Today was our last. We're done wasting time with things outside the curriculum. I have a job to do. I have content to teach. We have already wasted 300 minutes this year. Starting tomorrow, we will be done with Smiles and Frowns. The end of the semester is fast approaching and the state test is around the corner. We have more important things to do. Sorry."

"We don't get a say? pushed Isabella, her peers' heads nodding in unison as they muttered their agreement.

I paused, measured their eyes. "Fine. I'll give you a voice. Probably won't matter, but I'll give you a shot. Get out your Journey Journals and make an argument for why we should keep Smiles and Frowns."

Purposeful pens make a certain sound. And as the kids set to work in their journals, music arose from their instruments as they emphatically-aggressively-etched their dissent, pressing their pens deeply into the paper.

"Okay, what ya got?" I sighed with bored indifference.

Shelby, stabbing her finger into her page, "On November 17th, turning back to the entry in her journal, I told you I was thankful for you because you listen to us, because you care. I almost cried when I read it out loud, and now you're taking it away?"

Ainsley, pen raised above her head, "I will throw this Sharpie at you."

Jacob, leaning into his desk, "This is my outlet. I get so worked up in my day, and it's a great way for me to let off steam. I need this."

Kaiden, looking around the room, "I don't usually talk to these people, much less get to know them, but Smiles and Frowns has changed that."

Isabella, eyes pierced, teeth clenched, "This is our time for a voice. Where else do we get to talk about things that matter to us? What about when we were all upset about our access time being taken away from us, and we shared our frustrations? You can't do this. I am so pissed right now."

Annika, calmly, "It's such a refreshing way to start the period, especially here during 6th."

Many students at once, "We are a community."

Bethany, desperately bargaining, "What if we…," going on to present a list of options for doing it differently, instead of taking it away.

Me, smiling, "What if we keep doing it just as we have?"

Isabella, head cocked, mouth open, "Wait. What? You were joking? You lied to us? Now I am really pissed."

Me, sitting up and leaning towards the kids, looking at each, "Okay, I'm sorry that I misled you. I just wanted to see if you cared about Smiles and Frowns as much as I do. Obviously, you do, and that pleases me greatly. Smiles and Frowns is here to stay. I will never take it away. Promise."

Feeling a little mischievous yesterday, at the end of the period I told the kids during 5th and 6th that we were no longer going to do Smiles and Frowns. As you can see from our interactions above, it elicited strong responses from the kids. I did not relish misleading them, but I wanted to see if it mattered to them-really mattered. It does. And so now, it matters even more to me. Yes, it has cost me roughly 300 minutes of instructional time, but it is perhaps the most valuable time I have spent this year. I made a promise to myself and to my kids that we would start each day with them, using Smiles and Frowns. At the beginning of our journey, the kids, I believe, were indifferent about Smiles and Frowns because it was so out of the norm for them. But at this point in our shared journey, they have moved far beyond indifference. They have come to own it. It is theirs. It is mine. It is ours.

Note: Isabella and I are fine. Yes, she was pissed, but she forgave me. It was only a little lie.

```
Happy Wednesday, all.

Do. Reflect. Do Better.
```

360°2021

And the "Jackass of the Year Award goes to..." The dude in the donkey hat. It was a jerk move, one I still regret for the emotion was raw and real, and I played on that. Fortunately, the kids forgave me, but even so, I learned I couldn't do that anymore. There are less-jerky ways to get to authentic answers.

I now ask kids to share how they'd feel if we no longer did Smiles and Frowns. And their answers are no less-emphatic, though far less-emotional. They love Smiles and Frowns. They need Smiles and Frowns. They will fight for Smiles and Frowns. It is theirs. And this has been true year after year. And that is why it will forever have a place at the very front of our day, every day. I made a vow that we'd always start with each other no matter what, even worries of lost instructional time.

But I lost that worry long ago. It is the best decision I have ever made in the classroom. That's no lie, not even a little one.

better Builder

In my room, what would kids fight to keep?

____

____

____

____

Today, I will live in a world that I have created to make my kids feel empowered, challenged, connected, supported, valued, respected, and safe. For that, today is the test.

180°1.16.2018

Room. Our rooms are worlds. And we—want it or not, like it or not—are creators of those worlds, for we make choices that shape those worlds, worlds where our kids live and learn. *And feel.* As we know, kids will never forget how we made them feel. That is our blessing and our curse. And sometimes we cannot tell the difference between the two as we make our way, bearing our beautiful burden: the responsibility of our rooms.

How do I want kids to feel in my room? If I know that they will forever remember how they felt in my room, can I use that knowledge to better shape their experiences now and their memories forever? If I can, what will it mean for them, for me? Is it something I can capture? Is it something I can control? Is it something I should speak to the universe? What if I fail? What if I succeed?

There's no what if. There's only what is. I am responsible for my room. My choices shape my students' experiences in my room.

TODAY IN #MYROOM: PROJECT 180, DAY 80
JANUARY 16, 2018

In a few hours, I am going to venture down a new path, a path that I have thought a lot about, a path that I have prepared for, but a path that I have not traveled before. Fortunately, I will not go it alone. I will have twenty-four young souls along with me—they, too, new to this particular path. Today, we will take a tour along the select-and-support trail. Today, we will begin our grading conferences. Today, I will listen. Today, I will learn. Today, I will live in a world that I have created to make my kids feel empowered, challenged, connected, supported, valued, respected, and safe. For that, today is the test.

Over the weekend, thinking about this "world," I, on a whim, started a # movement on Twitter, #myroom. Movement may be too strong a word, but I wanted to challenge my Tweeps to think about their own rooms, their own worlds. And so I threw it out there into the Twitterverse, and though the response has been modest, it has gained some ground, and my teacher friends are chiming in. Of course, I felt obligated to jump into the challenge as well, sharing my own list for how I want kids to feel in my room. My goal here, really, is to create both an opportunity for reflection and accountability for myself. Before making public my purpose, I had to reflect deeply on what it is that I really want kids to feel while they experience life and learning with me fifty-five minutes a day. By making public my purpose, I am compelled to hold myself to account, to make sure my walk is matching my talk.

Tweets Tweets & replies Media Likes

Monte Syrie @MonteSyrie · 1d
#myroom challenge. I want my students to feel empowered, challenged, connected, supported, valued, respected, and safe. These are ever-present in my mind as I plan my experiences with them. They are my standards, my way for making sure my walk matches my talk. #myroom

7

Monte Syrie @MonteSyrie · 1d
Take the #myroom challenge. Complete the following statement. "In my classroom, I want my students to feel..." Share it with the world. When we make our paths public, we elevate ourselves. When we elevate ourselves, we may well elevate others. #myroom

And so, today, I walk. I will walk the path with whom I hope are twenty-four kids who feel empowered. They get to put their finger on their learning. They get to select and support a mark that they believe best reflects their learning journey in my class this semester. And I created that opportunity. I say that not to brag. I say that to advance my notion that we are creators of worlds, for we have the power of choice, and those choices that we make in our rooms become the worlds in which kids dwell, worlds in which they shine, or worlds in which they suffer. And that is the responsibility that comes with our choices. We wield a great and terrible power, a power that is brought to bear every moment of every day in our classrooms. And that is why I believe it is vital that we continuously reflect on our choices in light of the simple question, "How do I want kids to feel in my classroom?" My own reflections, thus, cast light on both my successes and my failures. Kids shine in my class. But kids suffer, too. And , for that, all that I can do is do my best to do better. Do. Reflect. Do Better.

Today, I do. It will not be perfect. I will need to no doubt make changes. But it will be real-a mix of wins and fails. And as I reflect on the twenty-four conversations today, and the hundred-some to follow, I will find ways to get better. In these moments, I want my kids to feel empowered. But that does not mean I simply acquiesce to their selections. Power is not merely measured in freedom. Power is truly measured against resistance. As I wrote last week in my Do I Like My Kids Too Much post, I have to check my feelings a bit for I am vulnerable to them, and I have to provide the necessary "professional resistance" so that we arrive at a place of meaning. Today, that is our path. And to be honest, I am nearly giddy with anticipation. I know-though there will be some disappointment-that the kids are going to blow me away today. They will shine, and I will bask proudly in their light. I am inclined to record a few, but I always worry that the camera will diminish the authenticity I seek. We'll see. Either way, it's going to be thrilling. Never have I been excited for "grading." Never.

Happy Tuesday, all.

Do. Reflect. Do Better.

360°2021

Caught in a moment, I started a movement. A modest movement. Okay, maybe a minor movement. But the idea of #myroom took root.

I did not expect it. It was reflection run wild (my terminal condition) as I was revving up for our semester select-and-support grading conferences. And, in that moment, I was caught up in the hope that such an event would leave my kids feeling empowered by the choice I had made to give them the pen. But I also imagined that they might feel more, and I would learn as much as I came face to face with them. Face to face. No hiding. No behind the scenes grading done *to* them, but only making sense *with* them. It was for them. But it was as much for me.

#MyRoom would become my self-standards, the expectations I would set for myself, judged by the feedback that I solicited from them. I would share with them how I wanted them to feel in my room, and then I would ask them how I was doing. In my room.

better Builder

In my room, how do I want kids to feel?

___

___

___

___

___

...but we concede that it will never be a perfect marriage, so we just keep tweaking, trying to honor not only our approach but also our kids and parents.

180°1.30.2018

Revisit. It was time to go back. A semester in the books, it was time to go back and revisit our work. We had DOne. We were REFLECTing. And now it was time to DO BETTER. The business of better.

Skyward, our required online grade book, continued to be problematic, despite our efforts to shape it to our needs. *We* knew it going in. The *kids* were discovering it coming out.

Skyward was designed with traditional grading in mind, and so, it does what it was designed to do–well. Maybe too well. No matter our efforts to manage and mitigate the primary function of Skyward, it still managed to mitigate our mission to minimize grades.

And this was a problem. A problem for us. A problem for our kids. A problem for our parents.

Communication had been a key component to navigating our new waters for the first half of the year. But with such a drastic departure from the conventional, even consistent communication seemed to fall short as parents and kids defaulted to the familiar–points and percentages in Skyward.

THE BUSINESS END, PART ONE: PROJECT 180, DAY 91
JANUARY 30, 2018

"But it's a 'D.' On Skyward, it's a 'D.'"

During our recent grading conferences, I gave kids a chance to offer recommendations/suggestions to our grading approach. Most shared that they liked it just the way it was. Many made no suggestions. Some suggested that we change the 3, 2, 1 scale because on Skyward, our online grade book, a 2 registers as a D. Some even went on to offer alternatives ranging from 5-point to 10-point scales. In fact, a few offered rather detailed plans with corresponding rationales. I was impressed, and I listened, but I respectfully declined their offers, thanking them for their input. Here's why.

To be fair, they are not wrong. It does show up as a D on Skyward. I, too, find this bothersome and unfortunate. If a parent is not adequately familiar with our approach, then this could be problematic, especially if their child is unable to sufficiently explain the approach. Of course, this is not necessarily the result of our not trying on our end to be communicative with parents about our approach, but we do acknowledge that what we send home does not always get home, so when the situation arises, our hope would be that a parent contact us, so we have an opportunity to explain. Still, one's knowledge of our approach does not change the bump in the road that Skyward is. It's a problem. Can't deny that, for it is neither readily nor conveniently adaptable to our approach. So, we have had to make do as best we can. And that making do, if you will, is about educating parents and students to think differently about grades. No, small task.

My gradeless colleagues, Jenna Tamura and Madeline Alderete, and I have been in and out and around this issue. We know the glitches that exist and persist as we bring our approach and Skyward together. And we have tried to make it work as best we can, but we concede that it will never be a perfect marriage, so we just keep tweaking, trying to honor not only our approach but also our kids and parents.

With this in mind, here are some tweaks that we have made to our approach for second semester.

We will no longer report practice on Skyward. We made this change for a couple of reasons. First, some background. Going back to earlier in the year, we discovered that if we did not enter a "counted" score, then our grade book would not show up on the student or family end. So, we decided, for better or worse, to go ahead and enter both practice and performance as "count" scores (both 3-point scales). This was not ideal, but it would give parents a sense, albeit only an approximate sense, of progress. And though it never really created too many issues with parents, we were worried that it might create false positives-or negatives, especially with the addition of practice scores.

For instance, a kid who had only done marginally well on performances but had diligently completed all practice, might have a percentage that communicated a "higher grade" than what the performances (the only evidence kids could use to support their selected grades in the end) reflected. Conversely, a kid who had scored 3's on all performances but did not complete all practice, may have a percentage that communicated a "lower grade" than what the performances reflected. And in the end, it is-and was-about the performances. Practice did not come into play during our grading conferences. So, with that in mind, we have decided to no longer include practice in Skyward. But there is more to it than Skyward.

Practice is important. Our approach to

learning relies on it. In the end we are asking kids to perform, and to support that, we have to give them practice. But we have decided to approach practice differently. As we reflected on the learning from semester one, we came to recognize that the most powerful learning moments for our kids came from their performances. It was here that they were growing, and it's no wonder, for it was here that they were getting the necessary nutrients to grow. They were getting feedback. Even more, they were given, through additional required and redo performances, the opportunity to apply what they had learned from the feedback. And as we made our way through our grading conferences it became apparent as kids pointed to their evidence that the performances were key to kids' growth. So, I had a thought. Performance as practice…

To be continued… Tomorrow, in Part 2, I will explain. But I'm out of time this morning. Sorry.

Happy Tuesday, all. Sorry for the uninspiring, incomplete post this morning. I guess that's what happens when one sits down with no idea of what he's going to write

```
about.

Do. Reflect. Do Better.
```

360°2021

"Revisit" became and remained a regular part of the 180 journey. But in the land of Do, Reflect, and Do Better that's to be expected and accepted, I suppose. Better necessitates revisiting. And revisiting Skyward continued–continues–to be necessary. I've revisited it so many times over the years that I am really more of a resident than a visitor. And I have become okay with that, especially with my recent (last 2 years) campaign to rename it as not my gradebook but rather a tool to record and report learning. Most recently, I have come to call it a Learning Tank, where kids keep an eye on their gauge, seeking to keep it at least 70% full, as we work together through the feedback/response process to get it to 100%. But that's another book, perhaps, waiting in the wings. For now, you can read about it on the 180 blog.

So that means I am getting ahead of myself, jumping from year two to year six. But, regardless the year, I've learned that it's really about *when* I'll revisit Skyward.

better Builder

In my room, what do I need to revisit?

____

____

____

____

____

Of course, it is entirely possible that I will be calling this a folly in some future post, but for now it is how we will seek to optimize learning in our classrooms.

180°1.31.2018

Revise. With revisit comes revision. And this revisit required some minor and major revision to how we would approach learning in the days ahead.

It was, indeed, more than a Skyward problem, though Skyward had earned, and would continue to earn, a place at the revisit table. There was a bigger problem to manage. We had a practice problem–our practice with practice. But problems in the better business become opportunities. Here I saw an opportunity not only to revamp and revise our use of Skyward (the minor) but also to revamp and revise our use of practice in the learning process (the major).

How do we continue to better the learning experience for our kids? This was the question that began the work, and it was the question that would continue the work. And when work is driven by questions, then the work needs answers...well, betters. This is a book of betters, remember, from the journey of better. And here I stumbled upon a big better–-a daring different–halfway through year two, and revision simply became the business of better.

THE BUSINESS END, PART TWO: PROJECT 180, DAY 92

JANUARY 31, 2018

Yesterday, I posted Part One . Today, I will pick up where I left off, sharing the changes that we have made to our grading approach at the mid-year point.

Performance as Practice

Hear me out. First, our "completion" approach last semester was folly. Our intentions were good, and we do think there is some value in "doing to learn," but since there was rarely, if ever, any feedback with the practice (simply a not-enough-time issue), it played only a minor role in our kids' growth. Second, it still perpetuated a bit of a carrot/stick stigma that we have been seeking to avoid. Because it was entered into Skyward and because it showed up as not done and/or it lowered the "approximate grade" if incomplete, it seemed to take us back to the compliance-based days of old, not the commitment-based days we were seeking to create in our classrooms. So, we sought change; we sought our next better.

Convinced that our best learning opportunities were coming from our Performances, we began to wonder and think aloud about how the implications of that truth could impact our approach moving forward. With reporting practice completion now off the table and recognizing the impact of Performances on learning, we knew we would have to find a way to get more

Performances in front of our kids, but we also knew that it would have to be different from our previous approach.

Last semester our basic approach involved our putting practice in front of the kids to prepare them for Performances. It made sense. In life, we practice to prepare. Beyond the real-world logic of it, we were also trying to be mindful of our kids' potential performance anxiety. No coach throws her players into a game, expecting them to perform without sufficient practice. So we planned out our practice, doing our best to ensure that kids had enough practice before we asked them to perform. Again, we believe our intentions here were good, but because we did not provide sufficient, if any, feedback (time issue), good intentions were not creating the results we were hoping for, and in the meantime, Skyward was filling up with lots of numbers, but those numbers meant little, and they were resulting in misleading representations of grades. Something had to change. And it started with my "What if…"

"What if we approached it from a performance-as-practice angle?" I proposed to my gradeless colleagues.

"What do you mean?" they asked.

"Well, here is what we know…"

We know that our practice approach is not producing the results we are looking for, and reporting completion is skewing our kids' learning stories.

We know that there is value in our Performances. This is where the learning is happening.

We know that we want there to be more Performances this next semester.

We know that those Performances create a valuable feedback loop.

We know that our Performances pen and provide the details of each student's learning story in our classrooms. We just listened to and learned from those stories in our grading conferences.

We know that our approach consistently puts kids in front of similar Performances, allowing them to apply what they have learned from our feedback.

We know that our kids' performance anxiety is being addressed through our retake and correction policies.

We know that practice is necessary, but we also know that we need to find a better way to use it.

"So, then, what if…"

...we present our approach to our kids as, "In our classes, you will learn by performing. We will use Performances as the means to learn. You will perform. You will get feedback. You will perform. Repeat. In our classes, we DO; we REFLECT; we DO BETTER"?

...we commit to one Performance per week, maybe even have a designated Performance day?

...we continue to acknowledge and address anxiety by even more earnestly encouraging retakes?

...we, instead of front loading practice, just jump straight to Performances? Of course, we will make sure kids know how to take the Performances, and there will still be some introductory activities, guidance, and practice, but let's consider practice on the back end. What I mean is, what if we created a system where kids made choices about practice, based on feedback? What if we had a system in place where a kid could access specific types of practice that target where he needs help based on what he has learned from his Performance?

...we basically did away with the notion of summative assessments? I mean, we already have on some level, but if we just simply framed everything around the notion that all Performances are formative. And they are, aren't they? And what's cool, and what can and will exist is our belief that learning happens at a different pace for each kid and learning never ends. We can create that for our kids. The only thing in our way is time, but we know we can monkey with that a bit, too-as we have. Nothing is final. Learning does not end.

What if? Many what if's to discover and discuss as our journey conversations continue. We have not found the way, but we are ever chasing to better our way.

For now, A "2" will still be a "D" in Skyward (going back to yesterday's post). We have already had that conversation with our kids, explaining that our marks are communication, not grades. And we will continue to have that conversation, asking them to let go of the past, to embrace their present, and to trust that we are doing our best to do better for their futures. One better at a time.

Happy Wednesday, all. Sorry for the long post.

Do. Reflect. Do Better.

360°2021

So many revisions since. So many. But as I look back at this particular revision, I now know it marks a pivotal point in the way of the 180 journey. Indeed, **180°1.31.2018** is a significant waypoint, for the fork it presented, then, undeniably pointed the way to where I am now.

As such, I am *not* now calling this "a folly in some future post." To be sure, the future is now, and I find this decision no folly. In fact, I find it to be of great fortune, for we heeded what we learned from those first grading conferences with our kids. As the kids were capturing and telling their stories, we were writing our story, and any story eventually finds itself along the revision route. And this particular route of revision provided the foundation for more exploring, revisiting, and revising.

Changing practice to performance helped more widely open the door to assessment ***AS*** learning. It paved the path to creating learning experiences for the sole purpose of initiating the feedback/response process. Folly? No. A fortune.

better Builder

In my room, what needs to be revised?

____

____

____

____

____

If a kid's learning necessitates a little inconvenience, then I will endure it. My responses to kids' mistakes should not be governed by my inconvenience.

180°2.20.2018

Reasonable. I suppose I, as many, could probably reason my way out of or into anything. We often rationalize the convenient, making convincing cases–if only to ourselves–that what we are doing is acceptable, appropriate, necessary. We want to believe, *we have to* *believe*, that we are doing the right thing. And to bolster that belief, we rationalize our realities.

For too many years, I found myself rationalizing the punitive practices I employed. If kids turned it in late, there had to be a penalty. If kids were late to class, there had to be a penalty. If kids didn't read the directions, there had to be a penalty. *Had to be.* I was convinced. And the more I thought it, said it, the more convinced I became—convinced I was full of shit.

There didn't *have to be.* And I knew it, but I didn't act on it as early in the journey as I should have. Fortunately, for me, my condition—reflection—eventually righted my rationalizations, and I used my ability to reason—through reflection—to reach a more reasonable road, leading to better.

SHE MADE A MISTAKE: PROJECT 180, DAY 104
FEBRUARY 20, 2018

Once upon a classroom, I would have taken points away for such an egregious error. The directions were clear. I wrote them. I spoke them. But she did not read them. And she did not listen to them. There would have been no other conclusion to make. For, if she had read and listened, she would not have been so far off target with her response. And so, I could not have let go such a mistake.

Directions matter. In some instances, they could mean the difference between life and death. If the plane lands in water, one may well need to use her seat cushion as a floating device. And in many instances, they could mean the difference between getting the job or getting into college or not. If the application calls for three letters of recommendation, then one will not succeed with only one. Real situations. Real consequences. And it is such considerations of reality that led me to punish such errors in the past. If I did not, then she would never learn to follow directions. In the real world, there is no room for such errors.

I am in a different classroom now. I no longer take points away when kids make such mistakes, and trust me they do; that has not changed, probably never will. On a recent Performance, I had two young ladies misunderstand the directions. I wrote them clearly. I believe I spoke them clearly, for one-hundred-ten other students followed them, but for some reason these two did not. Instead of summarizing a selected scene, they summarized the entire movie, which then impacted their scene analyses, and so I could not assess their work, and consequently, they will have to redo the Performance. That simple. No need for additional punishment. I am not assessing their ability to follow directions. I am assessing their ability to summarize and analyze a selected scene from a movie.

They made a mistake. It was an understandable mistake that could have been avoided by carefully following directions. They completed the Performance as did all the other kids; they just did it incorrectly. In truth, they did more than their peers, for it takes more time and thought to summarize an entire movie than just a scene. Unfortunately, their additional work was for naught, and they will have to redo, so I can assess them on the specified targets. And I think that's a reasonable consequence for their mistakes. I do not need to attach an additional punishment for their error. I wrote both a quick note at the top of their performances pointing out their mistakes, telling them they would have to do a retake.

Yes, it will take more time for them and me. Mistakes often exact a cost of time, and in that I think there is a lesson. My time? Well, if mistakes are necessary to learning, then my time will be well spent, for the girls are learning.

But what about the inconvenience? What about it? If a kid's learning necessitates a little inconvenience, then I will endure it.

My responses to kids' mistakes should not be governed by my inconvenience. I cannot talk the talk about valuing mistakes as part of learning, and then complain about or punish the kids because their learning inconveniences me.

She made a mistake. I am glad she did. Hope it's not her last.

Happy Tuesday, all.

Do. Reflect. Do Better.

360°2021

In true 180 fashion, I now tend to rationalize the *inconvenient.* I expect and accept that I'll be inconvenienced. My work, our work, is human work, and humans...well, we are rarely convenient. That's the truth in our work, a truth we can either work against or with. I have learned to work with it.

How? Essentially, I got over myself. Yes, I think I still give good directions. I think I write them well. I think I speak them well. But that's the problem. *I think.* And as I have learned to think better (to reason), I've learned that "I think" is naively narrow. Just because it's true on my side of the room does not mean it's true on their side of the room. It's not whether I think my directions are clear; it's whether they think they are clear. So, I found a way to give better, even foolproof, directions: the humble offer to clarify as many times as necessary. I tell my kids my directions are as clear as they see them. "Please let me clarify."

better Builder

In my room, how do I deal with the inconvenience of working with humans?

____

____

____

____

____

Old realities cling. New realities struggle to take hold.

180°3.20.2018

Redirect. I don't fail kids. Well, I don't put "F" marks on transcripts. In truth, I don't know if I fail them. Maybe I do. Maybe I fail them insofar that I am not able to meet or support all their learning needs. *Maybe.* So, I wonder, and I worry. And as such, I refuse to let my failure become their failure. No F's.

Even so–even though I tell my kids they cannot fail my class–the "F" still finds its way into our day-to-day. Enter Skyward, my old enemy who is stubbornly set in his ways and has a different say. He cannot let the "F" go. And though I try to cajole and manipulate him into doing otherwise, he still favors the mark as it readily appears on the screen when kids' percentages dip below sixty percent. I don't fail kids. But Skyward does. And that leads to problems on occasion, but problems love solutions. So, I have continued to work out new solutions to persistent problems.

Here, it required my redirecting kids' perceptions of what the "F" meant.

F=FIND ME: PROJECT 180, DAY 124
MARCH 20, 2018

"Sy, I got beef with you."

"Well, good morning, Dev. What's up?"

I was meeting with my grade-level team in another classroom when Dev found me early yesterday morning.

"Well, it's not with you personally," he continued, "but have you seen my grade? I mean, I know it's not my 'grade' but I can't have an F, Sy."

"Let's go see what's going on, Dev." And we walked across the hall to my room.

Funny how, despite one's efforts to get kids to see "grades" differently, there still remains vestiges of the Freak out from their traditional experiences when they see an F on the online grading screen. Thinking I had perhaps moved us past such moments with multiple explanations and reassurances to kids and parents about what the "grade" means on the screen, I was a bit disappointed but not surprised by Devin's response to his "grade" on Skyward. Old realities cling. New realities struggle to take hold.

"Sy, you know I gotta have my bike. If I have an F, then I can't ride my bike. And that's not an option. I gotta ride my bike," Dev persisted on the way to my classroom.

He's right, I do know. He tells me and the rest of the class every day during Smiles and Frowns. Not a day goes by that he's not sharing something about maintaining his many bikes or pulling off some gnarly new tricks at the skatepark. I know. I also know because I, too, need my bike. Bikes. That was our connecting point. Dev was new to my class at semester, and he was not quiet about wanting to transfer back into my colleague Jenna Tamura's classroom. He liked her. He was comfortable with her. But he said he'd give me a chance. And so, for a few days, Dev took me and my class for a test ride. Somewhere along the way, he learned about my love for two-wheel wonders and apparently that sealed the deal, for he stayed. And I am glad. I am glad I passed Dev's test.

Anyway, back to my room and Dev's beef. In a matter of minutes, we settled his grievance. He was missing two performances, which I knew, for I had just updated the online grade book the night before. One, I was able to give to him, along with a fresh stack of resources, to take home. The other, I told him he could take during class later that day. And just like that, all was right in Dev's world again. He would not lose his bike. He was not "failing." But he did need to follow up; he did need to "find" me, so we could set things straight. And he did. He found me.

And that's what I am now going to start telling my kids that an "F" means: Find me. It does not mean you are failing. It means you need to find me. It means that your grade needs attention. And until we connect, we can't do much about it. But once we do, there are many things we can do. There's always possibility. There's always opportunity.

But these require connecting. And while I'd like to think that I am closely connected to all my kids at all times, it is simply not the truth. There are too many of them, and there is too little of me. And that, along with my adult ADHD and my not-so-impressive organizational skills, results in our losing touch every now and then along the trail. But I stay on the trail. Yes, I sometimes explore that curious path that "bends into the undergrowth," but I never stray from the trail. And in that, I try to be the beacon. I try to be he who brings some comfort and supplies some aid out here in the great expanse of my and my kids' wandering. I try.

Yesterday, Dev found me. And so did many other kids. We emailed our learning reports home to parents. So, yesterday was a good day to be found. Yesterday was a good day to peddle possibility and offer opportunity. It's what I do. It's why I am out here. But I can't do it all. The kids have to help. They have to Find me. For I get lost sometimes, too.

Happy Tuesday, all.

Do. Reflect. Do Better.

360°2021

Whether it's **F**ind me or **F**ill your learning tank (the present meaning in my room), the new meanings have not yet fully replaced the old meaning soundly stuck in the minds of my students: *you are failing*. And no matter how much I try to "F" that up by redirecting my kids' perceptions, old realities cling.

And maybe that's okay. Maybe the urgent, conditioned concern created by the appearance of an "F" in Skyward is to some advantage. Maybe there is value in the "**F**lag." Afterall, upon seeing the red flag, kids *do* come find me, and once they do, we work together to fill their learning tanks. So, though I care not for the fret of failure it invariably and unnecessarily causes for my kids, it does call attention to what needs attention: their learning.

So, maybe I need to redirect my own thinking about F's fabled place at the table. It can serve, perhaps. I cannot, it seems, even this far down the road, escape the reality of grades, but I can find a way to frame them.

better Builder

In my room, how do I redirect perceptions when misunderstandings occur?

____

____

____

____

...it stops short of presenting the reality of relationships in the classroom: relationships are work. All relationships are, even our best and most important ones.

180°5.21.2018

Relationships. If relationships are indeed everything, then everything needs to be about relationships. They need to be the thread that connects, the fabric that forms, the tie that binds. I began the year here (see first post) by going all in on relationships, steadfast in my belief that all things started and ended with this "importantest" R of all. And here near the end, my all-in investment was delivering the dividends my plan had projected, the returns I had predicted: a connected community.

It was a reality well-known and lived by my kids and me. We did the work. We knew the impact. We had spent the time (well over a 1,000 minutes) committing to connections through Smiles and Frowns: our relationship ritual, something so routine that we began to take for granted its power to transform and connect a classroom. From the inside, the power was clear, but what about from the outside? Would others see the power and promise? And if they could–or could not, did it really matter?

My supervisor did, and, yeah, it mattered–well, some.

RELATIONSHIPS BUT MORE: PROJECT 180, DAY 163
MAY 21, 2018

Though I stand firmly behind the assertion that everything in the classroom depends on relationships, I think it's important to acknowledge that one cannot simply chant "Relationships. Relationships.

Relationships," and expect everything to magically fall into place, like "Ta Da!" Of course, when talking about my own classroom and the successes-and failures-I've had, I have offered the relationship chant. In fact, I catch myself doing it all the time, and while there is certainly something to it, it stops short of presenting the reality of relationships in the classroom: relationships are work. All relationships are, even our best and most important ones. And just as my relationships with my wife, Mom, best friend, children, and the list goes on require constant attention and effort, so do my relationships with my students.

And though I beat my drum to this all the time-and will continue to do so, it all begins with how we want people to feel. I stand by that. I live by that, for it is the feelings from that "connectedness" that foster the relationships we have with those around us. How I make you feel will ultimately determine the nature and strength of our relationship. So, when I think about the kinds of relationships I want with my students, I consider how I want and need them to feel to create the classroom culture that I desire.

In my classroom, I want you to feel…
Connected
Empowered
Respected
Valued
Challenged
Supported

I have shared these before. And I will likely share them again, for they are my standards; they are how I judge my success. And while I daily reflect on my meeting-or not meeting-these standards, there is a lot of preparatory, behind-the-scenes planning and front loading that goes into creating the culture of "my room." Below are the rights and routines that I handed the kids at the beginning of the year. I want them to feel valued and connected, so I refer to them as members of our learning community. I don't call them "rules." I want them to feel respected, I call them rights and responsibilities. Further, I want them to feel empowered by the notion that they have rights, that they have the right to expect certain things from their education, and they can and should call me out when their needs are not being met. I could continue my analysis, but here's my point: I am very intentional about creating culture, about developing real relationships with my kids. It's so much more than chanting "relationships!"

I do have great relationships with my kids, but it is a lot of hard and consistent work. I have had a number of people recently inquiring about my entry task, Smiles and Frowns. And I am thrilled by their interest in my approach, but I would gently caution that it's not just a sideshow or cute activity, it's a deeply embedded routine that fits the full scheme of my desired classroom culture. Of all that I have committed to this year to bring about student success in my room, it has been the top priority from day one. I decided 163 days ago that my kids' feeling connected would get prioritized over everything, and I best do that with Smiles and Frowns. Recently, in my end of the year evaluation, I was pleased that my supervisor noted and complimented my work.

Component 1.3: Understanding Students' Interests and Backgrounds

The teacher builds positive relationships with students by understanding students' interests and background.

"Thank you for taking the time to do smiles and frowns. I know it is difficult to take time away from 'academics,' but I know you are well aware of the value of getting to know about student's lives outside of class. It's strange, because I've had moments during weeks when I've thought to myself, 'I could share that during smiles and frowns.' This practice gives you a quick reference for how a student might be acting in class. When they are having an 'off' day, you're aware of that before class begins. Nice job keeping the pace quick so that this is helpful, but doesn't overtake class."

I am pleased that she sees the value in my taking time to be connected to my kids. It is not an accident. It is an investment. And it has paid dividends this year. Relationships and all the work that goes into them have the power to impact student success, academically and behaviorally. Not arrogantly-yes, kids like my class; yes, I am popular. Yes, my class looks and feels different from a traditional classroom. And I think some teachers begrudge that and think that I am only doing it to be popular among the kids, but I think they misunderstand, and I think they don't really see or know what goes on in my classroom. I have written zero referrals this year, and once again over 90% of my kids met or exceeded proficiency standards on the Smarter Balanced Assessment. The latter, I don't really care about, but some do-likely the same some who think that Smiles and Frowns is akin to sitting in a circle singing Kumbaya. I am sorry that they do not see. I am sorry that they do not see the impact that relationships can have on student success. We don't need rules and rigidity to create success. We just need to connect with kids on a human level. I think it is that simple. Truly.

Rights

As a member of this community, you have the following rights.

I have the right to feel safe.

I have the right to learn.
I have the right to ask as many questions as I want.
I have the right to make mistakes and not fear penalty.
I have the right to "prove" my learning in various ways.
I have the right to feedback as an essential part of my learning.
I have the right to access my teacher for help whenever possible.
I have the right to eat and drink in class.
I have the right to express that my rights are not being granted or protected.

Responsibilities

Beyond your rights, you will also have responsibilities as a member of our learning community.
I have a responsibility to get to class on time. If I am late, I will not disrupt the class. I will quietly apologize and sit down. I understand that if my being late becomes a habit, my teacher and I will have to find a solution.
I have a responsibility to know and honor the routines of this class.
I have a responsibility to monitor my behavior so I do not disrupt the learning of

my community members.
I have a responsibility to self-regulate my use of electronic devices in this room. I will keep my device stored out of sight until the Brain Break or when I have been given permission to use it as a tool. I understand that if I cannot self-regulate, my teacher will ask me to keep my device on her desk during class. I may have it back during Brain Break. I will also have future opportunities to prove I can self-regulate.
I have a responsibility to be a great listener. This means, I will not talk while others are talking; I will visually track/connect with the speaker; and I will use gestures to demonstrate that I am listening.
I have a responsibility to self-regulate my leaving the room. I may go to the bathroom when I need to, but I need to work at keeping my leaving to a minimum.
I have a responsibility to take ownership for my learning. It is my learning.
I have a responsibility to be sensitive to and respectful of others' viewpoints. In short, I have a responsibility to be kind.I have a responsibility to clean my space before I leave for the day.

Interventions for when I do not meet the obligations of my responsibilities.

Reminder(s)

Conversation(s)

Parent Contact

Office Referral (It is unlikely that I will ever get to this point.)

Happy Monday, all. Sorry for the long post. Have a splendid day.

Do. Reflect. Do Better.

360°2021

She saw the tip of the iceberg. And why would she have seen much more than that? A few times in the classroom, a few conversations about her observations, doesn't really allow for much more. In fact, it amounts to little more than a formality in the grand scheme–a drive by, a glimpse, a snapshot. Not saying that's good or bad, and I am certainly not saying that the system's fault is her fault–it's not, but I am saying that there's more–so much more–at play here than a quick check-in activity.

First, it's not a check-in activity. It's a connection strategy for every human in the room.

Second, it's really not difficult to take time away from academics. Well, it *was* difficult, I suppose, in the early stages of using Smiles and Frowns when I was admittedly conscious of the time it was taking, but as I came to see the results it was producing, it became difficult to let academic time take away from connection time.

She saw. She—sincerely—filled in the form. But there was more. So much more.

better Builder

In my room, what might others not see that lies beneath the surface?

____

____

____

____

____

Give the kids a try-again button. Let them retake assessments. Little to lose. Possibly much to gain.

180°5.29.2018

Retakes. In the business of labeling and sorting kids, retakes ruin the reason for testing: ranking. In the business of challenging and supporting kids, retakes redefine the reason for testing: learning.

When we change the way we look at things, then the way things look changes. When I quit looking at assessments through grading goggles and started looking through learning lenses, I re-imagined my work with kids. If I focused on grading, I was focusing on sorting and labeling, fixing kids in place. When I focused on learning, I was focusing on challenging and supporting, moving kids along. Things looked differently, so things worked differently.

We have to challenge kids for their growth. We have to support kids for their growth. Our job is their growth. And we communicate this in our general call for growth mindsets. They have to believe they can grow. Or they become fixed in the places we place them (with grading), developing fixed mindsets. Their belief in growth often stems from the room we give them to grow. When we limit opportunity, we limit growth.

CONSIDER THIS: PROJECT 180, DAY 168
MAY 29, 2018

Funny how many R's there are in education. For years, long before I was a teacher, I remember hearing the three R's: reading, writing, and 'rithmetic. And for those years, long before I was a teacher, these seemed to prevail as the core to an educational experience, and even today they prevail as the targeted areas for annual yearly progress (AYP) as evidenced in standardized testing requirements. In Washington, kids have to pass the math and ELA tests to graduate. But there are other R's that matter. And though it doesn't start with an "R," it passes the sound test. Art. My wife, the art teacher, reminds me of its importance all the time, but it doesn't take much reminding; she's right. Art matters. A lot. Another R that matters a lot, maybe more than all, is relationships. It is the "R" that I push the most, for it, I believe, is as close to being the magic key in education as anything. All my success and/or failure in the classroom has come from the relationships I have–or don't have–with my kids. Relationships matter most, so I push them. But I also push another R, at least I am going to today. Retakes.

I believe we have to re-imagine learning. I have said numerous times and in numerous ways that we have a lot to learn about learning. That said, I know less than more, but one of my "places of knowing," especially as I have experimented with grading over the last several years, is that we have to move away from the one-and-done approach to learning as we rush through too much content, moving from unit to unit, test to test, calling this learning, labeling and sorting kids as winners and losers. This weekend, inspired in part by what some of my kids shared with our guest Rachael Kettner-Thompson (Tweep and fellow ed rebel), I tweeted a thread on the importance of allowing retakes.

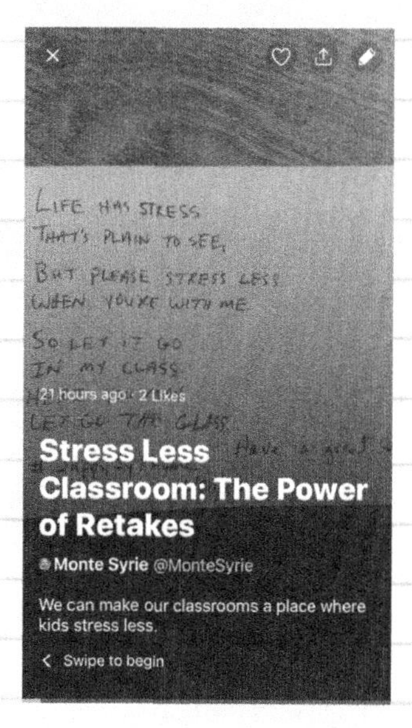

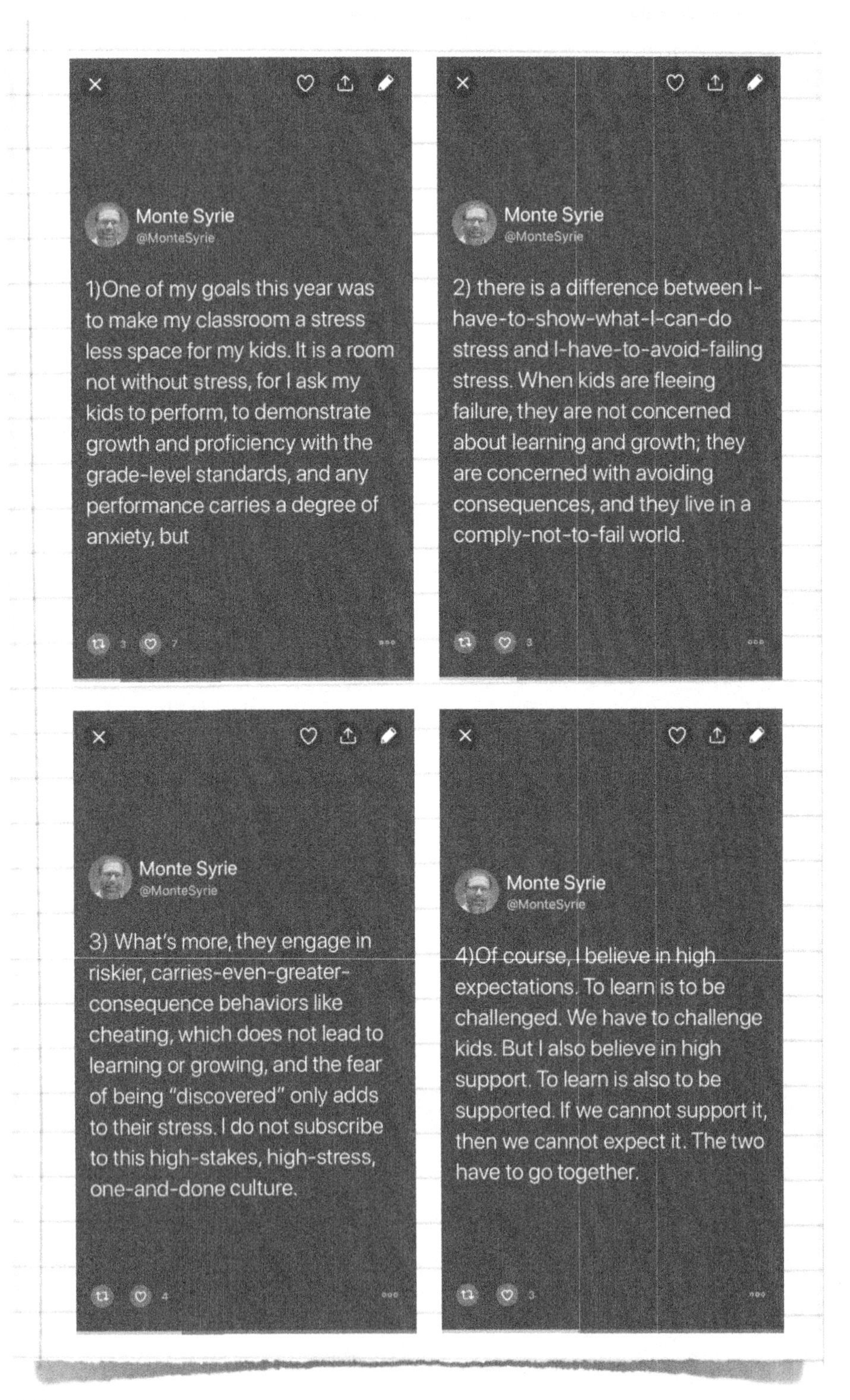
Monte Syrie
@MonteSyrie
1)One of my goals this year was to make my classroom a stress less space for my kids. It is a room not without stress, for I ask my kids to perform, to demonstrate growth and proficiency with the grade-level standards, and any performance carries a degree of anxiety, but
Monte Syrie
@MonteSyrie
2) there is a difference between I-have-to-show-what-I-can-do stress and I-have-to-avoid-failing stress. When kids are fleeing failure, they are not concerned about learning and growth; they are concerned with avoiding consequences, and they live in a comply-not-to-fail world.
Monte Syrie
@MonteSyrie
3) What's more, they engage in riskier, carries-even-greater-consequence behaviors like cheating, which does not lead to learning or growing, and the fear of being "discovered" only adds to their stress. I do not subscribe to this high-stakes, high-stress, one-and-done culture.
Monte Syrie
@MonteSyrie
4)Of course, I believe in high expectations. To learn is to be challenged. We have to challenge kids. But I also believe in high support. To learn is also to be supported. If we cannot support it, then we cannot expect it. The two have to go together.

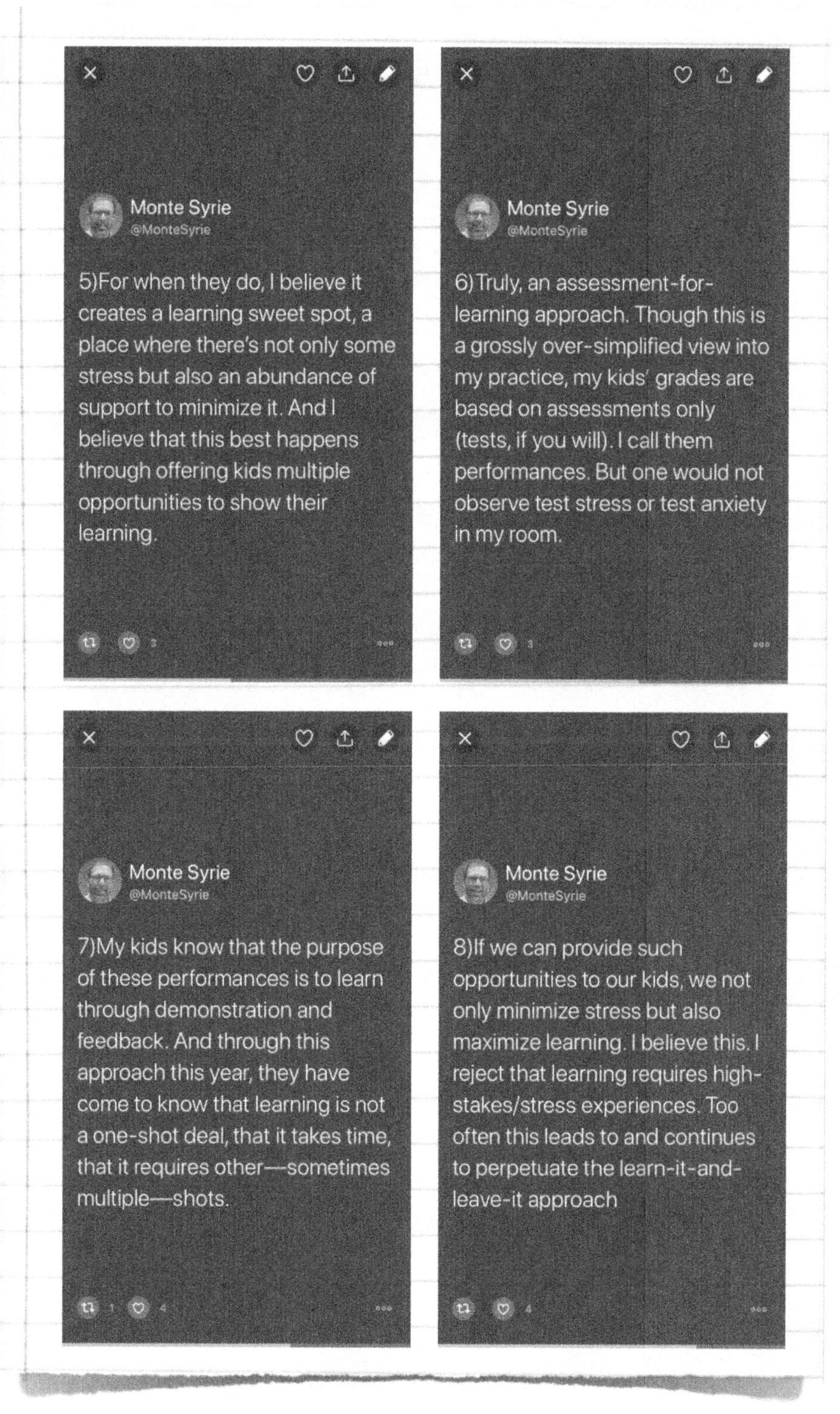
Monte Syrie
@MonteSyrie
5)For when they do, I believe it creates a learning sweet spot, a place where there's not only some stress but also an abundance of support to minimize it. And I believe that this best happens through offering kids multiple opportunities to show their learning.
Monte Syrie
@MonteSyrie
6)Truly, an assessment-for-learning approach. Though this is a grossly over-simplified view into my practice, my kids' grades are based on assessments only (tests, if you will). I call them performances. But one would not observe test stress or test anxiety in my room.
Monte Syrie
@MonteSyrie
7)My kids know that the purpose of these performances is to learn through demonstration and feedback. And through this approach this year, they have come to know that learning is not a one-shot deal, that it takes time, that it requires other—sometimes multiple—shots.
Monte Syrie
@MonteSyrie
8)If we can provide such opportunities to our kids, we not only minimize stress but also maximize learning. I believe this. I reject that learning requires high-stakes/stress experiences. Too often this leads to and continues to perpetuate the learn-it-and-leave-it approach

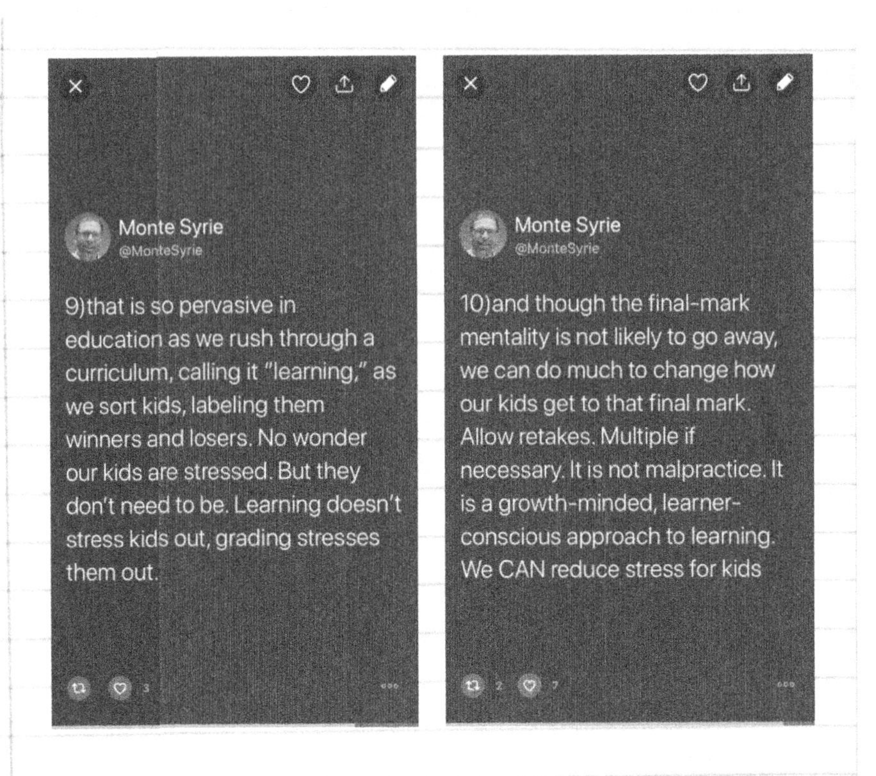

I believe that this is yet again, despite myriad factors outside our rooms and control, something that we CAN do in OUR rooms. As you reflect on this year and think ahead to next, please consider adding another R to your repertoire. Give the kids a try-again button. Let them retake assessments. Little to lose. Possibly much to gain.

Do. Reflect. Do Better.

360°2021

I still know less. Better assumes we don't know enough. Better makes us look at the world and ourselves differently so we work differently. We have to. One take is never enough, for if it were, we all would have stayed in our past places, and that for me is a scary thought. When I think about all the takes from my past, I cringe. *If I had remained stuck in those places…*

Fortunately, I learned to look again at my takes on the world, my takes on the work. My work has been full of retakes and redos because my work has been about learning. I gave myself the room to grow, the opportunity to experiment, the freedom to fail so that I may try again.

And it is the same path I present to my kids, who are all on their own better journeys. And I bank on those betters. I know there's better ahead, and I even tell them before they "take" the test that they will likely "retake" the test. It's simply a matter of learning.

better Builder

In my room, what is my take on retakes?

____

____

____

____

____

It really was a **year of R**evelation. And while it is unlikely that the R's I encountered will make it on to any official lists of the "R's in education," they will remain (have remained) on my list as regular, repeat routes along the 180 journey, for it is along these routes (**R**elationships, **R**eality, **R**eflection, **R**eturn, **R**epeat, **R**eal, **R**evolution,

Revolt, **R**oom, **R**evisit, **R**evise, **R**easonable, **R**edirect, and **R**etakes) where, as I further distanced myself from the grips of grading, I came to see my real role in the classroom: human helper.

better Builders

1. In my room, how do I build community?
2. In my room, how do I reconcile my ideals and realities?
3. In my room, what do I wonder and worry about?
4. In my room, how do I create "return-to-learn" opportunities?
5. In my room, what's worth repeating?
6. In my room, how do I keep it real?
7. In my room, what do I want my students to want for their own children's education?
8. In my room, what would kids fight to keep?
9. In my room, how do I want kids to feel?
10. In my room, what do I need to revisit?
11. In my room, what needs to be revised?
12. In my room, how do I deal with the inconvenience of working with humans?
13. In my room, how do I redirect perceptions when misunderstandings occur?
14. In my room, what might others not see that lies beneath the surface?
15. In my room, what is my take on retakes?

better Between

SUMMER 2018

Though not as big as the previous "better Between: Summer 2017," this second summer still had me dreamin' and schemin' about my next betters around the bend. And here, after the **year of R**evelation, my reflections' realities had me confessin' and guessin' as I took a turn inward, where better really begins. To truly see without, I had to truly look within. And whatever I found, I would have to face, for better must come from an honest place. And that is where I found myself in this space between.

Though it may seem counter-intuitive and counter-productive, I am going to let kids do work from other classes in my room.

180°6.28.2018

As I have found, more often than not, deep reflection and honest introspection lead to open confession. In fact, this entire book, at times, feels like a years-long professional confessional. I have sinned. I am sinning. I will sin. I have confessed. I am confessing. I will confess. I have atoned. I am atoning. I will atone.

My atonement? Better. I have found better. I am finding better. I will find better.

And here, at this juncture in the journey, from the recesses of reflection, I was compelled to make a confession. I had to come clean so I could atone, so I could do better.

But this particular classroom crime had layers. It was no simple sin, for I was complicit. I had for too long turned a blind eye—outwardly and inwardly. Outwardly, I did not want to confront them (my kids), for inwardly, I did not want to confront myself. So, I let things lie, but all the while I was living a lie with my blind eye.

It was time to open my eyes. Better isn't blind.

A MATTER OF PRIORITY: REFLECTIONS FROM THE 180 CLASSROOM

JUNE 28, 2018

Reflection's Reality: A Summer Series from the Project 180 Classroom

Confession. Kids do too much work from other classes in my room.
Confession. In general, I allow it, but in principle, I am not okay with it.
Confession. It's one of my frustrating fails from this past year.

I did. Really, in this case, **I did not.** I have been **reflecting**—*more like agonizing*—on it for months. And so now, if I am going to live up to my "Do. Reflect. Do Better." standard, then I have to do **better**.

Last week, as I processed a Twitter conversation by some of my tweeps, Joy Kirr, Scott Hazeu, and Nicholas Emmanuele, my ruminations presented a possibility of better.

In an end of the year blog post, Joy Kirr, a middle-school ELA teacher and the author of *Shift This*, shared a detailed, honest reflection from her gradeless classroom.

And while many things caught my attention, one line in particular resonated, revealing one of my own struggles.

"Students prioritize other classes first."

Other classes first. When one does not grade practice, when one does not penalize late work, when one does not impose rigid deadlines, when one does not punish behavior with grades, and when one does not adhere to the one-and-done approach to moving through the curriculum, he is going to face the reality of his class sliding down the priority scale. Of course, it is not a surprising reality, for he set that stage, but that does not mean it's not a disappointing reality. Of course, he wants kids to make his class a priority.

Of course, I want kids to make my class a priority. And I am not alone. Others who offer the flexibility found in a gradeless classroom do, too, but they are not going to compromise principles for compliance. They choose flexibility. It is a student-considerate approach.

Nicholas Emmanuele, an ELA teacher from Pennsylvania, chooses to make his classroom a "doomless" classroom.

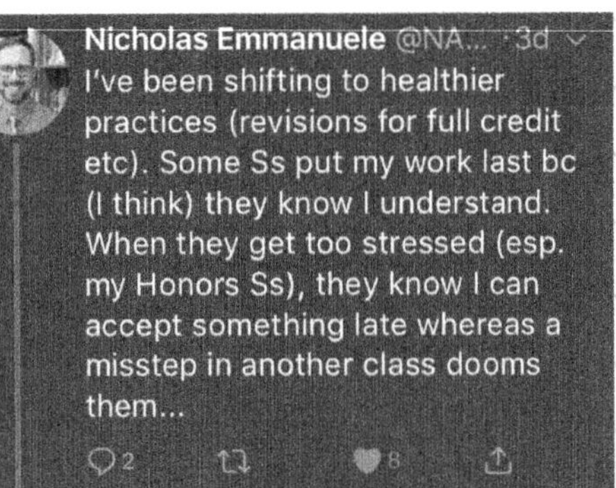

Scott Hazeu, a Canadian high school ELA teacher with the coolest beard ever, shared his own ruminations about the prioritization of work, raising an important question.

"…a problem or an old habit/feeling of control that needs to die?"

Scott Hazeu @scotthazeu · 3d
Been chewing on this post for weeks. Honest question: Is the fact that Ss might use the flexibility of a T in a grade-less classroom to "prioritize" work from other classes a problem or an old habit/feeling of control that needs to die?
7 9

This one cut deeply. Truth always does. Of course, this is not the first time I've been cut by this particular blade. I have reported on my own self-inflicted wounds as I have shared in numerous posts the realities of trading power for influence and the realities of freedom from flexibility in the gradeless classroom. I was already thinking of changes for the coming year when Scott's question sealed the deal. And I came up with a plan.

A Matter of Respect or Priority?

Though it may seem counter-intuitive and counter-productive, I am going to let kids do work from other classes in my room. I am going to publicly invite them to work on their math and science assignments in my class. Let me explain.

As I mentioned in my confessional above, kids do too much work from other classes in my room. They do. And they do for all the reasons that were raised explicitly and implicitly in the tweets above. And while it would be easy-too easy-to make this a matter of respect, I think there's something else at play. I am not suggesting it has nothing to do with respect. It does. It does seem disrespectful on the surface, and it is hard not to take it personally. It is my class. My class. But that hints of ego. And my wanting to control how my ego feels does not necessarily make my kids disrespectful. Some of my very favorite kids, with whom I feel a deep sense of mutual respect, took advantage of my flexibility this year.

But I don't think they were being disrespectful, though my ego may have suggested otherwise at the time. They were prioritizing. They assessed the situation. They made a judgment call. It wasn't about me. It was about them. They knew that I would take their work late, but they knew, too, that they would be "doomed" (thank you, Nicholas) if they did not have their math assignment done before next period (Sorry math peeps. Nothing against math, but most assignments that kids "prioritized" were math). And now that I can emotionally detach from the situation, I can see that it was a matter of priority, not respect.

But, as I also mentioned in my confessional, I am not really okay with this-in principle. In principle, I want my kids to take advantage of the opportunities to learn in my class, and I want them to commit to the responsibility of this opportunity.

In general, we make a tacit agreement when kids enter our classrooms. When you are in my room, you will work on my work. Of course, some agreements in some classes are more explicit than tacit, giving rise to specific consequences when the agreement is not upheld, and more often than not, those consequences take the form of punishment. I have found in my own "agreement" that things have been too tacit, and as such, I feel I have little recourse when I find kids working on work from other classes. So, I wanted to find a way to make our agreement less-tacit, but in a way that I could remain true to my own principles and not punish kids.

As a rule, I have little interest in compliance. My real interest lies in commitment. So, how do I get kids to commit? I believe that answer is found in ownership. One of the guiding principles in the 180 classroom is student ownership, which invites responsibility. Priorities are a part of responsibility. I want kids to own their priorities. I want them to take responsibility for their priorities. And that requires a level of honesty. And that is another guiding principle in the 180 classroom. I don't want to "play school" with my kids. I don't want to operate under the pretense of ostensible roles. I want to authentically experience life and learning with them. I want things to be real.

So, earlier when I said that I would invite them to do work from other classes in my room, I was being honest. I will. There was, however, a "but." But I want them to be honest, too. I want them to own it. I don't want them to hide it. And I don't want to pretend like I don't see it. We have to be honest with each other. I want them to come to me and say, "Sy, I have to get my math done." That is the first step of taking responsibility for their priorities. But their doing so, does not take their responsibilities for my class off the table; it just shuffles the list. They still have to get to my work. That will be our agreement. The first two will be "freebies" (see below). I will trust that they will get it done on their time. The "next times" will require a trade. Time for time. If John needs 15 minutes to finish his math, he will then owe me 15 minutes of his time. He will have to come in during lunch or before/after school. Another guiding principle in the 180 classroom is to grant grace when I can and find fair when I cannot. The Lifeline is grace. The trade is fair.

This ticket entitles you to use a lifeline. Using the ticket does not excuse you from the responsibility of class requirements. Its use is an agreement that the you will trade the day's class time and meet the requirement(s) on your own time. Each ticket can only be used once. Thank you for taking ownership of your learning. Enjoy your lifeline.

I will give each kid two tickets per semester. They may use them at any time. No questions asked. Once they have used their tickets, they will have to barter with me. Importantly, I too will have two tickets to spend. There are days when my priorities get shuffled also. So instead of "playing school" and keeping kids busy while I secretly take care of other priorities in my life, I will be real with my kids. I will spend a ticket when I have to. I will take responsibility for my priorities. I will be real in hopes that my doing so creates an authentic experience for all of us.

And that really is the goal of the 180 classroom. To find better. To find different. And yes, this is different. Probably too different for most, and for some perhaps a different that borders on "malpractice," but if doing the same was the answer, I wouldn't be seeking better, and you probably wouldn't be reading this post. We have to dare different at times if we want to get better. I just want to get and make better.

Of course, it's going to take more than a ticket to create the "better" I desire. I also have to continue to seek better ways to provide more meaningful learning experiences for all my kids. I have to do better. And I will. I have more new "betters" to share, but I will save those for another post. For now, I will be content in my finding this latest better regarding priorities—just another better to learn from, so I can chase the next one. Always a next one.

Do. Reflect. Do Better.

360°2021

If I can't/won't own my teaching, then I can't/won't expect my kids to own their learning. As such, in the 180 classroom, better—any better—begins with me. I cannot clearly see "out" until I first look in. And this was a big, "look-in" moment for me, for an honest look in can lead to uncomfortable discoveries, not the least of which is coming to grips with the fact that most things are not about me. And while that may be a "duh!" admission for many, for me, one who's always had a healthy ego, it's a hard hit, especially when one comes to discover that looking in isn't the same as looking good, that owning isn't blaming. So, the paradox. It's not about me, but it begins with me.

Here, as I said above, it would've been easy to make it all about me—my ego reeling from their lack of respect, which in turn would make it all about them. But I had sung that song far too long. It was time for a different tune—a song about us.

better Builder

In my room, how do I respond when kids do work from other classes?

____

____

____

I have doubts. But there's more at work here than one teacher's doubts about the system he works in.

180°7.21.2018

Jack and Jill went up a hill to fetch a pail of water. Why up the hill? Would the water not come down the hill? Everyone knows that water flows downhill. So, why didn't they just fill their pail the easy way? Why did they go up the hill? Maybe they had to. Not all water flows as a stream. Some water wells, instead, from a spring. Maybe that's why they went up the hill. They couldn't find the water down below where it *should have been*; they had to go to where the water *was*. They had to go to the source.

Nursery rhyme ruminations aside, there is a source from which to draw "water" in the classroom: the learner. We tend to find learning where we look for it. And for years, I had come to look for it where I thought it should be. And if–when–it wasn't, I rarely looked past my own notion of learning. After all, I was trained to look for learning. I *knew* where it should be, which was not always where it was.

GO TO THE SOURCE: THOUGHTS FROM THE 180 CLASSROOM
JULY 21, 2018

How do we know what we know in education? How do we know Jill learned this? How do we know Jack didn't learn that? How do we know this was a good lesson? How do we know that was a bad lesson? How do we know this is a good teacher? How do we know that is a bad teacher? How do we know this is a good program? How do we know that is a bad program? How DO we know this? How DO we know that?

Maybe we don't.

Maybe I don't. Maybe it's just me. But how do I know?

Seems when we don't know, we don't want others to know. So we seek answers. It's human. We want to know. But what if we can't know? I mean, really, what if we can't? What if in education, we can't know?

Oh, we try to know, especially if our "knowing" is necessary to hide what we don't know. I mean, we can't tell a parent we don't know if Jack is learning. We can't tell our supervisor we don't know if that was an effective lesson. We can't tell someone we don't know if he is a good teacher. We can't tell the school board we don't know if that program is successful. We have to know. We have to prove we know. And so, we measure.

We measure. When we want to know if an essay is effective, we create a rubric. When we want to know if a student has learned, we provide a grade. When we want to know if a teacher is good, we create an evaluation. When we want to know if a program is successful, we mine data. We measure to show what we know, to prove beyond doubt that we know. But what if there's doubt?

What if the same essay, using the same rubric was scored differently by a number of teachers? Does that mean we know? I have some doubts.

What if a student got an A on all tests but only got a C in the class because she didn't do the homework? Does that mean we know? I have some doubts.

What if a teacher puts on a show only when he is observed to be labeled good? Does that mean we know? I have some doubts.

What if a school or district fails fewer kids to increase graduation rates. Does that mean we know? I have some doubts.

I have doubts. But there's more at work here

than one teacher's doubts about the system he works in. When we measure, we rank. When we rank, we label. When we label, we sort. In short, when we measure, whether it's an intended outcome or not, we create a culture of winners and losers, a reality that we know can have grave implications for kids at the top and bottom. A kid who is labeled a poor reader in elementary school will come to believe that label, come to live that label. And by the time she reaches me at the high school, she has lived out the prophecy. When my own son comes to believe-despite my suggesting otherwise-that an A is all that matters, his heightened stress makes me hope in earnest that he gets an A- this next year as he starts his high school experience.

Of course, we will never get away from the measure. We have to show what we know. But maybe, in the case of kids' learning, we can take a different tack. Maybe we can know better by engaging those who know best: the learner. Let's ask her. And if we can't let it take the place of our measure, then maybe we can make it a complement to our measure. Either way, there may be some merit to the notion that if you want to know something, go to the source.

Kids know. They do. More than we believe, and the longer I have spent moving away from the measure and moving closer to the source, the more I have come to believe that if we want to know if kids are learning, we have to ask and listen. And that's why I have gone to and continue to refine my select-and-support grading. Kids select their grades and support their choices with evidence. We come to an agreement based on the evidence, but we also take into account our judgment, our gut. For each kid, each situation is different, and among the myriad measurements that exist in our system, the only thing I "know" is that there is no one, best means to measure each kid. This I know. And of that there's no doubt.

We should not only consider but go to the source when it comes to learning. Go to the headwaters. Ask her. She knows.

Do. Reflect. Do Better.

360°2021

Early explorers were obsessed with discovering the headwaters of the Nile. And for nearly three millennia the source eluded explorers as they risked life, limb, and reputation to definitively discover from where it all came. Even today, there remains disagreement about the definitive source (Rapp). *Even today there remains disagreement about the definitive source.* In another context, education (our Nile), despite knowing all we know, *there remains disagreement* about the definitive definition of learning (the headwaters of our work). And so, in the absence of answers, one must explore, especially when he comes to doubt long-held beliefs about what "should be," and he comes to wonder and worry about what he knows and how he knows. And as he explores, he comes to obsess about finding the source. So, he seeks the source. He has to.

Five-plus years later, I am still seeking the source. I may not be risking life or limb (there are limits to braving better). But maybe I am risking my reputation with a mad obsession to find the source. Too late to turn back now.

(Rapp, Joshua. "The Source of the Nile River: A Mystery That Spanned Three Millennia." Discover Magazine, 9 May 2021)

better Builder

In my room, how do I know what I know about learning?

____

____

____

____

____

And just like that a priority became a memory.

180°8.16.2018

I'm a great starter. But I'm a terrible pacer. This was true when I ran the 800 in high school track. This was true when I raced mountain bikes in college. Fast and furious was my trademark, but fast and furious, more often than not, led to dead at the end. And this, too, has been true in the classroom as fast at the front has led to fizzle at the finish.

And while this fizzle is less about pace and more about attention, I found myself once again not keeping up with my commitments, my priorities. And here, not for the last time, I found myself starting over with the Journey Journal.

As you may recall from "better Between: Summer 2017," I had come up with a grand plan for the Journey Journal. And though I knew I had not arrived at an end (an always and forever idea), I thought for sure I would see the thing to which I had devoted so much time and energy all the way through, but, of course, the fizzle found me.

UNPACKING 180, PART II: PROJECT 180
PROLOGUE, YEAR THREE
AUGUST 16, 2018

I tried.
I failed.
I am trying again.
I will succeed.
Until I fail again.

One of my biggest disappointments last year was my dropping the ball with our Journey Journals. Long story. Quit making a priority a priority. Time got on. Never got back to it. And just like that a priority became a memory. Kind of a painful one. So now I will seek to do better. Here's the plan.

Journey Journal
Expectations

- You will reflect every day. You will have the last 5 minutes of every period to do this.
- I will provide the "entry sheets." You will be able to complete six entries on a sheet, 3 on each side. You will store completed sheets in your portfolio.
- Entries should be approximately 50 words.
- Each entry should tell a story of sorts. It should stand alone; that is, to an outsider, each entry should give a glimpse of not only what you did but also why it matters.
- I will provide ideas and resources to help you enter into the reflective mode.
- The tone should be informal, reflective, conversational. You are telling *your* story. Be you.
- You will be encouraged to practice the "ways-of-a-writer" skills that we are currently emphasizing in class.
- You will share your entries: with a partner, with the class, with me. When we share our work, we make it real. When we share our work, we create community.
- You will keep track of your daily activity, circling the activity that best indicates the bulk of your work for that day. This will just be a recordkeeping component, a way to gather some data on the type and amount of work you are doing.
- Reflection is evidence of learning. Your journal entries will be part of your select-and-support grading conversation at the end of the semester. Remember, you must show that you are growing as a learner. Your Journey Journal is intended to help you capture your growth.
- You must help me make this a priority. Don't let me off the hook. We have to do this every day.

Tried to keep it simple and straightforward. One thing I have discovered is that it takes many kids a while to warm up to the reflective mode, especially when it comes to getting them to move beyond the "what" of things. I want them to get to the "so what" and "now what" of things in their entries. I will offer support and practice patience. I will present my "Story Stems" again this year to help them get started down their reflective routes.

Of note, perhaps, is that this year I will include their Journey Journals as part of the select-and-support grading process. Admittedly, this is a bit uncomfortable for me, as I do not want it to create compliance. As you know, I have little interest in that path. I prefer to travel down the commitment path. I don't want kids to reflect because they have to. I want kids to reflect because they want to, because they see the value it adds to their learning. So I will keep my eyes wide open to this as we journey forth. I will not give points. I will not penalize for missing entries. I will leverage commitment by engaging the kids about their reflections, both formally and informally. I will also leverage their commitment by pointing to the fact that we have no homework, only school work, and as part of their commitment, I expect them to

work when they are at school, when they are in my class. Reflecting is at the center of our work…well, at least that's the goal.

I am not using notebooks this year. Instead, I am using sheets. I know this may seem a bit old school, but I think it will make it more manageable and efficient. Why not digitally? Thought about it. But the reality remains: we still don't have continual, immediate access to tech, so I am going with paper. Here's the template we will use.

Journey Journal Entries

Date:
Work: Reading Writing Discussing Creating Presenting Collaborating Conferencing Viewing Practicing Performing
Entry:

We do. We reflect. We do better. This is my next better with Journey Journals. It's all I can do until I come to my next, "next better."

Do. Reflect. Do Better.

360°2021

Next never stopped. It just seems to be the race I run. I've never been able to settle into a comfortable pace, and I've never been able to settle for a routine route (at least not for very long). I get restless in my reflection. I think. I imagine. I innovate. I do to undo. Maybe I get bored. Is boredom the real drive behind better? Yes. No. Maybe. Regardless, I'm always after better. In fact, this year (21/22), I changed the Journey Journal halfway through. Here's my latest.

Learning-Level Commitment: A B C (Highlight One)
Monday Please list what *you did* during class today. What is your confidence level with our current work? (Highlight One) **Confident Somewhat Confident Not Confident** Please explain your confidence level: Please discuss what you read during Personal Reading today. Did you feel **Connected, Empowered, Valued, Respected, Challenged, Supported** in class today? (Highlight any that apply) Choose one from the list and explain why you did or did not feel this way. Who is someone in this class that you feel connected to? Overall, how was your experience in here today?

And though it's been "better" for a bit, I'm already dreamin' and schemin' my next.

So, then, is that the course–perhaps *curse*–of better? Yes, *my* better. I have come to expect and, more importantly, accept that this is the race I run. But my race isn't your race. You have your own pace; you run your own race. And when there's never a finish line, only a next leg, we just keep moving. That's the beauty of better. There's no race to be won, for our work is never done.

better Builder

In my room, how do I pace my year-long race?

____

____

____

____

The spaces between. Between years. Between months. Between days. Between hours. Between minutes. Each between becomes a moment, a place to pause, a place to reflect, a place to discover. A place to *better.*

And while the 180 journey *is* about the endless quest of ever-chasing better, it's no less about what we capture in those moments between, those moments before we hit the 180 spin again, where DO meets REFLECT, and DO BETTER waits its turn, its own brief *better* moment.

And so it goes. And goes. And goes.

better Builders

1. In my room, how do I respond when kids do work from other classes?
2. In my room, how do I know what I know about learning?
3. In my room, how do I pace my year-long race?

Year Three

HELPING HUMANS

I arrived at Year Three much changed, for things had changed—*much.* Two years of exploring the gradeless realm had changed how I viewed the work, which, of course, in turn, changed how I viewed my students, how I viewed myself. Grades gone, I came to see the humans in the room, the humans in the work. And once one reaches that point in his journey (seeing humans), he can never not see them again. Our work is first and most human work, and we…well, then, we are helpers of humans.

Sometimes life gets in the way. Sometimes we all need some grace. Sometimes we need a lifeline.

180°9.19.2018

Humans need flexibility—for the purpose of priority, for the reason of responsibility. So, with that purpose (priority) and that reason (responsibility) in mind, I came up with a Lifeline, which I discussed at length in the preceding "better Between" chapter ("A Matter of Priority").

And here, fifteen days into year three, it became a matter of priority to present the plan to my kids, for old human habits were happening:

they were doing work from other classes in my class. So it was time to put the plan in place.

As will all things, frames matter. So, I was careful, thoughtful, and intentional with the frame. I didn't want this to be about shaming kids for having priorities. I wanted it to be about the responsibility of managing priorities. I wanted to make real my belief that self-regulation requires room–flexibility, not rigidity. So, we had an honest–real–conversation about priorities, responsibilities, and opportunities to frame the Lifeline. And that (opportunity) is really the reason, I suppose, for offering the Lifeline in the first place. We would have an opportunity to learn.

LIFELINES: PROJECT 180, DAY 15
SEPTEMBER 19, 2018

It's my curse. I'm flexible to a fault. I know this. I own this. I am this. I give my kids too much freedom. And though I believe such flexibility is necessary to create situations that promote responsibility, it sometimes bites me in the butt. One sizable chunk from my derriere comes in the form of kids' doing work from other classes in my class. And while I have grudgingly turned a blind eye in the past, it has never really sat well with me, and this summer I vowed to come up with a plan to address this issue. I presented the idea in one of my Reflection's Reality posts this summer, A Matter of Priority.

Basically, I decided to marry my flexibility to my priority. I still want to give kids room, freedom, grace, but I want them to understand the responsibility that comes with the flexibility I grant. I want them to understand that we both have priorities and sometimes those priorities don't match, and things get out of balance. That's going to happen. So, when it happens, I have come up with a system that will eventually set things right again, allowing for flexibility, priority, and responsibility to work in concert. Yesterday, I introduced the plan to my kiddos.

The Lifeline

Sometimes life gets in the way. Sometimes we all need some grace. Sometimes we need a lifeline.

My class is not my kids' lives. It is but a small part of their lives. And sometimes the other parts of their lives get in the way of their lives in my fifty-five-minute world. They have priorities. We all have priorities. And sometimes we live at the whim of those priorities, and such whimsy is not always easy for others to understand. I try to understand such whimsicality-another curse.

Yesterday, I gave each kid two lifeline tickets for those times when their whimsy visits and they need a break. Here's the basic premise.

This ticket entitles you to use a lifeline. Using the ticket does not excuse you from the responsibility of class requirements. Its use is an agreement that the you will trade the day's class time and meet the requirement(s) on your own time. Each ticket can only be used once. Thank you for taking ownership of your learning. Enjoy your lifeline.

Kids may use their lifelines to attend to the other parts of their lives they bring with them. This could be the monster math test they have the next period or the bad day that just won't let go. They may use them on any day. No restrictions.

They only get two per semester. If they do not use them, they may carry them over to the next semester.

A lifeline does not excuse or exempt them from the work in the class. It just buys them some flexibility.

Two lifelines may not be enough for some to make it through the semester. Life doesn't come in standardized models (despite what we perpetuate in school). So, in addition, I offer another lifeline of sorts: time for time. If John needs to spend fifteen minutes on his math assignment that's due the next period, then he owes me fifteen minutes of his time. This is an honor system that lives or dies with kids' honoring their commitment. One no-show by John, then he loses access to this particular lifeline. Why not just tell kids no? I could. But I believe their minds will likely be elsewhere anyway, and I don't want them stressing out. I just want them to own it by working with me in these situations, not trying to sneak and do their work from other classes.

Crazy? *Maybe*. Better fixed by a stronger hand? *Not convinced*. Different from other teachers? *Intentionally*. Better requires change. Change necessitates different. So, I do different. Better? *Only until I find my next better*. Always chasing better.

Happy Wednesday, all.

Do. Reflect. Do Better.

360°2021

And…they didn't use them. Oh, some did. They needed them. They used them, all four (2 per semester). But most never put into play their Lifelines.

I did not expect this. I expected them to cash in early and often, figuring many would use them up long before the end of the semester, forcing me to face my flexibility faults, fearing I would grant more because…well, my forever fault. But I never had to cross that bridge, for I never came to it. Kids didn't use their Lifelines.

So, then, they weren't necessary? No, they were absolutely necessary. They still are. I still issue them, and kids still—largely—don't use them, but I believe the option to use them is as meaningful as the actual action. They create a consciousness. Kids think about priority. They think about responsibility, both of which are opportunities created from flexibility. They have the room to regulate. And that is why I still offer them. Humans need room to think about themselves, to learn about themselves. So, in my room, I give room.

Humans need flexibility.

better Builder

In my room, how far am I willing to stretch?

___

___

___

___

___

Maybe all we're doing is adding to kids' experiences as they make their ways through our classrooms.

180°9.27.2018

Humans need experience. Not for the first time, I found myself wondering (worrying) about what learning is–and isn't. And while we seem to cling to traditional means–*and ends*–for answering the learning question, I wonder–a lot–if we really do answer the question: What is learning?

I wanted to know. So, I began to look into my own learning, which eventually led to my own teaching. And I arrived at two questions. First, what have I learned? Second, what have they (my students) learned? And I got stuck on the word "learned."

And why wouldn't I get stuck there? "Learned" suggests an end, an arrival. And as I reflected more deeply about my experiences, as learner and teacher, I found no ends, only steps along the way. I hadn't arrived. And I certainly hadn't arrived at my understanding of learning, for if I had, I wouldn't have been writing this post in which I wrestled with the learning question.

So, I grabbed on and grappled. What had I learned? What had they learned (all of them over the years)?

Nothing was learned.

WHAT YA LEARNING? PROJECT 180, DAY 21
SEPTEMBER 27, 2018

What are you learning?

Seems a fair question. Seems maybe the only question.

But what's the answer? Is it as simple as a teacher-generated learning target that is posted in the front of the room? If a student is able to recite the target, is that evidence that she is learning in that room? If a student can hold up a number on her fingers at the end of the lesson, indicating where she is situated in the learning target, is that evidence that she is learning in that room? Or…

Or is it more complicated than the ritual routine that plays out in so many classrooms, where outsiders drop in and attempt to put a finger on what is and what is not learning?

But what is learning? Is it the score on the end-of-the-unit test? Is it the standardized-test score at the end of the year? Is it the percentage in the grade book? Maybe it's grander. Maybe it's an arrival, a moment of clarity, an epiphany that screams, "I have learned."

I think of my own learning as a teacher. And I try to put in targets.

I can meet the needs of all the students in

my classroom.

I can motivate all the students in my classroom.

I can get all the students to grade-level achievement in my classroom (with all 86 standards).

Or

By the end of (insert time marker), the Teacher Will Be Able To (TWBAT)…

…meet the needs of all the students in my classroom.

…motivate all the students in my classroom.

…get all the students to grade-level achievement in my classroom (with all 86 standards).

First, I neither "can," nor will I "be able to," regardless the time marker: lesson, unit, day, year, decade, career.

Second, it seems absurd, artificial, contrived…well, silly.

Third, I am reminded every lesson, every unit, every day, every year, every decade, and-I imagine-in my one career that there will be no arrival. I will never stand atop the mount and declare, "I have arrived. I have learned."

No, I won't. But I will declare after every lesson, every unit, every day, every year, and I imagine at the end of my career, "I am learning." I entered my career learning. I live my career learning. I will leave my career learning. I am learning. I am experiencing.

Experiencing.

Maybe that's it. Maybe the question is "What are you experiencing?" Semantics? Maybe. But there may be more to it, too.

Ever wonder why we have to "reteach" things? Things that kids "learned" the year before. Things they learned earlier in the same year? Maybe they didn't learn it as an end. Maybe they learned it as a step. Maybe all we're doing is adding to kids' experiences as they make their ways through our classrooms. They enter our rooms somewhere along their learning; they dwell with us in their learning; and they leave us in their learning. Their learning.

In the end, I don't know. My learning suggests that there is no simple answer to "what are you learning?" And I certainly have not found that it resides in the rote routine of a target. That is not to say that targets are bad, but it is to say that they are not enough. In my room they are not enough to drive me or my students deeper into the realm of our experience, making sense of ourselves, making sense of our worlds.

And so, one will not find a learning target in my room. But if one looks, if one stays, they may find learning in the daily experiences that I create for my kids as we make our ways to our own mounts on the horizon where we will someday declare, "I am learning."

Happy Thursday, all.

Do. Reflect. Do Better.

360°2021

And I am learning. So are my kids. For I, they, we are experiencing, so we have to be learning. *We are learning.*

One will still not find learning targets on the board–they're still not enough, and I refuse to act as if they are (if only it were that simple). But one *will* find something that I have begun this year: teaching targets, which stem from my experienced opinion that teaching is responding, that teaching is supporting.

Teaching Targets

Today, I will support your experience with ______________(insert standard) by meeting you where you are in your learning.

Of course, there's more to it than this, but this captures the gist of how I'm trying to shape learning and teaching in the 180 classroom. I will share more in Year Five.

But this is no arrival. It, as all, is but a step from my own learning about learning–my own "experiencing," where I just try to meet each kid, not all kids, in their learning experience, which becomes my learning experience, which becomes our learning experience.

Humans need experience.

better Builder

In my room, how is learning experienced?

____

____

____

____

____

Sadly, in building that trust, for many, I am not starting at zero; I am starting from a trust deficit.

180°9.28.2018

Humans need trust. It is perhaps *the* factor in all interpersonal relationships. Without trust there is no relationship. Without a relationship there is no real work. We need to do real work with our kids. So, we need to build real relationships. Therefore, we need to focus on the factor that is key in all relationships: trust.

Amateur arguments aside, we know trust is a must. We know it in our personal lives, and we know it in our professional lives. We've known it all our lives. And so do our kids. It's human sense. We are born with it. And though trust is a must, it is not a given in our relations with the world. It is hard earned, and easily lost.

In the classroom, trust is also a must. The level of trust determines the level of relationship, which determines the level of learning. Kids will only go as far as their trust allows. So, we need to build trust. We need to earn trust. And for that, there's no easy road, especially when we dare different.

LET'S TALK: PROJECT 180, DAY 22
SEPTEMBER 28, 2018

"Best two words ever, Sy. 'Let's talk.'"

Smile on his face, earnestness in his eyes as Mark (name changed) responded to my comment and his score of "1," an indication of a "far miss" on a performance in my classroom.

I like two things about this. One, he was not deflated by the judgment. Two, he sees the value in our having a conversation about his learning.

Though I am trying to get better at writing fewer comments for the sake of efficiency, I still find myself not only wanting to explain my position on my kids' performances but also wanting to set their minds at ease. Of course, this time of year, in these early, pivotal moments, I find myself working overtime to undo what's largely been done to them over last decade (and still continues) in their school experience: the stressful reality of "assessment of learning," which is generally a one-stop, one-shot judgment in a race through the content onto a "permanent mark" on their record. As such, a large part of that undo is framing the purpose of assessment differently, with a word swap: of for as. I want my kiddos to regard our performances, our assessments as learning. Assessment as learning. It's not just what happened on the assessment, but importantly it's what happens after the assessment: the feedback, the discussion, the intervention, and the opportunity to redo. And of all, I believe it's in that discussion where the learning happens. And so, I seek to create opportunities for that to happen. Sometimes, when the learning is big, I simply respond with a "let's talk." It, I think, is the most respectful, powerful thing I can do for my kids. For my kids. I serve them.

Yesterday, I served Tom (name changed) as he worked his way through a messy redo. But with each talk and back-to-the-drawing-board opportunity, we got closer. Closer to the target. But also closer to the truth: learning is not a product; learning is a process. As well, we got closer to each other. Kids are reluctant to trust my approach. And why wouldn't they be reluctant? It's not what they've been conditioned to expect in their transactions with other teachers. But I seek not transaction here; I seek connection. And I believe with each conversation we build a connection, and when we are connected, we can trust. Kids will do great things when they trust. Sadly, in building that trust, for many, I am not starting at zero; I am starting from a trust deficit, which has accumulated over the years. Still, I have hope, so that my kids may have hope. So I work to build each day.

Yesterday, I shared my unease at this juncture of trust building. I know some of the kids were disappointed with their results, and I implored them not to get discouraged, that we would get through this together.

As Rosa (name changed) left yesterday, she paused, "Sy, I don't think we should be sad. It's just a chance to get better."

Yes, Rosa. Thank you for the music, kiddo.

Happy Friday, all. Have a great weekend.

Do. Reflect. Do Better.

360°2021

I think maybe when we say relationships are the most important thing in our work, we are really saying trust is the most important thing in our work. Trust is the thread in human connectedness. We need trust. Kids need trust. They need to trust us when they are at their best, and they certainly need to trust us when they are at their least. In the 180 classroom, I ask them to trust in my service and support on the journey to their better. And that requires a commitment to each. If we are going to meet kids where they are, we need to see them for who they are. We need to know them, so we can show them that they can rely on us, that they can trust us.

And that is not easy, especially for those kiddos who've come not to trust the system to see and meet their needs. And that is the deficit of which I spoke. Kids become numb, fearing to feel the real–the vulnerability–necessary for trust. And they hide.

Humans need trust.

better Builder

In my room, how do I build trust?

____

____

____

____

____

I have kids. Kids have needs. I have feed.
My kids will eat–as much as they want.

180°10.2.2018

Humans need feed. Teaching fuels learning. It is the necessary nutrient for growth. What is my–*our*–job if not to help our humans grow? We host the learning opportunities in our room. We set the table. We feed the need.

As I moved deeper into the gradeless realm, I came to see feedback differently because I came to see my students differently, which ultimately led me to see myself differently.

The essence of teaching is responding. It is found in the sweet spot where teachers meet learners. It is where our purpose is most pure. It is where we help kids grow ahead with the feed they need: feedback.

The more opportunities I created for feedback, the more I felt like I was existing in the essence of the work. So, I began creating opportunities for the sole purpose of creating feedback opportunities. And as I did, I discovered kids—humans—are indeed hungry to learn and grow. So, as the host, I had to ensure there was plenty and more in store to feed the need of each guest at my table.

FEEDBACK, FAIRNESS, FEASTS, AND A BIT OF FLIPPANCY: PROJECT 180, DAY 24
OCTOBER 2, 2018

How much is too much? Seconds? Thirds? What about thirteenths?

(Mostly) finished up our first round of performance retakes and corrections yesterday. Generally, these occur outside of class on kids' own time, but for this first performance, I provided class time because-as planned-there were many who had to retake it. I knew they would. I put it in front of them with minimal preparation, for I have come to believe that kids learn from performance situations, for it is from there-a feedback opportunity-that learning takes place, and I believe that we have to create the need for feed.

So, with performances in hand, kids came to the table to eat. Some nibbled. Some gorged. For all, the goal was to feed their need.

As I have shared, my scoring is simple. A "3" indicates hitting the target [meeting the standard(s)]. A "2" is a near miss. And a "1" is a far miss. A "2" presents kids with a correction opportunity, small adjustments based on my feedback. A "1" presents a retake opportunity, which in most cases means completely starting over, requiring both feedback and interventions (reteach, further, examples, review of criteria, clarification of expectations, etc.). And from there the feast begins, the goal to get all kids to a 3.

And for some kids, that requires multiple trips back through the chow line. Thirteen trips? Well, not sure anyone quite made that many trips, but several got close. In truth, I don't care how many trips they make as long as they are hungry for more. I have plenty to spare, and I can't abide the thought of a hungry kid (see Project Feed Forward).

But such opportunities to eat one's fill

raises questions. Is it fair? Am I giving them too much help? Are they really learning? Can they do it without feedback? Do all kids deserve a 3? I don't know. But I have some thoughts from the table I set.

Is it fair?

To whom? The kid? Or the kid sitting next to him?

The kid. If learning is the goal and to get to the goal he has to have the necessary "fuel" to get to the end, and I have the fuel, then how could it ever not be fair? The journey is a bit different for each kid, regardless my approach. I can't ration fuel based on an average need. I have to fuel each according to his end. So am I giving some kids more fuel than others? Yes.

The kid sitting next to him. Who? Oh, you mean the kid with his own needs, his own learning? His own learning. Next question.

Am I giving them too much help?

Sorry, what's the question? Flippant self aside, how do we explain to a kid that we have no more to give if they need more to get there? If there's a need, then we have to feed. Right?

Are they really learning?
That's the question isn't it? Not sure anyone in ed has cornered the answer.

Can they do it without feedback?
Is it learning if they do? What if they do it for feedback? Don't we do for feedback? Isn't that a real world thing?

Do all kids deserve a 3?
No. But they certainly deserve an opportunity. The 3 is not a treasure to be guarded and granted to a deserving few. It is a measure to be pursued and attained by any who seek it, and if she needs a little more to get there, then…well, that puts us back to the original question.

I have kids. Kids have needs. I have feed. My kids will eat-as much as they want.

Happy Tuesday, all.

Do. Reflect. Do Better.

360°2021

Five years later, I am still trying to be the host with the most. I am still trying to meet each in that sweet spot, that pure place where teaching and learning come to life, where the essence of the work exists in responding to–*feeding*–the learners at my table.

Still trying. As with all my discoveries in the 180 classroom, there are still betters around the bend. In year three, where I came to see more clearly the humans in the work, I made an important discovery. I *did* come to see things differently: my kids, myself, my feedback. When one frames his work in human terms, he has come to terms–if you will–with his work. I had come to terms. I wasn't simply a talker on topics, a deliverer of directions, a giver of grades; I was a feeder–a backer–of growth. I was one human helping other humans. And with that, I had found the frame for the work–the messy, imperfect work. To be sure, no gallery masterpiece but a candid pic from the human album.

Humans need feed.

better Builder

In my room, how do I feed learning?

____

____

____

____

____

Of course, my prejudice towards this approach is neither warm nor quiet. It's BS. And I tell the kids it is.

180°10.26.2018

Humans need support…to be challenged. How do we raise the rigor in the classroom? We raise the support. We come from a place of high support so we can present a place of high expectations. We create a *vigorous* experience for both teacher and learner. If I'm not invigorated to rise to the challenge of my expectations, why should I expect my kids to be invigorated to rise to the challenge? Challenging work is invigorating work. Invigorating work is authentic work. It drives the teacher. It drives the learner. It drives us. It's not something we do to kids. It is something we do with and for kids. I raise my support, so I can raise my kids. It's "we" work. It's our work.

"Rigorous" work, on the other hand, seems to come from a place that obviates the "we" in the work. It too often creates an "it's-on-you" experience for kids, and a "hands-off" excuse for teachers. Rigor should be an all-hands-on-deck, we-swim-together expectation. No sinking ships. No drowning in excess. If we have to tread, we tread together.

WHAT DO YOU NEED? PROJECT 180, DAY 41
OCTOBER 26, 2018

Kids had a challenging performance yesterday. And in the 180 classroom, challenge necessitates support. Heck, in any classroom, it should necessitate support. We should not expect what we cannot-in some

FOR TODAY'S PERFORMANCE …

… REMEMBER, IT'S SIMPLY A CHANCE TO DEMONSTRATE YOUR LEARNING. THAT'S IT.

… DO YOUR BEST. IT'S ALL ANY OF US CAN EVER DO.

… REMEMBER, YOU WILL ALWAYS HAVE A CHANCE TO DO BETTER. ALWAYS. PROMISE.

-SY

cases, will not-support.

But doesn't every teacher support what they expect? I'd like to think this true, but my ears tell me differently as I listen to kid after kid share stories of being tested on things that were never covered in class, things that come as a complete surprise. Mystery. Gotcha.

Of course, my prejudice towards this approach is neither warm nor quiet. It's BS. And I tell the kids it is. And I wish-I wish-they and their parents would call teachers out on it. Kids should know, always know, what to expect on an assessment. I'll even go one further, they should know, too, how they are going to perform. Shouldn't they? In many "gotcha" classrooms there is often a disconnect between the homework and the test. Sold as if it's pertinent practice, "homework" too often fills the grade book with points rather than the kids with confidence. Shouldn't practice lead to confidence? And if it doesn't, what's the point?

Don't get me wrong, "doing" has its place, serves its purpose, but "doing to do," rarely if ever produces the necessary confidence, much less growth, in our kids' learning experiences. Doing is necessary. Can't give kids feedback until they do, but if there's no feedback that follows, no "this is why you missed the target," joined with "this is how you need to do it next time," then there's likely no learning occurring. And if there's no learning occurring…

Please know that I am not coming from a place of "having it all figured out." I have not "cornered" learning in the 180 classroom, but I am chasing it. And while I dream of a day that I do finally corner and catch it, I know it's a goose chase, for every kid learns differently, and just as I catch it with one, it will have escaped with another. And so, the chase continues-eternally.

So what's my point? Just this. Let's come at it as if we don't know definitively what learning is for all kids. Let's concede that, and then let's approach it from how can we best serve each in her own struggle to grow. Serve them. Challenge them (gosh yes, we have to). But support them. Serve them. No gotcha. No mystery. Give them time. Give them resources. Give them redo opportunities (there are redos in the real world btw). Give them feedback. And then give them more feedback.

I told my kids yesterday, and I am going to begin telling them more frequently, "I am here for you. You are not here for me. I am here for you. I serve you. What do you need?"

That's what I am about. Yesterday, sixth period, Martin likened me to a mom, poking a bit of fun at my ardent pleas to let me know what else I could do for them. Mom? Okay. I can live with that. Everyone knows moms are the best. Thanks, Martin.

Happy Friday, all.

Do. Reflect. Do Better.

360°2021

I know. Trust me, I know. I've let the pendulum swing a bit too far; in that, I'm too supportive—in certain contexts. In the context of labeling, sorting, and ranking kids, I am not just flexible to a fault; I am a failure from flexibility. I will own that. I have to, for I reject this reality in the classroom. It is not my job to create win-lose situations in the classroom. That's an unintended consequence of a system that lost sight–I believe–of its original noble goal: to educate our youth. But even that misses the mark, lacking the luster of what is our calling: helping humans grow.

Okay, I have maybe framed it unfairly to my own advantage, where I once again rationalize my flexibility, but I can't do it any differently. I can't, I won't, subscribe to this notion that we have to rigidly rigorize our rooms to rationalize things on the other side, either. I do subscribe to the notion that a balance can be struck, but that begins with elevating support, then challenge.

Humans need support.

better Builder

In my room, how do I elevate my support?

____

____

____

____

____

I. Don't. Care. Not anymore. It's my room, and I will help kids.

180°11.7.2018

Humans need help. We all reach a point, I suppose. We reach a place where we're tired of the between, the back and forth, the wonder and worry, and we just say eff it, and we pick a path. I had reached a point. I had reached an eff-it moment in my journey, and so, I picked a path.

I *was* tired of the between, stuck in the middle of my own angst over right/wrong, good/bad. My head, of course, had a hand in it. *Dude, you can't help them so much. It goes against the grain.* My gut (heart, same thing–kinda) also had a hand in it. *Dude, you* ***can*** *help them so much. It goes against the grain.* "Against the grain." My kinda path. So, I went with my gut–again.

Over the years I've discovered, more often than not, the only difference between what's possible and impossible is a choice. In my room, that's my choice. And though I had actually–quietly–made the choice long before this eff-it point in my journey, I'd be quiet no more.

HELP: PROJECT 180, DAY 49
NOVEMBER 7, 2018

"Can't avoid it any longer, Mr. Sy."

"No, 'spose not, kiddo."

She had turned it in blank. Well, she never even started. I knew-we knew-there was no point. Her anxiety had come to haunt, so I just told her we could do it another day, maybe during the next day's Access Time we could sit down and work through it together. But that day came and went (the ghosts still lingered) and so did three other Access Time opportunities. But yesterday, will intact, she decided we needed to get Performance #4 done. So we did.

We cleared off the corner of my desk; she pulled up a chair; we gathered our materials, and we set to work.

We set to work. But I didn't walk for her, I walked with her. She needs me to. She is plenty able but her needs are a little different, so I meet her at her needs. She gets easily confused and frustrated; her anxiety creeps along, settles in, and she shuts down. So we walk at her pace.

"Okay, kiddo, let's go to the passage. Read it and look for the universal theme(s) that Elie is addressing."

"Loss of Faith."

"Great. Now, what is Elie saying about the loss of faith."

"Um, well, in dark times, people question their faith, and…"

"Okay, let's write that down."

And she did, or she tried, and then she stopped. Wringing her hands, she began to recite "d," "b" making symbols with her fingers.

"Dyslexia, I asked."

"Yeah, she sighed. Elementary was awful. Teachers yelled at me all the time."

Yelled. All the time.

"But you seem to be dealing."

"Yeah, I just gotta slow down and focus. My fingers help. My dad taught me that."

And so, we made our way, my giving little nudges here and there, her working with her hands to find her focus and avoid her anxiety. And many minutes later, her Performance was done. And done well.

With help. And, of course this brings questions. Is it learning? Did she do the work? Did I do the work? If we did the work, is it then invalid? Can she earn a 3 on the Performance since I helped her? Is it fair to the other kids? Will this prepare her for the future when she may not get help? Is teaching helping or is teaching testing?

Teaching has to be helping, right? If helping is not teaching, then why does it feel right? Testing has never felt right. Never. It's always felt that it was something I was doing to the kids. Not with the kids.

Yesterday, I walked with her. I helped her. I taught her. And I think that is the essence of my job. Help.

Sadly, I cannot help all my kids in all the ways they need help all the time. But I will try. It's all I can do. As for the other questions and criticisms that may come with my giving such "help," I don't care.

I. Don't. Care. Not anymore. It's my room, and I will help kids. That is my purpose. That is my why. And as the outside world puffs and proffers under the pretense of what is and isn't "good teaching," I will be here helping kids. I think it's that simple.

Happy Wednesday, all.

Do. Reflect. Do Better.

360°2021

I still think it's that simple. Teacher. Student. Students need help. Teachers give help. I was hired to help. Teacher is synonymous with helper. I teach, so I help–the humans in the room, not the students in the room.

What's the difference? And how can I say, "not the students in the room"? When I see the humans, I see the students, for humans are students of existence, and as such, I have to help them in the state of their existence (where they are cognitively, socially, emotionally). If this is not true, then my purpose is a lie. I've never only met kids academically.

Conversely, if I only see the students, then I may miss the humans, and if I miss the humans, then I miss the point–human help. *But that's what all teachers do. They help students.* Yes, but that "help" has limits, regulated by the need to label, sort, and rank *students*. And I decided to be done with that contrivance, that artificial allegiance to academia.

I help humans. Semantics? Maybe. But maybe more.

Humans need help.

better Builder

In my room, where do I draw the line on how much I help my kids?

____

____

____

____

____

You know nothing, Monte Syrie.

180°12.11.2018

Humans need direction. We get lost in our own ways. We get so focused on the present path we lose our way. We got lost in others' ways, too. We try to conform to the way things are, and we lose our way. We get lost in the way of things. And when we get lost, we need direction.

I have spent so much of my career lost in the way of things that those things got in my way. Of course, at the time, I didn't know I was lost. And even if I did, I couldn't admit it, for I was certain I understood the way of things. *I was certain*. I knew nothing, which means I have to accept that I know nothing—until I know better.

Fortunately, I came to know better (many betters), and here at this point of my journey, one of my betters came to visit, bringing with it the haunts of practice past, where a student's not following directions was something I could not, would not accept. It was the way of things.

THE WAY OF THINGS: PROJECT 180, DAY 69
DECEMBER 11, 2018

"No bad. Just where you are until we find our way, okay?"

Somewhere along the way we got our wires crossed. What I expected and what she thought I wanted were two different things, and, consequently, it affected her performance.

I said as much in my written feedback at the top of her paper, giving her the benefit of the doubt and taking some responsibility that I may have explained it inadequately. Even so, our conference began yesterday with her uttering, "I did bad."

But she didn't do "bad." She just needed clarification, for as we went through the performance (assessment), it was clear that she understood the "what," she had just gotten mixed up on the "how." And that's partly on me, yes?

Once upon a classroom, the conversation would have gone far differently. So differently, in fact, that I struggle to recognize the teacher I once was. Then, I would have simply said that she didn't follow directions. I said them. I wrote them. And almost every other kid followed them. So it was not my fault. It was hers. And there are consequences for not following instructions. It's the way things are. And she would have earned her "F."

Who does that? Well, clearly, I. But as I did, too many still do. But it doesn't have to be. I will never go back to that place, a place no longer imaginable. But even as I run away from that place where I once dwelt and dealt, I cannot deny that when I was there, I thought I was right. I knew I was right. You know nothing, Monte Syrie.

Even now, in a place far better, I know less than more. I have not the answers. I have not arrived at the magical land of ED upon a yellow brick road. I have no illusions that there isn't simply a man behind the curtain. But. But I no longer only look behind the curtain for answers, I look out into the room, the space and there I find who knows as well or better than I. The kids.

Oh, there in that place I still have a role. Always will. Somebody has to make it okay. No bad. Just learning. I can do that, and though I will no doubt look back someday and find fault in this space, too, I have to believe-I want to believe-I won't cringe knowing that I helped a kid find her way, instead of hiding behind the "way of things."

And so, that's what I did. I helped her find her way. No wicked witches. No wizardry. Just two humans working together as we seek

```
our way.

Today's Trail

Happy Tuesday, all.

Do. Reflect. Do Better.
```

360°2021

She needed clarification. She got lost in *my way* of things. She just needed direction, just as I have needed (time and again) clarification and direction when I get lost in my and others' ways of things. How human of her. How human of me. How human of us. We all need direction. We are all always lost, at least a little.

And it is with this assumption of being a little lost (sometimes, a lot lost) that I have embraced the 180 journey, the teacher's journey (the human's journey) of doing, reflecting, and doing better. I am lost until I know better.

I've gotten better at giving directions, for I assume that despite my initial directions, some kids will be lost. As I mentioned back in Year Two, my present practice is to humbly offer to clarify my directions as many times as necessary, which–I believe–is a *better* based on this experience with this kiddo from Year Three. She directed me to my better. She gave me direction. They all do. All the direction I need.

Humans need direction.

better Builder

In my room, how well do I give directions?

A long time ago I discovered that, most of the time, the difference between what's possible and impossible in the classroom rests with my decision.

180°12.30.2018

Humans need possibility. I imagine possibility as a fish tank, where the resident fish grows to fit the tank. The bigger the tank, the bigger the growth. The smaller the tank, the smaller the growth. It's an environmental effect. Our rooms, while not tanks, are environments, where kids will grow or not grow based on environmental factors, of which there are many. Of course, there are some we can control; there are some we cannot control. So, then, I focus on what I can control: my choices. And from that place of control, I have learned that possibility is a foundational factor, an environmental effect on the growth of my kids. So, I choose possible.

Of course, this wasn't always the case. I didn't walk into the room twenty-five years ago believing I wielded the power of possibility. Heck, I didn't even know I could make choices, and I certainly didn't understand the control/cannot control phenomenon of life or the classroom. I thought–imagined, really–that some outside force was pulling the strings, and I did things because "I had to."

TO A FAULT

DECEMBER 30, 2018

We all make choices.

I am sure it caught her off guard. I am sad that it stressed her out. I am glad she contacted me. Well, her mom did.

Yesterday, I got an email from a parent requesting that I change her daughter's presentation date. They have been on vacation since before break and now they will be on vacation after break, so consequently, her mom wants me to change the date because she won't be here when her presentation is scheduled. I have to make a choice.

Teachers have to make a lot of choices, even without kids, but add kids to the mix, and those choices rise considerably, for kids' choices impact our choices, which then impact their choices. And…well, lots of choices.

Of course, to stem the tide, we have policies in place which aim to minimize the number of choices we have to make and to create some consistency in our day-to-day dealings with our students. Consistency is key in the classroom. And so we do our best to provide consistent experiences for our kids. But sometimes it's difficult to be consistent. Life happens. Unforeseen's show up-longer vacations. And consistency crumbles. And we have to make choices. I have to make a choice.

So, I did. It was an easy one to make. I changed the presentation date.

First, her project was done before she went on vacation. She is a diligent student. Second, her partner selected the "lottery" date, which just happened to be the day we got back from break. It could just as well have been the last day of presentations. So, with those in mind, it was really easy to change the date, but even without those circumstances, I would have changed it.

Flexible to a Fault

Am I too flexible? Maybe. Probably. Okay, yes. I am too flexible. There I said it. I, Monte Syrie, am too flexible as a teacher. Always have been and always will be. Pretty set in that way, despite my claim. I have made a choice to be so. I have consciously made a choice to create a culture of possibility in my classroom. And so, to achieve that desired end, I have to be flexible.

A long time ago I discovered that, most of the time, the difference between what's possible and impossible in the classroom rests with my decision. Late work policy. My choice. Retake policy. My choice. Presentation dates. My choice. The list goes on. And as they are my choices, and as I seek to make things possible, I will not let my choices keep a kid from trying to make progress.

But is that fair to the other kids? She chose to go on vacation. She chose to extend her vacation. Shouldn't there be consequences for that choice? Well, a choice was made, but it wasn't hers. I am pretty sure that she did not call the airline to change the tickets or contact the hotel's front desk to reserve a few extra nights' lodging. But even so, she won't learn an important life lesson about choices and consequences if I move the date. Really? I am not about that. There is nothing wrong with moving a date when it can be done, and here it can be done. It's possible. So, I did it.

But what about consistency? Won't that undermine my standing with the other kids if I am not consistent? Well, not if I am consistently flexible. In that, I am consistent. And my kids know it. In fact, though she made it "official" by having mom email me the request, I have to believe she knew I would do it. So, why even email me, then? Well, I want to believe it was an act of consideration and respect. Further, I want to believe that she was so because she finds me so. Considerate and respectful. She is not taking advantage of me. She is experiencing life with me. And oftentimes life forces us to make decisions that affect others. Her choices. My choices. Our choices.

In the end I believe in a culture of possibility through flexibility. And I have found few students or parents who object. Interestingly, the few people who do offer some objection are fellow teachers, for I am "failing to teach them the lessons of the real world." Not sure about that. But I am certain of my choice, and I will own it, even if it's a fault.

Do. Reflect. Do Better.

360°2021

Room to grow. *The bigger the tank…* Well, turns out the classroom-as-fish-tank metaphor doesn't fit. Some quick research, as I was writing this, put to rest the long standing myth–based on a lack of understanding–that fish magically, or naturally, adjust their size to the tank. It's a bit more complicated than that. And so, I suppose, it goes that it's a bit more complicated than that in the classroom, too.

Of course, the literal size of the room has nothing to do with the growth of our students (good thing, given how inadequate the physical space is). But what about the figurative size of our rooms? Doesn't even the "mythical metaphor" work here? Doesn't the size of possibility impact our students' growth? Or let's take a different tack, what about the size of the *impossibility*? How many "impossible" policies (late work penalties, zeros, etc.) have stunted students? Seems "possible" plays a part. Further, it seems, since possible or impossible is a choice, that our choices play a part, too. For my part, then, I will choose possible.

Humans need possibility.

better Builder

In my room, how do I choose between what's possible and impossible?

Maybe instead of placing some future world on their shoulders, we should just simply help them with the one that lies on their shoulders right now.

180°1.10.2019

Humans need to feel real. When we make students feel like their present worlds are less-real than their future worlds, we distort and dishonor the reality of the human experience. And this approach creates distance. And when we distance ourselves from them by holding at arm's length the "real in their worlds," we distance ourselves from our present responsibility: their present realities. Distance negates responsibility.

We shouldn't get to decide what's real and what isn't, for our perceptions are flawed. And we take flaw to fatal fault when we perpetuate this notion of the real world as "motivation" in our work with kids. *"In the real world…"*

Though I believe such utterances can come from a place of good intentions, more often than not, they're rationalizations, justifications for punitive practices. *You can't miss deadlines in the real world.* You can. *There are no redos in the real world.* There are.

So, what gives? Why the real-world rationalizations? Many reasons, I suppose, but maybe it's easier for us to operate from the "future" than it is to participate in the present.

LIES ON THEIR SHOULDERS: PROJECT 180, DAY 81
JANUARY 10, 2019

In the real world…

Yesterday…

She had a panic attack.

He was up at 5:00 AM to do his chores, so he could get to zero-hour band.

She didn't have breakfast.

He met six different deadlines in six different classes.

She didn't do her homework because no one was at home to take care of her younger brothers and sisters.

He thought about suicide.

She didn't tell someone about sexual assault.

He wore the same clothes he had the three days before.

She was bullied on social media.

He missed the game-winning free throw.

She was medicated. Her anxiety is crippling otherwise.

He binged on the food he had hidden in his room. And then hated himself for it.

She silently endured racism.

He didn't "come out."

He did drugs again. He doesn't know how to stop.

They broke up. They didn't know how to make it work.

No one talked to her. They never do.

His mom died.

…in the real world.

Whether we think it or say it, when we warn kids with the "real world," it is an affront to their existence, to their humanity, to their reality. The kids, the humans above, attend Anywhere High School in Everywhere, World. And whether it was yesterday, today, or tomorrow their world feels real enough. Ask them. They'll tell you.

Nothing is more real than now. Yesterday's gone. Tomorrow's not here. All we have-young or old-is today. Now. Are there things we can bring to the attention of our young from our own experiences in the world? Of course. But the key here is that they are our experiences, not theirs. And even for us, each of us, that experience was different, so when we say "real world," whose world, which world are we talking about? We often seem to suggest there is a standardized, formulaic experience that is the real world. Maybe instead of placing some future world on their shoulders, we should just simply help them with the one that lies on their shoulders right now. Otherwise, we might be placing lies on their shoulders.

We have an opportunity to exist with and support kids as they make their ways through their worlds, worlds that are the most real they can be, for they are now. That's the "real talk" we should be having with them.

Happy Thursday, all. Sorry that my post was a little "edgier" than usual. Been on my mind lately. Had to get it out.

Do. Reflect. Do Better.

360°2021

If real is now, then we have to make now real. We have to make their "nows" real. We have to participate in their present. We have to lean in, for when we are closer to the thing, we accept the responsibility of the thing. If distance negates responsibility, then presence activates responsibility.

So, how do we do it? How do we get closer to and make more real their present realities, most of which seem to involve things outside our control? Well, to begin, we cannot control many of the things that impact their realities. We have to accept that. But, we can control how we see and respond to their realities. We have to believe that. And then, when we do, we have to put it to work. We have to exercise that which closes the gaps in the human experience, that which places us in the present of our work.

We have to exercise empathy.

Human work is empathetic work.

I cannot change my kids' realities. But I can honor their realities.

Humans need to feel real.

better Builder

In my room, how do I honor my kids' realities?

I thanked her—my arms raised in triumph—for uttering such an important truth.

180°1.23.2019

Humans need mistakes. We learn from them, and we need to learn, so, it goes, then, that we need to make mistakes.

We *seem* to acknowledge such wisdom in education. We spend a lot of time talking about mindset, grit, and the lot, but I wonder if mistakes really are welcomed guests in the classroom, if they really do have a place at the table, for it seems as if we've created a culture set on avoiding them, not embracing them.

At least, that was my experience in the "graded" classroom, where even then, I talked the talk, telling my kids mistakes were necessary steps in learning. "You have to make mistakes. It's how you learn." And I think I thought I was, if not inspiring them, then at least reassuring them that mistakes were part of the process. But as I look back now, I think I was more likely communicating, through action, "You have to make mistakes. It's how I grade you." For that's really what was going on. Mistakes more often meant losing points, not gaining learning.

GIVING MISTAKES A PLACE AT THE TABLE:
PROJECT 180, DAY 89
JANUARY 23, 2019

Mistakes should be greeted as welcomed guests, not intruders.

"MY BEST EVIDENCE OF LEARNING IS I AM NOT MAKING THE SAME MISTAKES; I AM MAKING NEW MISTAKES."

STUDENT RESPONSE TO "EVIDENCE OF LEARNING QUESTION" DURING HER SEMESTER GRADING CONFERENCE

@MONTESYRIE

Okay, by now, I am sure some of you are tired of seeing this, as I shared it and gushed about it on social media yesterday. Sorry. But it was such an important revelation for me. It's some assuring affirmation that what I am attempting to do with Project 180 might be making a difference in my kids' learning experiences. I needed this.

As most of you know, I have been conducting end-of-term learning conferences with my kiddos. In our conferences, the kids select a grade and support it with evidence. The primary evidence for their selections comes from their Performances (my name for assessments) that we keep in an evidence portfolio. The goal is for us to come to an agreement by the end of the conference, arriving at something that we are both comfortable with as a mark that best represents their learning from the semester. Jamie, the young lady whose wisdom I have been keen to share the last two days, didn't have to do much convincing. She had secured 3's (meeting standard) on all her Performances, either the first time or from feedback-driven retakes. I didn't expect her to select anything other than an A. The evidence was clear. Yet, as she offered up her evidence, she didn't really focus on what we both already knew-her Performance scores; she homed in on mistakes and retakes as her evidence of learning. When she offered the words above, I made her pause, rewind , and play them again, as I quickly scribbled them onto the back of a grade sheet in my grade book.

Inspired by the smile on her face and the wisdom in her words, I thanked her-my arms raised in triumph-for uttering such an important truth. We then went on to talk about the value in mistakes and how we learn with them and about her and her peers' comfort level with them in my room. Of course, the conversation led beyond my room where mistakes hold no such place in word or deed, and some only in word. Many teachers say they value and encourage mistakes in their rooms, but only kids really know the weight of those words in the end. In my opinion, for teachers to give weight and value, mistakes must be…

…met without alarm. They should be greeted as welcomed guests, not intruders. Our reactions to them matter.

…answered with actionable, I-can-improve feedback. Mistakes come with an appetite. The last thing we should do is starve them. We need to back them with feed.

…graced with the opportunity of a redo(s). This is a must. Actionable feedback requires an opportunity to create action, to encourage movement. Mistakes should be dynamic developments, not static sorters.

...part of the learning story. Kids need to reflect on such moments in their journeys. Mistakes need to look in the mirror; they have a remarkable appearance, a beauty if we behold. I use my Journey Journals for this. Jamie's wisdom was born there.

Please know I am not trying to preach this morning. I just think mistakes present us with invaluable opportunities. But I think those opportunities live and die with us. Our walk has to match our talk. We have to give mistakes a place at the table. I believe the head of the table.

Happy Wednesday, all. We are on two-hour delay with a block finals' schedule. Gonna be a strange day.

Do. Reflect. Do Better.

360°2021

This was a significant moment–indeed, a triumphant moment–in the journey. My arms are still raised. What wisdom for her. And what affirmation for me–well, for Project 180.

My kids were seeing mistakes differently. My kids were seeing learning differently. My kids were seeing themselves differently. My dream was becoming my reality. If we could get grades out of the way, then kids could find *their* way–to learning.

Of course, it's not exactly as simple as that, not every kid reaches the realization that Jamie did. For many, there remains a lot of unlearning, a lot of unconditioning when it comes to regarding the meaning of mistakes. It takes time and experience–new and different experience–to reach such understanding about mistakes, about learning, about themselves.

So, with the little time we have with our kids, we need to give them opportunities to see what can be when they make mistakes to learn rather than when they avoid mistakes to earn a grade. If we change the frame, we change the lens. If we change the lens, we change perception.

Humans need mistakes.

better Builder

In my room, how do I frame mistake making?

____

____

____

____

____

I dream of a new place in education, a place where help is the currency, where kids ask for help as not a sign of weakness but as a sign of power…

180°4.10.2019

Humans need…*to ask for help*. Yet another recurring reality (driving another recurring dream): kids don't/won't ask for help. I know I tend to grind on this one, but in truth, it grinds on me. *It grinds on me*, not that kids avoid asking for help–that's grindy, too–but more that we have created a place, a system–a society, really–where asking for help makes kids–people–feel stupid. Grinds my guts.

It has to. I am a teacher. And as I shared earlier, I believe teacher is synonymous with helper. If I am not helping, am I teaching? I don't think so. And if I am not teaching, then what am I doing? Talking? Assigning? Grading? That's certainly a part of the job, but it's not helping, which I believe should be the bulk of our job. And in my experience (both as student and teacher), it has not been. Oh, "help" was and has always been an option on the table, but we've always pushed it around the plate, as it were, and we've never really dug into it.

Time for better.

GOT HELP? PROJECT 180, DAY 134
APRIL 10, 2019

Somewhere along the way we got lost. We veered from the path and ended up in a place where "help" became anathema in education.

Maybe it's rugged American individualism. Maybe it's a hyper-competitive culture. Maybe it's a hide-weakness-at-all-costs attitude. Regardless, our kids tend to hide from help, and the farther they get into their journeys, the more they hide.

But why? And how? How did we get to a place

where our job is to help only to find ourselves operating in a space where kids are afraid to ask us to perform our primary function? If we are not helping, are we teaching? If kids aren't asking for help, are they learning?

Of course this is nothing new. I, too, remember hiding from help for the entirety of my experiences in school. And the only times I did ask for help was when I had reached a point of desperation and shouldered the shame, or I had a teacher who invited us to ask questions, who made "help" an accepted, expected part of the deal, but the latter was few and far between. Seeking help was never comfortable. Never.

Nothing new. Nothing has changed. Yesterday, I encountered a troubling experience with a young lady during fourth period. Troubling on two levels. One, she told me that asking for help made her feel stupid, Two-and this is most troubling, she was afraid to ask me for help. Me? Dang. And I work really hard-or so I thought-to make questions, to make help, necessary--a welcomed dynamic in our classroom. Here was the gist of our exchange.

She came out of hiding. She sought help. She got help. A lot. And I loved every minute of it. IT'S WHY I AM IN THE ROOM! No, it wasn't easy for either of us. Learning is work, work that requires help. So, it was deeply gratifying for me to be that for her. I hope she turned a corner yesterday. I hope she is less-afraid to ask for help. I hope all my kids are, and I plan to make a point-again-of telling them that they must ask me for help. Must.

I dream of a new place in education, a place where help is the currency, where kids ask for help as not a sign of weakness but as a sign of power, expecting no less from their teachers. Help should be an expectation, a living, breathing entity in every classroom. Of this I dream.

Happy Wednesday, all.

Do. Reflect. Do Better.

360°2021

"Please ask me for help. That's why I am here." I include this on every task I assign my kids. And when they do, I sincerely thank them for asking.

"Please ask me for help. That's why they pay me the big bucks." I often make this remark to my kids as we set to work, and we share a laugh.

"Another member inducted into the Help Hall of Fame." I, on occasion, loudly announce this to the class after helping a kid. Someday, I may actually create a Help Hall of Fame plaque to which I add kids' names.

"You need me!" I often gush when kids raise their hands while working, making a big deal out of getting to do my job. Of course, more often than not, they just want to use the restroom, of which I also make a big deal out of my disappointment.

Are such things helping? Yes, to a degree. The world doesn't change overnight. Dreams don't come true upon waking, but upon working. So I'm working.

Humans need to ask for help.

better Builder

In my room, are kids asking for help?

___

___

___

___

___

I believe if you ever imagined all the things that a kid could have stacked against him, he would materialize before your eyes.

180°4.11.2019

Humans need moments. I live for and live in moments. I look for the moments that will matter in my life. And once I find them, I long to linger in the moments that will matter for the rest of my life. Moments matter. To all of us. All our lives we find them, even—maybe especially—when we least expect them. And once we find them, we linger in them, for we need them. They mattered, and because they mattered, they became moments. We need moments.

We find them in our classrooms, too. We don't always know when they are going to happen, but we always know they have happened, for they give us pause; they remind us of the nobler things we do in our work, the things that really matter in our work, and nearly always—at least for me—those moments have been human moments, connections beyond the content and curriculum, connections with kids. Those are the moments that have mattered most for me. The moments I look for, live for, and as with this particular moment, linger in. *Moments.*

I'LL STOP THE WORLD: PROJECT 180, DAY 135
APRIL 11, 2019

"Deficient. Never used that word in my writing before."

"Yeah, I just used the word anathema for the first time in my blog post this morning, means something or someone that is strongly disliked."

"Anathema, that word just sounds like it means something bad."

We laughed, as he said the word aloud again.

We laughed. He laughed. That's a big deal.

He doesn't laugh. He barely, rarely smiles, and he certainly never does when schoolwork is the topic.

I want to describe him, but I can't describe him. Oh, I have the words. That's not the problem. It's just that the words break my heart, for I believe if you ever imagined all the things that a kid could have stacked against him, he would materialize before your eyes.

I see him every day, and my heart breaks for him every day. I do what I can to help, and he's come to let me more as the year has passed, but yesterday, he let me in, and I stayed as long as I could, maybe longer than I should have, for I never did get to the other kids who needed my help. But, as they no doubt sat and watched and listened to his and my moment, they, too, witnessed some beauty in the human connection I shared with this young man. It was understood, I think by all, that there was nothing more important than that moment. And they, with grace, let us be.

And so, for the better part of twenty minutes, I sat with him and worked patiently, painstakingly-for working with writers at times requires Herculean efforts-on his essay. I wrote. He wrote. We scribbled. Backspaced. Laughed at his huge-I mean huge-fingers fumbling around on the keyboard, as he muttered, "I don't type so good."

At some point, feeling like he could manage the rest on his own, I left him to wrap up the quickly closing period with the rest of my kiddos. And as the bell rang and the room cleared, he was there at my desk, shifting his weight awkwardly from one foot to the other.

"Just wanna say thank you for your help. No one could do what you do. So, thanks."

Plenty of others could and do, do what I do. But yesterday, I did what I did because I had to. I had a million other things to do, but I had to let the moment dictate, and I did. We stopped the world and melted into the moment. I may never get another moment with him quite the same, so I stayed. I lingered, finding myself fully present in a

```
moment while the world waited.

Happy Thursday, all.

Do. Reflect. Do Better. (and stop the world
every once in a while)
```

360°2021

I will never forget this moment, and I'd like to think that he will never forget it, either. I'd like to think the same for all my kids with whom I have shared such moments. I'd like to think that they, as I, find themselves on occasion lingering in the moments that have mattered.

I'd also like to think that as you've read about my moment, you have recalled your own moments (which, remember, is really the whole point of this book). I hope you have recalled the times when you, too, have stopped the world and melted into the moment. More, I'd like to think that you, too, need these moments. Our work *is* noble work, but it is also hard work, and in the mundanity of the day-to-day, we need our moments. They elevate us. They sustain us.

So, when we have the fortune of finding ourselves in such moments in real time, we need to pause, we need to linger, and we need to remember: it's not just about us. It's also about them.

Humans need moments.

better Builder

In my room, what moments have mattered?

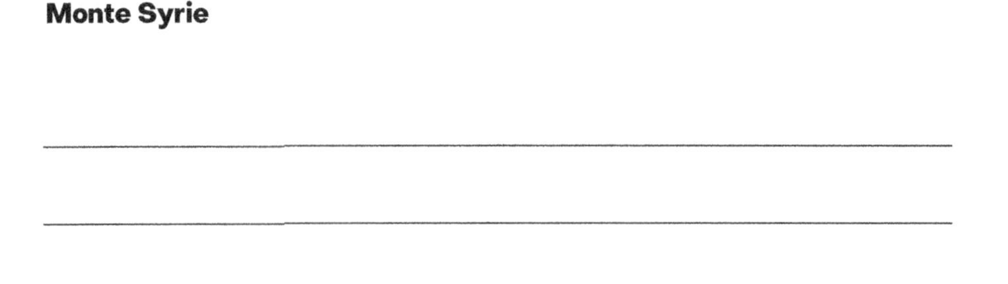

And while things have changed for the better—most of us believe—within our rooms, the rest of the world remains largely unchanged without.

180°4.16.2019

Humans need dreams. We have to have something to look forward to. We have to have some *better* to imagine to drive us beyond. We live in a world. We imagine a better world. We *dream* of a better world. Simply, we dream of better.

I dream of better. It's how the whole 180 journey began. I dreamt of a classroom where learning, not grading, was the goal. So, I got going on my goal, daring my dream by changing the reality in my world—taking grades off the table. I introduced my dream to my reality, and we got to work. Yes," we." Dream, reality, and me. We three had to work together.

I can't hang out in the clouds with my dreams. I can't stay stuck on the ground of my reality. Better is not a simple exchange. I can't just trade in my reality for my dreams. Those aren't the terms of better. It's an agreement, a reasoned, reflective response to bridge and balance the two. Here, I needed a bridge. Reality had me dreaming again—of better.

CHASING BETTER: DREAMS OF A FEEDBACK-ONLY CLASSROOM
APRIL 16, 2019

Always a Better around the Bend

Though I have been gradeless for three years now, in my earnest attempt to emphasize learning by de-emphasizing grading, I am still not satisfied with my approach, for it still relies on numbers which impact how my students "see" their feedback during their learning experiences. It seems, regardless of what I write or say, the number speaks first and most. I want to get away from this. (I know Ruth Butler speaks to and there exists a body of work to support this, but I have yet to read any of her work-I will, but it makes sense to me without her work. I mean that most respectfully.)

Over the past two years, I have used an approach I call "Performance Learning." Essentially, "performances" are assessments, the only thing I "grade." I use a 3 point system to mark performance: 3 = Met Standard 2 = Near Miss 1 = Far Miss. With each number I also provide feedback. For 2's and 1's, the feedback, indicates why they missed and what they need to do next time. "Next time" is key. With this "assessment-as-learning" approach, retakes are encouraged. Really, they are expected. My kids go into all performances knowing that for most of them it's a matter of when not if there's a next time. In general, this approach has been a positive, productive step for me as I have distanced myself from traditional grading. Even so, the approach is lacking. So, this is one of the reasons I am seeking better.

There are other reasons.

Data, Data, Who's Got the Data?

I have come to see learning as a story, a complex, idiosyncratic tale that is hard to pen, especially when we try to put it into standard numbers and letters. This is yet another compelling reason for my venturing into the gradeless realm three years ago. A grade never-I repeat never– felt sufficient; in truth, even more, it never really felt accurate. So, unsettled by this, I sought better. Still seeking better. That's why I am writing this, but at some point betters meet and it then becomes a question of whose better is better.

Things happen differently in the gradeless classroom. They have to. Nearly all teachers

I know who've gone "gradeless," are doing it in response to the inadequacy of traditional grading practices. It's the nature of the journey. We have to do things differently. And while things have changed for the better–most of us believe–within our rooms, the rest of the world remains largely unchanged without. And that interface between worlds presents challenges. Many of us have found ways to overcome these challenges, and we do so willingly because we believe in what we are doing. The extra effort is worth it. From explaining our work to parents to finding clever ways to manipulate our online grade books, we have found ways to make our "different" work–within our walls, but what about outside our walls? What happens when these worlds collide?

As many of you know, I am no fan of standardized testing. I find it a false narrative, at times deeply at odds with the stories we pen in our room all year long. Of late, as I have begun to more publicly and purposefully resist, the chances for these at-odds moments are likely to increase as I shrug the test and embrace instead the experiences in my classroom. I imagine there will be a disconnect, a discrepancy in the data. The outside data and the inside data will tell different tales. Such is the risk of different. Such is the risk that discourages many to do differently in the first place. I have risked much in the past, and I will risk much in the future, but risk is not without preparation. I was "prepared" when I went gradeless three years ago. I will be prepared with this next phase, evolution of Project 180.

A Tale of Two Experiences

The initial genesis of this most recent plan to do differently actually occurred during a recent PLC meeting where my team and I were discussing our findings from a common assessment, an argumentative letter (yes, I'm a sellout. It was test prep). And we arrived at this place where we were wondering about what our data revealed vs. what the SBA data might reveal. What if the two told different tales? And it got me to thinking about the value of qualitative data in telling kids' learning stories, thinking if the day ever came where we had to reconcile the difference in data, how could we relate, how could the kids relate their learning experiences in a way that could/

would stand up to the inquiry? We would have to have our act together. And I, in particular, for I do far differently than they, would really have to have it together. So, I started thinking.

Kids would have to present a compelling tale to stand up to the "truth" of standardized data. My kids already collect a portfolio of evidence all semester long, but I am not sure it is truly compelling, particularly to outside eyes.But that is a secondary, reactionary concern. More to the point, how can I create an experience where we can capture growth moments? That's the primary, for me. That's the tale I want my kids to write, that's the tale I want them to tell. But as I wrestled with how that manifests itself in kids' learning experiences, I always hit a snag. And then, finally it dawned. It's the numbers. It's the damn numbers. They tell the tale too short; they end the tale too soon. I have to get rid of the numbers. I have known for a long time that the sweet spot in learning is the feedback cycle, but I have also known, experienced, bemoaned that feedback gets tainted by numbers. So yesterday, I decided to devise a way to get rid of the numbers.

But I am not fully ready to share that yet, for I have a lot of processing to do. This is going to be a BIG different.

I wanted to share this to create some context for my change, to share my why before my what and how. I know holes exist in my thinking, that's the nature of chasing better-there are always holes, but this is what I have for now. My thinking moving forward is hovering around these questions/ ideas.

What is learning?

We learn from experiences.

Experiences provide feedback opportunities.

Feedback opportunities promote growth.

Growth is evidence of learning.

Learning is the goal.

So, our goal is to provide meaningful growth experiences so each student may learn.

What makes a "Growth Experience" meaningful?

```
Relevance
Choice
Agency
Standards
Criteria
Feedback
Support
Reflection
Self-Assessment

That's my rough shove of my idea into the
world. Any questions or feedback would be
welcomed and appreciated.
```

Do. Reflect. Do Better.

360°2021

Still dreaming. Still chasing. Still building bridges between dream and reality. And, really, that's where I've learned to live. On the bridge. In between.

Five years later, I am still trying to capture that place where the dream of a feedback-only classroom becomes–fully–the reality of a feedback-only classroom. I made some significant strides in Year Four, as you will see in that chapter, but here in Year Six, my dream is not yet fully realized. And maybe that's how it's supposed to be–*how it has to be.* There's always the dream of better.

My current dream is not all that different from the dream I dreamt back in Year Three. Really, it's a recurring dream where I find myself on the verge of something BIG, as I did here, but I cannot quite get it right. And that's perhaps because of the recurring realities in education, many of which I reject in principle (we are still seeking "truth" in standardized testing, even in the pandemic) but accept in practice as the means to a dream of *better*.

Humans need dreams.

better Builder

In my room, what dreams do I dream?

____

____

____

____

____

I will no longer 'hide' behind symbols, pretending they are an adequate language to communicate learning.

180°4.19.2019

Humans need to tell their stories. My plan for the feedback-only classroom was coming into being. I had been wrestling with the wonder of it for days, wondering how I would capture the learning experience, and I had finally found some clarity. The story.

If I could frame the idea of learning as a story, then maybe I could discover a way to help kids capture their stories more adequately, more authentically than we had in the past with numbers and letters. *The damn numbers and letters.* There had to be a better way.

So, I started sketching out a plan, using a plot diagram as a template, imagining the stages of learning were not really all that different from the stages of a story: exposition, rising action, climax, resolution. Learning is a story.

Their story. Our story. Our time together was not, could not, should not simply be something reduced to a letter or number—not ever, and certainly not during this foundational, formative stage of our young humans' lives. They had learning to live. They had stories to tell.

WRESTLING WONDER: PROJECT 180, DAY 141
APRIL 19, 2019

But how will we "catch" their learning?

Been wrestling with a lot of ideas the past few days as I dream and scheme about the creation of a feedback-only classroom. But, the most formidable opponent I've been grappling with is how I will capture the learning.

My thinking to this point has pushed me to consider "story" as my desired end based on the early and emerging rationale for creating this feedback-focused experience for my kiddos in the first place.

What is learning?
We learn from experiences.
Experiences provide feedback opportunities.
Feedback opportunities promote growth.

Growth is evidence of learning.
Learning is the goal.
So, our goal is to provide meaningful growth experiences so each student may learn.

Yesterday, I was able to make some headway with my messy thinking. I started with the end in mind, for in the end, I want kids to capture their learning as stories stemming from "growth moments." Here is what I roughed out in that regard.

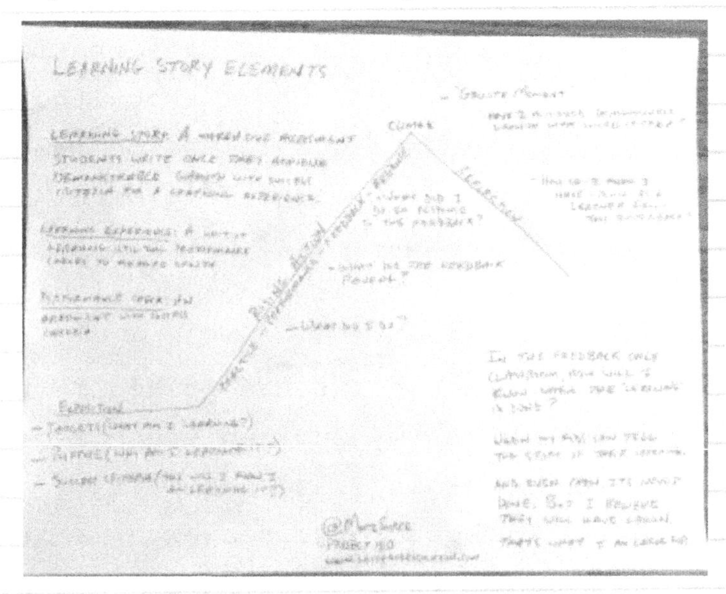

This–or some future, better draft of this–is what I hope will empower my kids to capture and tell their stories as we make our way through the feedback cycle to find their "growth moments." That is what I want; consequently, that is what I never really found with traditional grades, which purported to tell the story, but they were always a report too short. They never truly told the tale.

Numbers and letters get in the way, often creating ends before the learning has even begun. My belief-and certainly neither mine first nor exclusively-is that feedback is the stuff of learning. It is what compels and propels learners. But it also propels and compels teachers. I will no longer "hide" behind symbols, pretending they are an adequate language to communicate learning. Without them, I will be "exposed." I will have to be a better "feedbacker," ever mindful of the fact that I am co-authoring my kids' learning stories every time I open my mouth, or move my pen. And that is my next match, my next wonder to wrestle: the how of my feedback.

Happy Friday, all. For the most part, "done" with testing. So glad to authentically engage my kids today. Been an artificial week. Feel like we get our classroom back today.

Do. Reflect. Do Better.

360°2021

Still wrestling with the wonder of this one. Oh, as you will see in Year Four, I made strides with the story concept, but as better goes, I am still working on better.

I am still convinced learning is a story. I am still convinced that numbers and letters are an affront to the complexity and humanity of the learning experience. And I am still convinced that kids have to tell the tale—their tale. I will not stray from this path, to the story I am committed, but I am also always committed to chasing and building better. And with ever-present wonders like, "What is learning?" and "How will we catch their learning?" chasing, building, *and* wrestling are constant commitments, constant companions.

In fact, at present, I am trying—again—to frame feedback as the binding force between teaching and learning. Learning gives rise to feedback which gives rise to teaching which again gives rise to learning which again gives rise to teaching, and...well, you get the point. And that's the stuff of learning, of stories.

Humans need to tell their stories.

better Builder

In my room, what's the learning narrative?

____

____

____

____

____

But, really, she's neither strange nor weird; really, she's just misunderstood.

180°6.17.2019

Humans need to be understood. There is much I want my kids to understand by the time we reach our end. But, of all, I want them to understand each other, *and* I want them to understand themselves. Our time with them presents us with a unique opportunity to do more than develop their academic ability; it presents us with an opportunity to explore and discover *our* humanity.

We talk a lot about the importance of an educated society when we look to the purpose of education, focusing primarily on literacy and numeracy. And while that's certainly important, it seems not enough if that's the only end that drives our means. We miss a chance to develop empathy. Our society needs more than communication and computation; it needs compassion, but we can't get there if we don't know each other, and if we don't know each other, then we can never understand each other. And if we can't understand–have empathy for–each other, then we never fully realize the power and potential in our humanity.

We provide the first real opportunity.

MISS UNDER STOOD: PROJECT 180, DAY 176
JUNE 17, 2019

I imagine by her peers' standards she's strange. She keeps to herself. She has different interests. She says and does weird things. But, really, she's neither strange nor weird; really, she's just misunderstood.

Turns out, I have a lot of Ms. (and Mr.) Understoods in the classroom. Always have. Always will. We are all different. We are all strange. We are all misunderstood. It's the way of things. But I say this not as an admission of apathy. Rather, I say it as a recognition of reality. In our world, we misunderstand much. Of all, it seems we misunderstand each other. And why wouldn't we? We don't know each other. We can't understand what we don't know. So, then, to understand, we have to know. The goal has to be to know each other. In room 206, that is the goal.

In my room I want you to feel connected.

This is everything in my room. All else comes second. We work-deliberately and diligently-at this every day. No magic bullet. No shiny, canned, costly program. Just 31 people in a room connecting each day through Smiles and Frowns. I know I often talk about and talk up our daily ritual, gushing about its impact on our classroom community and culture, but it has been a powerful means to a powerful end, an end that I am witnessing from the front row. And from my perch, I am watching in real time "knowing" transforming into "understanding." And yesterday, was the best yet. For yesterday, Miss Under stood.

She has refused to share her work all year long. Trapped in her anxiety, scarred by bullies and teasers in her past, aware of her socially awkward standing, she has hidden in the shadows, barely showing herself. Occasionally, intermittently, she has shared a smile or frown, but she has never shared her work, which I have always found to be our misfortune, for her work is good-really good. And as we neared the end of this project and approached the presentation part of it, she and I had already reached an agreement that-as always-she would not have to share her work. But, then, yesterday, something happened. Miss Under stirred.

Maybe she was having one of her "less-bad" days (for her, good). Maybe she was inspired by her peers' sharing their work. Maybe she finally believed me when I told her that she had good stuff. Maybe it was merely a fluke. Regardless the reason, as the period began, and I was asking if anyone wanted to fill the two vacant spots in the presentation schedule, she spoke up.

"Sy, I guess I can go."

"Really?" (shocked)

"But only my poem."

"You sure?" I was still in shock.

"I don't know. Maybe. Maybe not" (anxiety coming to life).

"Let's let the others go first. And if you go, great. If you don't, all good."

And then, when it was time, she stood. Miss Under stood. And she shared not only her poem but all of her pieces. Afraid for her, I quickly scanned the room, worried how the kids might respond. But they-and I should have known better-regarded her as one of the "family," transfixed by the wondrous work the weird girl in the corner shared from atop her moment's mountain. It was a palpably surreal moment for me, for all of us. And at the end, I marveled as she read through her peers' kind comment cards, smiling bigger than I have ever seen her smile.

We won't soon forget what we now better know and better understand about Miss Under. We will all remember the day she stood. More, she won't forget either. She, I believe, better understands, too.

Happy Friday, all. Have a great weekend.

Do. Reflect. Do Better.

360°2021

Much of what sticks with our kids isn't tied to what we teach them. Lessons on gerunds and participles don't linger and last. Human experiences, on the other hand, tend to stick; they do last; they do linger. For in them, from them, we come to understand others; we come to understand ourselves. But, unlike lessons, we don't teach experiences; they happen with or without us. We are not the directors as much as we are the stage hands. We don't direct the play, but we do set the stage for the play, and the best set I have ever found for the human play is Smiles and Frowns.

It was the set, the stage, that led to the moment with this young lady, and it continues to be the stage that daily delivers the power and potential of humanity as kids discover others and themselves, discovering they belong, not because they are in the room, not because they are on the roster, but because they are members of the human race, and they understand.

Humans need to be understood.

better Builder

In my room, how do I set the stage for the human experience?

____

____

____

____

____

If I began Year Three changed, I ended it forever changed. I couldn't see my students, myself, *our* work the same ever again. I had become, simply, a helper of humans. And that remains the simple place from which wells my work. But simple isn't always easy. And, when it comes to helping humans, it's never easy. As teachers, we know meeting all students' needs is at best a mess. As humans, we know meeting each human's needs is the messiest of messes, but we help anyway. Teachers. Humanity's helpers.

better Builders

1. In my room, how far am I willing to stretch?
2. In my room, how is learning experienced?
3. In my room, how do I build trust?
4. In my room, how do I feed learning?
5. In my room, how do I elevate my support?
6. In my room, where do I draw the line on how much I help my kids?
7. In my room, how well do I give directions?
8. In my room, how do I choose between what's possible and impossible?
9. In my room, how do I honor my kids' realities?
10. In my room, how do I frame mistake making?
11. In my room, what dreams do I dream?
12. In my room, are kids asking for help?

13. In my room, what moments have mattered?
14. In my room, what's the learning narrative?
15. In my room, how do I set the stage for the human experience?

better Bends

DO. REFLECT. DO BETTER.

And here we reach a bend, but not an end. For as we now know, better never ends. It only bends. And here at this bend of Book One, I will bid you adieu until our journeys join again in Book Two.

And as we part, dear friend, at this bend, I hope you have found differents to dare and betters to brave. I hope my journey ignited your own journey, which I believe is really our journey: a teacher's journey, a perpetual path of **DO**ing, **REFLECT**ing, and **DO**ing **BETTER**.

See ya around the bend,

better Builders

APPENDIX

Year One: The Year of the A

1. In my room, why do I do what I do?
2. In my room, what "leap(s)" am I ready to make?
3. In my room, what are the rules for grading?
4. In my room, do I teach from a position of power or influence?
5. In my room, what does choice look like?
6. In my room, what helps me find my way when I get lost?
7. In my room, how can I work with kids?
8. In my room, how can I use criticism to help me grow?
9. In my room, how do I respond to my own fear and insecurity?
10. In my room, do I push the pendulum?
11. In my room, what am I willing to leave behind as I move on to better?
12. In my room, what frontiers am I exploring?
13. In my room, how can I be a better passenger?
14. In my room, how can I help kids discover the "treasure" in themselves?
15. In my room, how confident am I that I can change the world?

better Between: Summer 2017

1. In my room, how do I deal with the "Dilemma of Do" (kids' doing/not doing work)?
2. In my room, what propels the learning?
3. In my room, how do I put people first?

4. In my room, how do I capture the learning journey?
5. In my room, what do I want kids to discover?
6. In my room, what do I want parents to know?
7. In my room, how do I frame the rules?
8. In my room, who's the expert?

Year Two: The Year of the R

1. In my room, how do I build community?
2. In my room, how do I reconcile my ideals and realities?
3. In my room, what do I wonder and worry about?
4. In my room, how do I create "return-to-learn" opportunities?
5. In my room, what's worth repeating?
6. In my room, how do I keep it real?
7. In my room, what do I want my students to want for their own children's education?
8. In my room, what would kids fight to keep?
9. In my room, how do I want kids to feel?
10. In my room, what do I need to revisit?
11. In my room, what needs to be revised?
12. In my room, how do I deal with the inconvenience of working with humans?
13. In my room, how do I redirect perceptions when misunderstandings occur?
14. In my room, what might others not see that lies beneath the surface?
15. In my room, what is my take on retakes?

better Between: Summer 2018

1. In my room, how do I respond when kids do work from other classes?
2. In my room, how do I know what I know about learning?
3. In my room, how do I pace my year-long race?

Year Three: Helping Humans

1. In my room, how far am I willing to stretch?
2. In my room, how is learning experienced?
3. In my room, how do I build trust?
4. In my room, how do I feed learning?
5. In my room, how do I elevate my support?

6. In my room, where do I draw the line on how much I help my kids?
7. In my room, how well do I give directions?
8. In my room, how do I choose between what's possible and impossible?
9. In my room, how do I honor my kids' realities?
10. In my room, how do I frame mistake making?
11. In my room, what dreams do I dream?
12. In my room, are kids asking for help?
13. In my room, what moments have mattered?
14. In my room, what's the learning narrative?
15. In my room, how do I set the stage for the human experience?

ABOUT THE AUTHOR

Monte Syric has been chasing better in the classroom for 25 years. His long journey to better began in Royal City, Washington in the fall of 1996 where he was a middle school ELA teacher for 7 years. In 2003, he had a chance to move back to his hometown of Cheney, Washington to teach high school ELA at his alma mater. Today, he is still there at home chasing better, one step at a time.

Ever an advocate for challenging the status quo in education, Monte started Project 180 in the fall of 2016, a journey he has documented on his daily blog. Unsettled by the notion that things in education have to be because they've always been, he set out to find better for himself and his students, discovering along the way the promise, potential, and possibility in the humanization of the educational experience. He hopes his discoveries from his "do-reflect-do better" approach to education, and life, inspire others on their own journeys to better.

Do. Reflect. Do Better.

CODE BREAKER LEADERSHIP SERIES

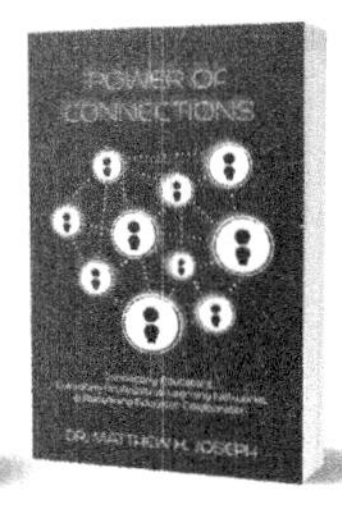

CODE BREAKER KID COLLECTION

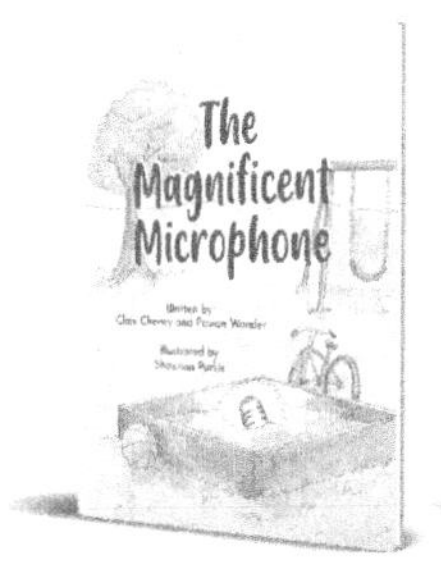

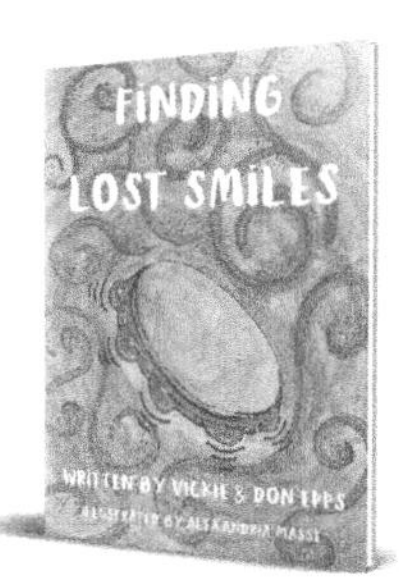

THE X FACTOR LIBRARY

Code
BREAKER
www.codebreakeredu.com

Made in the USA
Monee, IL
24 April 2023

32368288R00233